ELIZABETHAN
EROTIC
NARRATIVES

Titian, *Venus and Adonis* (Madrid, Museo Prado; ca. 1554).   Photo Museo Prado.

ELIZABETHAN EROTIC NARRATIVES

Irony and Pathos in the Ovidian Poetry of Shakespeare, Marlowe, and Their Contemporaries

WILLIAM KEACH

RUTGERS UNIVERSITY PRESS
New Brunswick, New Jersey

Library of Congress Cataloging in Publication Data

Keach, William, 1942-
  Elizabethan erotic narratives.

  Includes bibliographical references and index.
  1. Narrative Poetry, English—History and criticism.
2. English poetry—Early modern, 1500-1700—History and
criticism. 3. Ovidius Naso, Publius—Influence.
I. Title.
PR539.N3K4   821'.03   76-25487
ISBN 0-8135-0830-4

To Sam Keach

CONTENTS

ILLUSTRATIONS

Preface

The purpose of this book is to clarify the expressive possibilities and the literary significance of a group of late Elizabethan poems which have not received the kind of attention they deserve. As will be explained more fully in the Introduction, I have restricted my focus both thematically and historically: I want to show how, and to what extent, the ambivalence of Shakespeare's *Venus and Adonis* and Marlowe's *Hero and Leander* is central to other immediately contemporary Ovidian narratives. Underlying my approach is the conviction that the best writing about sexual love characteristically embodies a convergence of the beautiful and the disconcerting, the tender and the violent, the passionate and the comic, the seriousness of desire and the fun of titillation.

I first read the Ovidian narratives of Shakespeare, Marlowe, and their followers with Christopher Ricks at Worcester College, Oxford. That experience eventually led me to undertake a dissertation on Ovidian poetry at Yale under the direction of Richard S. Sylvester. To both these teachers and advisers I owe a great deal. Of the many friends and colleagues who subsequently helped me with criticism, information, and encouragement, I should particularly like to thank Maurice Charney, Donald Cheney, Thomas R. Edwards, Sheila Emerson, Daniel F. Howard, John Huntington, David Kalstone, Gloria Kury, Kenneth Lewes, George de F. Lord, Bridget Lyons, John O'Connor, John Richetti, and Donald Weinstein. I am grateful to the Rutgers University Research Council, and especially to its associate director C. F. Main, whose advice and support were invaluable. With the assistance of the Research Council and of Rutgers College I was able to spend two summers and the autumn of 1973 working at the British Library and at the Warburg Institute in London. The staffs of both these institutions and of the university libraries at Rutgers, Yale, and Princeton were always more helpful than they had to be.

My editor at the Rutgers University Press, Edward McClellan, made this book better than it would have been otherwise and taught me more than he would be willing to admit. It was a pleasure to work with him.

Some of the material in Chapter IV appeared in "Marlowe's Hero as 'Venus' nun,'" *English Literary Renaissance*, 2 (1972), 307-320. I wish to thank the editors for permission to reprint.

Note on Texts and Translations

Quotations of the poems under special consideration in this study are taken from the following editions:

Thomas Lodge, *Glaucus and Scilla,* from *Elizabethan Minor Epics,* ed. Elizabeth Story Donno, New York, 1963.

William Shakespeare, *Venus and Adonis,* from the New Arden edition of *The Poems,* ed. F. T. Prince, London, 1960.

Christopher Marlowe, *Hero and Leander,* from the Revels Plays edition of *The Poems,* ed. Millar MacLure, London, 1968.

John Marston, *The Metamorphosis of Pigmalions Image,* from *The Poems of John Marston,* ed. Arnold Davenport, University Press of Liverpool, 1961.

John Weever, *Faunus and Melliflora,* from *Faunus and Melliflora (1600),* ed. Arnold Davenport, University Press of Liverpool, 1948.

Francis Beaumont, *Salmacis and Hermaphroditus,* from *Elizabethan Narrative Verse,* ed. Nigel Alexander, London, 1968.

I have used modernized texts of *Venus and Adonis* and *Hero and Leander* because this is the normal practice with Shakespeare, and there seemed no reason not to extend it to Marlowe and to take advantage of the excellent Revels Plays edition. Only old-spelling editions of the other poems are widely available, but I have regularized *u* and *v, i* and *j,* and *s* in all quotations.

All quotations of Shakespeare's plays are from the Arden edition, general eds. Harold F. Brooks and Harold Jenkins; all quotations from Spenser are from *The Works of Edmund Spenser: A Variorum Edition,* ed. Edwin Greenlaw et al., 10 vols., Baltimore, Md., 1932-1957. Quotations of Ovid are from the Loeb Classical Library editions: *Metamorphoses,* trans. Frank Justus Miller; *Heroides and Amores,* trans. Grant Showerman; *The Art of Love and Other Poems,* trans. J. H. Mozley. The English prose translations, based primarily on those in the Loeb editions but modernized in idiom and brought more closely in line with the literal sense of the Latin, are my own. (I have followed the usual method of rendering the Latin historical present with the English past tense.) Sir Arthur Golding's version of the *Metamorphoses* is a great monument in sixteenth-century literature and was certainly read by the authors under consideration, along with Ovid's own words. But Golding's verse often strays far from the Latin to enforce its pervasive moralizing and allegorizing perspective and to achieve the regularity of its "fourteeners." In cases where I have referred to Golding, I have used the Macmillan edition, ed. John Frederick Nims (London, 1965).

I have used the following standard abbreviations for well-known journals and reference works:

CE	*College English*
CL	*Comparative Literature*
DNB	*Dictionary of National Biography*
ELH	*Journal of English Literary History*
ELR	*English Literary Renaissance*
HLQ	*Huntington Library Quarterly*
JEGP	*Journal of English and Germanic Philology*
MLQ	*Modern Language Quarterly*
MLR	*Modern Language Review*
N & Q	*Notes and Queries*
PMLA	*Publications of the Modern Language Association of America*
PQ	*Philological Quarterly*
R.-E.	*Paulys Realenzyklopädie der klassischen Altertumswissenschaft*
RES	*Review of English Studies*
SEL	*Studies in English Literature, 1500–1900*
SP	*Studies in Philology*
SQ	*Shakespeare Quarterly*
STC	*Short Title Catalogue*

Introduction

Although the erotic mythological narrative poem has long been recognized as one of the characteristic expressions of late Elizabethan literary culture, there is no single book in English devoted to it. The reason for this is clear enough: of the many poems written during the so-called "vogue" of the Ovidian narrative, only Shakespeare's *Venus and Adonis* and Marlowe's *Hero and Leander* have been accorded any claim to major importance, and even they have seemed to require nothing beyond a substantial chapter or essay. For considerations of the genre as a whole, most readers have been satisfied with the summary treatments in literary histories and anthologies, in studies of Shakespeare and Marlowe, and in books and articles focused on other or larger subjects. This study does not challenge the traditional preëminence of *Venus and Adonis* and *Hero and Leander*: in fact, one of my main concerns will be to substantiate their status as major achievements of English Renaissance poetry and to show to what extent they create, rather than simply represent, the Elizabethan version of this kind of poem. But I shall also be concerned to show that the very qualities which make *Venus and Adonis* and *Hero and Leander* so provocative are to be found more consistently in other Ovidian narratives of the period than is generally acknowledged. The broad literary-historical judgment governing the entire study is that Ovidian narrative poetry has a distinctive importance in English Renaissance literature and that the fundamental issues it raises need to be examined in greater detail.

For some time now critics have noticed a range of apparently dissonant elements in the Ovidian narrative: comedy abruptly juxtaposed with or superimposed upon tragedy; irony entwined with romantic sentiment and pathos; conventional moral perspectives evoked in the midst of piquant eroticism; dramatic colloquial speech framed by elegant verbal artifice. The fact that classical scholars have recently begun to call attention to analogous dissonances in Ovid's own poetry suggests that a revaluation of Ovid's influence on the mythological narratives of Shakespeare, Marlowe, and their contemporaries would be useful. Even in the freest and most inventive departures from their mythological sources, these poets display an ironic literary self-consciousness and an urbane awareness of the human contradictions projected in their subjects which make them "Ovidian" in more than just a superficial sense.

Our belief that the Elizabethans did not read Ovid with the presumed objectivity of the modern Latinist has often led us to use the adjective "Ovidian" in a vague way which has little to do with the actual experience of Ovid's poetry. I have therefore begun with a non-specialist's attempt to obtain a more precise conception of what "Ovidian" ought to mean. Chapter I is devoted primarily to Ovid's own poetry. It is concerned secondarily with the immediate environment of the Elizabethan epyllion, an environment in which the proverbial backwardness and medievalism of sixteenth-century English culture merge with a literary sophistication and self-consciousness as intense as that of any contemporary Continental country. My main contention will be that while there is a playfully subversive element in the responses of many late Elizabethan "Ovidian" poets to the prevailing moral, allegorical, and pedagogical traditions, there is also a sensitivity to the contradictory human expressiveness of Ovid's poetry which the traditional approaches often obscured. The alternative to Sir Arthur Golding's moralized Ovid is not, as is so often assumed, mere "neo-pagan" indulgence and "Italianate" frivolity.

The term I have used throughout the book to refer to the deepest poetic connections between Ovid and Elizabethan "Ovidian" poets— *ambivalence*—is both dangerously abstract and suspiciously fashionable. But I can think of no better word to refer to the tonal and thematic complexity with which I am concerned, and I can only hope that the details of the argument will give *ambivalence* a specific content adequate to the use I want to make of it. It was reassuring to me—and it may be so to the reader as well—to know that Fowler, after warning us that *ambivalent* and *ambivalence* are terms "invented by psychoanalysts in the 20th C. to mean the coexistence in one person of opposing emotional attitudes towards the same object," goes on to observe that the "words are new, but not the condition they describe." He quotes from Ovid's presentation of Medea ("video meliora proboque, / deteriora sequor"—"I see the better and approve it, but I follow the worse," *Met.* VII. 20-21) to support his guarded approbation (*Modern English Usage*, 2nd ed., rev. Sir Ernest Gowers, p. 22).

Another problem of terminology arises with the word *epyllion*. An entire chapter might have been devoted to the validity and appropriateness of this term, especially since the recent debate among classicists about its applicability to those Hellenistic and Roman poems which constitute the most important sources of the episodes in the *Metamorphoses* makes the question more than simply a matter of generic terminology. But necessary decisions about the length and critical scope of this study have meant that only a brief defense of my use of the term is possible. We may begin with the fact that classical scholars have continued to find *epyllion* (Greek ἐπύλλιον, , diminutive of ἔπος, , hence *versicle* or *short epic poem*) useful for referring to what is admittedly a heterogeneous group of Hellenistic and Roman poems, in spite of the attacks on its historical and critical validity by, most notably, Walter Allen, Jr. C. S. Lewis, in his *English Literature in the Sixteenth Century Excluding Drama* (1954), seems to have been the first to apply *epyllion* to the Ovidian poems of Shakespeare, Marlowe, and their contemporaries, and the term has acquired some degree of currency in this context. But many readers of Elizabethan literature remain wary of it because of its ambiguous status as a classical literary category and because of the misleading connotations of its rough English equivalent, *minor epic* or *little epic*. I do not wish to claim, in response to this wariness, that Elizabethan Ovidian narrative poems form a rigorous genre based directly upon ancient prototypes. They are not consistently derived from the Hellenistic and Roman poems often referred to by classicists as *epyllia* in the way, say, that the Renaissance pastoral eclogue is derived from the poems of Theocritus and Virgil. But these Elizabethan poems are sufficiently like one another and sufficiently indebted to one another to be grouped under a single name, and they are closer to late classical *epyllia* than to any other kind of poem. The term has recently been used by Elizabeth Story Donno as the title of the best short account of the Elizabethan genre (in volume II of the *Sphere History of Literature in the English Language,* ed. Christopher Ricks, 1970), and it has been applied by Guy Demerson (in *La Mythologie Classique dans l'oeuvre lyrique de la "Pléiade,"* 1972) to the French mythological narratives which, as Sir Sidney Lee pointed out long ago, provide the most significant Continental precedent for the Elizabethan *epyllion*. There is also, one might as well admit, the question of convenience: *epyllion* is simply much handier over an extended stretch of writing than *erotic mythological narrative poem* or even *Ovidian narrative poem*. The term is problematical, but with careful obviation of misleading connotations, the combined factors of critical convention, poetic similarity, and convenience outweigh the liabilities.

This is not a comprehensive history of Ovidian narrative poetry in the Elizabethan period. I have not attempted to bring out the interest of such minor works as Thomas Heywood's *Oenone and Paris* (1594) and Thomas Edwards' *Cephalus and Procris* and *Narcissus* (1595). Nor, more importantly, have I dealt at length with George Chapman's two great contributions—*Ovid's Banquet of Sense* (1595) and the "continuation" of

Hero and Leander (1598). The absence of an extended discussion of Chapman may seem a major omission to some readers; the reason I offer in anticipatory reply is that his poems represent a different and separable perspective on Ovidian poetry from the perspective with which I am mainly concerned. One might well have grouped Chapman's two poems with Michael Drayton's *Endymion and Phoebe* (1595) into a separate section devoted to what could be described as a counter-movement within the mythological poetry of the 1590s, a counter-movement which reacted against the witty and often subversive erotic ambivalence of Shakespeare and Marlowe by infusing the epyllion with serious philosophical symbolism and moral idealism. The difficulty is that all three poems, and particularly Chapman's, are so extraordinarily complicated that an adequate discussion of them would have doubled the size of the book. Anyone familiar with Frank Kermode's analysis of *Ovid's Banquet of Sense (Bulletin of the John Rylands Library*, 44 [1961], 68-99) and with D. J. Gordon's seminal essay on "Chapman's *Hero and Leander*" (*English Miscellany*, ed. Mario Praz, vol. V [1954], 41-91) will be aware of the intricacy of these poems and of the critical issues they raise. Two recent dissertations on Chapman's poetry, A. R. Braunmuller's "Art's Commiseration of Truth: *Hero and Leander* and Chapman's Major Tragedies" (Yale, 1971) and John Huntington's "The Early Poems of George Chapman" (University of California, Berkeley, 1972), promise that we will soon have an even fuller sense of Chapman's achievement. If I have therefore restricted my treatment of Chapman to passing references and brief, generalized comparisons, I have done so with an awareness that he is a major participant in what Nigel Alexander aptly refers to as the "Ovidian debate" of the 1590s (*Elizabethan Narrative Verse*, p. 17).

Finally, let me say just a word about Spenser, who is himself, in a very different way from Shakespeare and Marlowe, or from Chapman for that matter, an Ovidian poet. Although there are specific references to Spenser's poetry throughout this study, I have reserved a direct assessment of his relation to the epyllia of the 1590s for the Conclusion. I offer this Conclusion as a suggestive and provocative (as opposed to exhaustive and definitive) view of a complicated moment in literary history: my hope is to end the book by opening the argument out rather than by closing it off.

PART ONE

Exploration and Achievement in the Elizabethan Epyllion

Chapter I

Ovid and "Ovidian" Poetry

❦

. . . the sweete wittie soule of *Ovid* lives
in mellifluous & hony-tongued *Shakespeare*. . . .

Francis Meres, *Palladis Tamia* (1598)

Lavinia, wert thou thus surpris'd, sweet girl?
Ravish'd and wrong'd as Philomela was,
Forc'd in the ruthless, vast, and gloomy woods?
See, See!
Ay, such a place there is where we did hunt
(O had we never, never hunted there!),
Pattern'd by that the poet here describes,
By nature made for murthers and for rapes.

Shakespeare, *Titus Andronicus* (ca. 1593-1594)

In 1968 a prominent American classicist began a review of Brooks Otis's *Ovid as an Epic Poet* with the observation that "Ovid's *Metamorphoses* is the most difficult major poem the Graeco-Roman world has bequeathed to us."[1] Since the mid-1950s, when L. P. Wilkinson's *Ovid Recalled* (1955) and the bimillenial celebration in 1957 of Ovid's birth initiated a major critical revaluation, numerous studies have addressed themselves to the elusive complexity of Ovid's poetry. But with very few exceptions, this complexity has not been adequately recognized in studies of Ovid's influence on poetry of the English Renaissance. Elizabethan epyllia and the poets who wrote them are habitually called "Ovidian," but little effort has been made to say what the adjectival form of Ovid's name ought to mean. Few writers have even acknowledged with D. J. Gordon that for the Renaissance its meaning is rich and complicated.[2] Of course, if one is content to use "Ovidian" to refer to nothing more than the borrowing of narrative material from the *Metamorphoses* and to an interest in eroticism which Elizabethan "Ovidian" poets share with Ovid in some general way, any attempt to examine the term more carefully may seem pointless. But if one suspects that the relationship between Ovid's poetry and the Elizabethan epyllion goes deeper than this perfunctory use of

3

"Ovidian" assumes, then some investigation of what the term should mean becomes imperative.

I want to establish as clearly as I can in this first chapter those aspects of Ovid's poetry which I presuppose in applying "Ovidian" to the epyllia of Shakespeare, Marlowe, and their contemporaries. It is not my intention here or in subsequent chapters to deny the importance of the traditional medieval and Renaissance attitudes towards Ovid found in earlier mythological poetry, in moralized and allegorical commentaries, in mythographical treatises and dictionaries, in emblem books. These attitudes are often relevant to our reading of Elizabethan epyllia, even— perhaps especially—when that relevance is indirect and ironic. It does seem to me, however, that in the case of the epyllion traditional medieval and Renaissance sources have often been wrongly invoked to the virtual exclusion of Ovid himself. Granting the methodological differences between literary criticism and art history, my approach here is similar to Svetlana Alpers' in her recent study of Rubens' *Decoration of the Torre de la Parada* (1971). She shows that in these mythological designs for the hunting lodge of Philip IV of Spain, conceived and executed during the 1630s, Rubens was primarily inspired by Ovid's own poetry rather than by the standard illustrated editions, that he responded to and adapted Ovid with great sensitivity and creative freedom, and that his adaptations are essentially fictional and dramatic, rather than allegorical, in their appeal. My contention will be that Elizabethan poets of the 1590s were also exploring Ovid's poetry, both in English translation and in the original Latin, with a new imaginative intensity, and that the influence of medieval and previous Renaissance adaptations and commentaries should be understood in relation to the Elizabethan poet's response to his primary source.

No poet suffers more from a rigidly schematized critical approach than Ovid. But for the purpose of clarifying our idea of "Ovidian" we may distinguish three large, interrelated issues which are particularly important in understanding what the authors of Elizabethan epyllia saw in Ovid and how they responded poetically to what they saw. To begin with, there is Ovid's attitude towards ancient myth itself. The tone of Ovid's mythological episodes and allusions is as much a part of the epyllion-writer's source, I would suggest, as are the basic details of the narrative. It is often Ovid's self-conscious way of presenting an already familiar myth that is the interesting influence to watch. Secondly, Ovid's view of erotic experience, however varied in its development from the *Amores* through the *Ars Amatoria* and *Heroides* and into the *Metamorphoses*, can nevertheless be discussed in terms of certain prevailing features. The most important feature—the one which subsumes all others—is ambivalence: a constantly active and poised awareness that sexual love can be humorous, grotesque, and animal-like in its savagery as well as beautiful, emotionally compelling, and an essential part of what it means to be human. Finally, there is Ovid's stylistic virtuosity, the quality for which he was most often praised by the Elizabethans. Here again one has to take into account significant variations in the poetic technique of "sweet-lipp'd Ovid,"[3] from the archly sophisticated elegiacs of the *Amores* to the loftier and more stylized epic hexameters of the *Metamorphoses*. But Ovid's extraordinary verbal ingenuity pervades his entire oeuvre, and it held a special fascination for Elizabethan writers who had been trained as schoolboys to see Ovid as a supreme stylistic model.

It goes without saying that each of these aspects of Ovid's poetry underwent considerable transformation in the process of being adapted to the idiom and the expressive conventions of late sixteenth-century poetry. It is a critical commonplace, for instance, to point out that Elizabethan "Ovidian" poets felt free to introduce "anachronistic" images and ideas from their own environment. And in every epyllion conspicuous departures from the Ovidian source are as important as the metaphorical patterns and rhetorical strategies borrowed from it. But more often than not these adaptive transformations and departures are themselves extensions of the Elizabethan poet's exploration of his Ovidian subject. One must also remember that Ovid's influence could be exerted from different parts of his oeuvre at the same time. The Elizabethan epyllion-writer will frequently elaborate a moment from an episode in the *Metamorphoses* in a way which reflects his familiarity with the witty informality of the *Amores* or the *Ars Amatoria*, or with the impassioned rhetoric of the *Heroides*. The eclectic indirectness of Ovid's influence on the epyllion makes it all the more important that we have a clearer grasp of what the basic dimensions of that influence are.

Recent studies of Ovid's poetry all agree in emphasizing the sophisticated distance from which he regards the gods and goddesses of ancient myth.[4] Ovid no more "believed in" the literal or supernatural existence of Jupiter and Juno, or of Venus and Adonis, than did Shakespeare and Marlowe. To appropriate a valuable distinction expounded by Frank Kermode in *The Sense of an Ending*, Ovid treats the ancient tales of the gods and goddesses not as *myths*, but as *fictions*.[5] In a well-known but often misread passage in the *Ars Amatoria*, Ovid appears to attribute a rather cynical pragmatic value to believing in the gods: "It is expedient that there should be gods, and since it is expedient let us deem that gods exist" (I. 637). But the passage in which this line occurs shows that the speaker's cynical expediency here is itself merely part of a more comprehensive artistic irony governing Ovid's attitude towards the ancient gods:

> Nec timide promitte: trahunt promissa puellas;
>   Pollicito testes quoslibet adde deos.
> Iuppiter ex alto periuria ridet amantum,
>   Et iubet Aeolios inrita ferre notos.
> Per Styga Iunoni falsum iurare solebat
>   Iuppiter; exemplo nunc favet ipse suo.
> Expedit esse deos, et, ut expedit, esse putemus;
>   Dentur in antiquos tura merumque focos;
> Nec secura quies illos similisque sopori
>   Detinet; innocue vivite: numen adest;
>
>   (I. 631-640)

[And do not be timid in your promises: women are betrayed by promises; make offering to whatever gods you please. From on high Jupiter smiles at the perjuries of lovers, and bids the winds of Aeolus carry them away without consequence. Jupiter was accustomed to swearing falsely by Styx to Juno; now he looks favorably on his own example. It is expedient that there should be gods, and since it is expedient, let us believe that gods exist; let incense and wine be poured on the ancient hearths; carefree quiet like sleep does not hold them off; live innocently, divinity is close by. . . .]

Throughout his early poetry Ovid uses the gods and the myths about them as he does in this very passage, to fictionalize with unremitting irony the erotic motivations and modes of behavior which are his principal subject. In the *Metamorphoses* his approach to myth becomes more elevated and more subtly symbolic, but in many episodes he continues to see the gods ironically, even parodically.[6]

The exaggerated anthropomorphism which Wilkinson and others have seen as a major source of the comedy in Ovid's poetry is of primary importance to the Elizabethan epyllion. Lodge, Shakespeare, Marlowe, and their followers exploit this strategy over and over again. And since the Elizabethans found ancient myth in Ovid's poetry already infused with a wittily intensified anthropomorphism, they tended to take the technique even further and to humanize the gods and goddesses in more broadly comic terms. In the episode of Glaucus and Scylla, for example, Ovid introduces only the slightest hint of comic deflation at the end of Glaucus's account of his bizarre transformation into a sea-god. Yet this hint makes the reader aware of the way in which the entire speech, given the rhetorical situation, verges on the grotesquely humorous:

> hanc ego tum primum viridi ferrugine barbam
> caesariemque meam, quam longa per aequora verro,
> ingentesque umeros et caerula bracchia vidi
> cruraque pinnigero curvata novissima pisce.
> quid tamen haec species, quid dis placuisse marinis,
> quid iuvat esse deum, si tu non tangeris istis?"
>
> (XIII. 960–963)

[Then for the first time I saw this rust-green beard and this hair of mine, which I sweep through the wide sea, these huge shoulders and blue arms and these legs curving and tapering into a finny fish. And yet, what joy is there in this appearance, in pleasing the gods of the sea, in being a god myself, if you are not moved by these things?]

But when Lodge tells how the love-sick Glaucus in his epyllion pauses in recounting his misfortunes in love to "shake his heavie head, / And fold his armes, and then unfold them straight" (ll. 43–44), he is exaggerating this characteristically Ovidian device and bringing it much closer to overt mythological burlesque. Shakespeare extends the strategy of comically exaggerated anthropomorphism in a similar manner when he tells how Venus sweats in pursuit of Adonis (ll. 175–180), Marlowe when he tells how Neptune cavorts ludicrously in pursuit of Leander (II. 167 ff.).

Comic anthropomorphism may be the most conspicuous manifestation of Ovid's urbane detachment from the ancient myths, but it is not the only manifestation. Consider, for instance, his way of handling one of the fundamental aspects of genuine myth and mythopoeic writing: that mysterious interrelationship between mythological figure and nature which allows mythic and natural identities to merge and to be projected as a single undifferentiated reality. Even in the *Metamorphoses* Ovid approaches this aspect of myth with a self-dramatizing verbal virtuosity which is, in its ultimate poetic effect, anti-mythopoeic. In Book IV he describes the beautiful nymph Salmacis in terms which almost duplicate those he applies to the pool she inhabits:[7]

> . . . videt hic stagnum *lucentis* ad imum
>   usque solum lymphae;
>
> (IV. 297–298: my italics)

> *perspicuus* liquor est; stagni tamen ultima vivo
> caespite cinguntur semperque virentibus *herbis*.
>
> (IV. 300–301: my italics)

[Here he saw a pool of water clear to the very bottom. . . . it was clear water. But the edges of the pool were ringed with fresh turf and grass that was always green.]

> nunc *perlucenti* circumdata corpus amictu
> mollibus aut foliis aut mollibus incubat *herbis,*
> (IV. 313–314: my italics)

[Now, her body wrapped in a transparent robe, she lay down on the soft leaves or on the soft grass.]

The artfulness of these descriptions is not being displayed merely for its own sake. As we shall see when we come to consider Beaumont's *Salmacis and Hermaphroditus,* it is important to the way in which the water symbolism functions in this episode that Salmacis should be linked metaphorically to her pool. The point, however, is that the reader's attention is engaged not through any appeal to a supernatural identification of the nymph with the pool, but through the metaphorical and rhetorical ties between the two descriptions. The total poetic effect depends, moreover, upon an awareness of simultaneous similarity and difference: Salmacis is significantly like her pool, but she is also significantly human in her pride and self-indulgence. In the line immediately preceding the description of her robe of water-like transparency, we are told that she uses the water as a mirror to admire her own beauty:

> et, quid se deceat, spectatas consulit undas;
> (IV. 312)

[And looked in the mirror-like waters to see what became her.]

This kind of clever toying with the mysterious internal connections of myth is deeply characteristic of Ovid. The reader is constantly made aware of the self-consciously ingenious verbal artistry through which the supernatural identities of myth are converted into the fictional identities of poetry.

The most brilliant adaptation in the Elizabethan epyllion of Ovid's exploitation of ambiguous mythical identity is Marlowe's account of Neptune's antics as Leander swims across the Hellespont. The passage in *Hero and Leander* is indicative of the way in which Ovid's mythological wit informs Marlowe's reworking of Musaeus:

> He watch'd his arms, and as they open'd wide
> At every stroke, betwixt them would he slide.
> (II. 183–184)

Rosemond Tuve urged us not to make too much of this passage, arguing that Elizabethan readers accustomed to the conventional poetic substitution of Neptune for the sea would have immediately translated Neptune's lovemaking into an account of the caressing flow of the water.[8] But Clifford Leech describes more accurately Marlowe's recreation of the Ovidian strategy at work in this passage: ". . . we have the double sense of the movement of the water and of the god's amorous pranks."[9] Like Ovid, Marlowe plays mythical and fictional identities off against one another; the mysterious convergences of myth are recalled and then exploited as occasions for arresting verbal and symbolic ingenuity.

An effect closely related to the ambiguous differentiation of mythological figure and natural phenomenon occurs in those transformations in the *Metamorphoses* in which a god takes the form of an animal in order to pursue his lustful purposes, or in which a mortal is transformed into an animal, plant, or some other lower form of life. Ovid will often allow the two states of existence—untransformed and transformed—to coexist. The poetic result may be grotesquely comic, as when Jove takes the form of a bull to woo Europa:

> sed quamvis mitem metuit contingere primo,
> mox adit et flores ad candida porrigit ora.
> gaudet amans et, dum veniat sperata voluptas,
> oscula dat manibus; vix iam, vix cetera differt;
> et nunc adludit viridique exsultat in herba,
>
> (II. 860–864)

[But, although he seemed gentle, she was afraid at first to touch him. Then she went closer and held out flowers to his snow-white lips. The lover was delighted and, until his hoped-for pleasure should come, kissed her hands. Only with great difficulty could he wait for the rest; and now he played and cavorted on the green grass. . . .]

In the preceding book, with the metamorphosis of Io into a heifer, the effect of allowing transformed and untransformed identities to coexist is less humorous and more disturbingly grotesque:[10]

> et conata queri mugitus edidit ore
> pertimuitque sonos propriaque exterrita voce est.
> venit et ad ripas, ubi ludere saepe solebat,
> Inachidas: rictus novaque ut conspexit in unda
> cornua, pertimuit seque exsternata refugit.
>
> (I. 637–641)

[And when she tried to complain, a moo issued from her lips, and she was afraid and terrified by the sound of her own voice. And she came to the banks of her father Inachus's river, where she often used to play; but when she saw in the water her gaping jaws and her new horns, she was terrified and fled, frightened by herself.]

In the following chapters, particularly in the discussions of *Venus and Adonis* and of *Salmacis and Hermaphroditus*, we shall see how the Elizabethans followed Ovid in exploiting the ambiguity of transformation and metamorphosis, an ambiguity brought about by the existence of permanence, continuation, or (in the case of Shakespeare's Adonis) symbolically significant similarity in the context of outward change. What I want to emphasize here is that this technique, like the exaggerated anthropomorphism and the interplay of mythological figure and natural phenomenon, presupposes a self-consciously ironic detachment from the myths being recounted.

Ovid felt free to alter and elaborate the ancient myths as they came down to him, and even to invent new aspects of his mythological narrative, as long as the most important elements of the traditional version remained intact. This freedom to invent and elaborate is of great importance for the Elizabethan epyllion. In fact Elizabethan poets go beyond Ovid in their fondness for creating their own mythological variants. Central to this freedom of invention in both Ovid and the Elizabethans is the etiological tradition of providing causal explanations for natural and human phenomena by means of myths and fables. Ovid himself inherited the etiological tradition from the Hellenistic poets, above all from Callimachus, whose *Aetia* was one of the most popular books of later antiquity.[11] Ovid's exploitation of etiology in the *Metamorphoses*, however, is even more clever, subtle, and ironic than that of Callimachus in the *Aetia*. The reader may not even think of the story of Apollo and Daphne as an explanation of how the laurel wreath came to have its symbolic significance as the crown of the great poet, so skillfully has Ovid woven the etiological motif into his tale. Yet he has Apollo himself make this motif explicit:

> cui deus "at, quoniam coniunx mea non potes esse,
> arbor eris certe" dixit "mea! semper habebunt
> te coma, te citharae, te nostrae, laure, pharetrae;
> tu ducibus Latiis aderis, cum laeta Triumphum
> vox canet et visent longas Capitolia pompas;
>
> (I. 557–561)

[Then the god said: "Since you cannot be my bride, you will at least be my tree. My hair, my lyre, my quiver will always bear the laurel. You will accompany the generals of Rome, when joyful voices sing their triumph, and they are seen in their long processions to the Capitol. . . ."]

Ovid adds a characteristically ironic touch to Apollo's paean by having the laurel tree respond to the god's words in a way which suggests the continuing consciousness of the metamorphosed Daphne:

> factis modo laurea ramis
> adnuit utque caput visa est agitasse cacumen.
> (I. 566–567)

[The laurel waved her new-made branches and seemed to nod her head-like top in consent.]

Among the Elizabethan Ovidians Marlowe is especially alert to the possibilities which etiology affords for spinning out one's own mythological variants. He often exploits it on a much smaller scale than is characteristic of Ovid, and the sheer delight in mythological invention is more obvious. But he also uses it for extended episodes: the "digression" of Mercury and the country maid at the end of the First Sestiad, for instance, is offered as an explanation ("Harken a while, and I will tell you why," I. 385) of the enmity between love and destiny. Marlowe's extravagant mythological inventions represent a remarkable extension of the freedom Ovid exhibits in this direction. And the etiological conceits and digressions of *Hero and Leander* provided the major inspiration for writers of later epyllia to create their own versions of established myths.

I have been emphasizing the comically ironic and playfully inventive manifestations of Ovid's sophisticated detachment from ancient myth because these qualities are so prominent in the Elizabethan epyllion. But there is another side to Ovid's handling of myth—a darker side which springs from an awareness of the violence and terror inherent in these narratives even after they have lost their original supernatural or religious significance. Charles Segal has written very perceptively about this darker side of the *Metamorphoses:*

"*Lascivia*[12] is the word which Quintilian uses to characterize the art of Ovid (Inst. Or. 4.1.77, 10.1.88 and 93). No one would deny that the term is well chosen. But for all its levity, the *Metamorphoses* has a grim and sombre side. Penetrating beneath Ovid's fluent grace of language and versification, his charm of narrative, his wit and abundance of invention, his apt turning of rhetorical *topoi*, one finds a poem pervaded by violence, cruelty, and arbitrary suffering. . . ."[13]

It is this grim side of Ovid's approach to myth, coupled as it is with sophisticated irony, comedy, and playfulness, which makes the *Metamorphoses* so enigmatic.

Nowhere is the enigmatic conjunction of the witty and the painful more apparent than in the metamorphoses themselves, which are inherently violent—a destruction of existing form and identity.[14] Time and time again Ovid narrates these moments of violent, painful transformation with a display of verbal cunning which leaves the reader in the most ambiguous of positions. Consider, for example, the following lines in which Ovid's narrator comments on the plea of one of the daughters of Helios and Clymene as she and her sisters are being changed into trees:

> cortex in verba novissima venit.
> inde fluunt lacrimae, stillataque sole rigescunt
> de ramis electra novis, quae lucidus amnis
> excipit et nuribus mittit gestanda Latinis.
> (II. 363–366)

[. . . the bark closed over her last words. From it tears flowed which, hardened into amber by the sun and dropped down from the new-made branches, the shining river received and sent on to be worn by the brides of Rome.]

The ambiguous merging of original and transformed identities (the tears clearly belong to the daughters, yet Ovid says they fall "from the new-made trees," "de ramis . . . novis") and the irony of making Helios himself responsible for turning the tears into amber ("sole rigescunt") are characteristic Ovidian maneuvers. The transformation of the tears into amber suggests metaphorically the way in which the reader's sense of the gruesome actuality of the metamorphosis has been stimulated in line 363 ("cortex in verba novissima venit") only to be distanced by the elegant image of the last line and a half (the omission of an explicit reference to the tears first changing into resin is an important aspect of Ovid's manipulation of the reader here).[15] The horror of physical transformation lingers in the mind as we watch ourselves being carried into a realm of sophisticated, urbane allusion. An examination of the metamorphoses of Actaeon (III. 193–252), Callisto (II. 477–495), and Scylla (XIV. 59–67) will reveal comparable instances of this simultaneity of violence, pain, and grotesqueness on the one hand and of ironic distance, verbal wit, and comedy on the other.

Segal is right to say that "this mixture of violence and urbanity presents a genuine problem."[16] Is Ovid merely subverting the reader's expectations of a unified response and catering to a taste for the bizarre and the morbid, or is he using his ambiguously rendered fables of metamorphosis to some more positive artistic purpose? An analogous problem will arise in our consideration of Elizabethan epyllia. It is relatively easy to talk about the Elizabethans' indebtedness to the ironically distanced and witty dimension of Ovid's handling of ancient myth; the real difficulty comes in trying to evaluate their comprehension of the darker aspects of his poetry. In the poems of Lodge, Edwards, and Beaumont one encounters an Ovidian "mixture of violence and urbanity," but one sometimes finds it difficult to see any coherent thematic significance in the clever juxtapositions of dissonant elements. With Shakespeare and Marlowe, as with Ovid himself, the "mixture of violence and urbanity" is even more disturbingly ambiguous—but it is also more coherently expressive of important perceptions about human erotic experience. *Venus and Adonis* and *Hero and Leander* are deeply Ovidian both in their resistance to the confines of traditional thematic exegesis and in their resistance to being dismissed as mere sophisticated poetic entertainment.

One of the features of Ovid's poetry which allows his urbane ambivalence to become more deeply expressive is his unobtrusive use of symbolic description and imagery. Nothing could differ more from the rigid allegorical and moralizing impositions of so many of Ovid's medieval and Renaissance interpreters than the deftness and openness of his own handling of symbolic detail. His account of the flower which Venus causes to spring from Adonis's blood at the end of Book X of the *Metamorphoses* provides a disturbingly beautiful instance of these qualities:

> sic fata cruorem
> nectare odorato sparsit, qui tactus ab illo
> intumuit sic, ut fulvo perlucida caeno
> surgere bulla solet, nec plena longior hora
> facta mora est, cum flos de sanguine concolor ortus,
> qualem, quae lento celant sub cortice granum,
> punica ferre solent; brevis est tamen usus in illo;
> namque male haerentem et nimia levitate caducum
> excutiunt idem, qui praestant nomina, venti."
>
> (X. 731-739)

[So saying, with fragrant nectar she sprinkled the blood which, touched by it, swelled as when clear bubbles rise up from yellow mud; and no longer than an hour's time had passed when a flower sprang up of blood-red color, like that borne by pomegranates, which hide their seed under a resistant skin. But brief is the enjoyment of this flower, for so weakly and lightly attached is it, and destined to fall, that the very winds which give it its name shake it off.]

Much that is haunting about *Venus and Adonis* grows out of Shakespeare's poetic response to Ovid's evocation here of an unyielding yet vulnerable beauty seen in relation to an almost visceral physical immediacy and to an inexorably destructive natural force. This kind of symbolic suggestiveness pervades the *Metamorphoses,* and it is important not because it compensates for or counteracts what Quintillian referred to as Ovid's "lascivia" by giving the poetry clear conceptual significance, but rather because it extends the ambivalence so central to Ovid's urbane humor and irony in a way which unobtrusively enlarges our sense of the human turbulence and pathos latent in the ancient mythological fictions.

Ovid's approach to erotic experience is inextricably bound up with his approach to ancient myth. In the *Amores,* the *Heroides,* and the *Ars Amatoria,* as we have already seen, myth is used primarily to dramatize erotic and amatory themes. In the *Metamorphoses,* this interrelationship may be stated in reverse: sexual desire figures prominently in almost every episode in which the gods and goddesses are the protagonists. The very idea of metamorphoses may have deep-lying psycho-cultural connections with sexuality.[17] Additional perceptions about Ovid's fictionalizing of myth will emerge as we direct our attention to his presentation of sexual love. But as a critical strategy, separating the issues of myth and sexual experience will help us clarify some of the more elusive aspects of Ovid's writing, and it will enable us to take into account those aspects of Ovid's handling of erotic and amatory themes in the elegiac poems which are not directly involved with myth but which nevertheless exert a recurrent influence on the Elizabethan epyllion.

Ovid's handling of erotic experience in the early elegiac poetry, although not without its darker, complicating elements, is essentially comic. In the very first poem of the *Amores* Ovid intimates that "love will be treated not seriously, but in a half-humorous, detached, Hellenistic spirit."[18] He complains that Cupid himself is responsible for having stolen away a metrical foot from the epic hexameters he intended to write ("risisse Cupido / dicitur atque unum surripuisse pedem," (ll. 3–4) and for the subject matter to which his elegiacs will give expression:

> lunavitque genu sinuosum fortiter arcum
> "quod" que "canas, vates, accipe" dixit "opus!"
> (I.i.23–24)

[He stoutly bent moonshape the sinuous bow against his knee and said:
"Poet, take that which you will sing about in your work!"]

Though comedy and wit are more prominent in some parts of the *Amores*
than in others, they are never entirely absent. The entire work, filled as it
is with "paradox, conceit, exaggeration and a sort of insinuating *savoir-
faire*,"[19] may be seen as a burlesque of the Augustan elegiac tradition.
    These qualities are all vividly present in the second elegy of the third
book, in which the speaker attempts to seduce his mistress at the horse
races and manages in the end to win at least a tantalizing promise:

> Risit, et argutis quiddam promisit ocellis.
> "Hoc satis hic; alio cetera redde loco!"
> (III.ii.83–84)

[She smiled, and with speaking eyes promised something. "That is enough
for here—give up the rest in some other place!"]

This particular poem also provides a direct anticipation of Ovid's
pseudo-didactic treatise on love, the *Ars Amatoria*.[20] One of the best-
known passages in the *Ars Amatoria* cleverly echoes *Amores* III.ii and
explains why the horse races are an especially advantageous place for
seduction:

> Cuius equi veniant, facito, studiose, requiras:
>   Nec mora, quisquis erit, cui favet illa, fave.
> At cum pompa frequens certantibus ibit ephebis,
>   Tu Veneri dominae plaude favente manu;
> Utque fit, in gremium pulvis si forte puellae
>   Deciderit, digitis excutiendus erit;
> Et si nullus erit pulvis, tamen excute nullum:
>   (I. 145–151)

[You should ask eagerly and quickly whose horses are entering: and do not
delay—whomever she favors, you favor too, no matter who it is. But when the
crowded procession of competing youths passes by, applaud the rule of Venus
with favoring hand. And if by chance it should happen that dust falls on your
lady's lap, let it be flicked off with your fingers: and if there is no dust, flick it
off anyway. . . .]

The sensibility behind both the *Amores* and the *Ars Amatoria*, though
differently projected, is consistently that of the witty connoisseur of erotic
experience. However passionately beautiful and tormenting sexual love is

to those directly involved in it, to the sophisticated observer it inevitably seems amusing. It is when the speaker of the *Amores* comments as an observer on his own erotic intrigues that the comic dimension of these poems is most conspicuous. And since the speaker of the *Ars Amatoria* is always the wry, experienced observer, Ovid's writing here is more pervasively comic than anywhere else in his oeuvre. Of course Ovid's real genius lies, as we shall see, in his ability to present erotic experience from both perspectives, from that of the participant and from that of the observer. But because this latter perspective is especially important for the epyllion-writers of the 1590s, the witty nonchalance so characteristic of Ovid's early elegiac poems deserves particular attention.

The comedy and wit of Ovid's approach to erotic experience undergo a complex transformation in the *Metamorphoses*. Comedy and wit are still important, particularly in the first two books, where, as Otis remarks, "divine majesty or dignity . . . is deflated at the first touch of love. The epic style of life simply cannot maintain itself under erotic stress."[21] Otis is referring specifically here to Apollo's passion for Daphne, and it is true that at moments this passion is made to appear humorous. But it is also disturbingly grotesque and painful, all the more so because of the touching urgency of Apollo's love:

> Hanc quoque Phoebus amat positaque in stipite dextra
> sentit adhuc trepidare novo sub cortice pectus
> conplexusque suis ramos ut membra lacertis
> oscula dat ligno; refugit tamen oscula lignum.
>
> (I. 553–556)

[Phoebus loved even this form, and, placing his hand on the trunk, he felt the heart still fluttering beneath the bark. And embracing the branches as if they were human limbs, he kissed the wood; but even the wood shrank from his kisses.]

Throughout the *Metamorphoses* one finds erotic passion presented in terms of this oscillation between or simultaneity of the comic and the grotesque. Erotic comedy in the *Metamorphoses* is constantly verging on the grotesque, and, vice versa, the grotesqueness of violent lust is often made to seem laughable. Thus Ovid's comedy comes to assume a somewhat different role than it had in the *Amores* and *Ars Amatoria*. In the face of this recurrent qualification of the comic by the grotesque, the witty sophistication of the earlier elegiac poems evolves into something much less reassuring, much more deeply problematic.

In trying to come to terms with the troubling violence and grotesqueness of the *Metamorphoses,* Wilkinson and other scholars have examined the degree to which Ovid was influenced by the "predilection of Hellenistic poets for stories of monstrous or forbidden love."[22] The episodes in which Jupiter and other gods assume animal forms in order to pursue the mortal objects of their lust involve, however indirectly, the idea of sexual relations between human beings and beasts, a not uncommon theme in Hellenistic fiction. We have already seen how Ovid exploits both the comedy and the grotesqueness of such episodes in the story of Europa in Book II, and one could single out other examples— Jupiter and Leda, Pasiphaë and the bull. It would be wrong to assume, however, that Ovid's interest in these episodes involving a bestial transformation of the sexual pursuer is primarily sensationalistic, as it was in the poetry of most of his Hellenistic predecessors. The thematic import of these episodes turns upon an awareness of the fundamentally animalistic dimension of sexual experience, a dimension which Ovid compels his readers to acknowledge along with the comedy and the emotive lyricism of love. The mere mention of Shakespeare's Venus and of the animal imagery associated with her should be sufficient to indicate the importance for the Elizabethan epyllion of Ovid's concern with sexual desire in its grotesque, animalistic manifestation.

Two other subjects common in Hellenistic literature may be mentioned here in connection with Ovid's interest in "stories of monstrous or forbidden love." One of these is incest. A number of episodes in the *Metamorphoses* deal with incest, and Ovid's handling of the grotesque possibilities of such stories may be seen in his account of the love of Myrrha (Adonis's mother) for her father Cinyras. Myrrha's own words establish, ironically, the link between incestuous passion and animal lust:

> coeunt animalia nullo
> cetera dilectu, nec habetur turpe iuvencae
> ferre patrem tergo, fit equo sua filia coniunx,
> quasque creavit init pecudes caper, ipsaque, cuius
> semine concepta est, ex illo concipit ales.
> felices, quibus ista licent!
>
> (X. 324-329)

[Other animals mate with no discrimination: there is no disgrace for a heifer if her father should mount her; a horse makes his own daughter his wife; the goat goes in among the flocks he has sired, and even the bird conceives from him by whose seed she was conceived. Happy creatures, who are allowed such behavior!]

The authors of Elizabethan epyllia show no particular interest in Ovid's tales of incest, although the Jacobeans, not surprisingly, do: William Barksted's *Myrra, the Mother of Adonis; or Lustes Prodegies* appeared in 1607. The Elizabethans were, however, interested in another category of tales concerning deviant sexuality which most Ovidian scholars have treated as "stories of monstrous or forbidden love"—namely, tales concerning homosexuality.

Most of Ovid's commentators have been anxious to show that he repudiated homosexual love. "It does him credit," Fränkel writes, "that, in contrast to the other poets and the whole body of society of his time, he demurred at homosexual love, and offered a characteristic reason for his heterodoxy."[23] The "reason" cited by Fränkel appears in a passage from Book II of the *Ars Amatoria:*

> Odi concubitus, qui non utrumque resolvunt;
> Hoc est, cur pueri tangar amore minus.
> (II. 683–684)

[I hate copulation which does not satisfy both; that is why the love of a boy appeals less.]

Wilkinson offers a somewhat more balanced and open-minded assessment of Ovid's attitude towards homoeroticism, but he too is less helpful on this issue than on other aspects of Ovid's poetry. The "infrequency and restraint" with which Ovid deals with homoeroticism, he argues, suggests a positive decision on Ovid's part not to emphasize a theme which held a special prominence in the poetry of his Hellenistic forerunners.[24] Wilkinson mentions Jupiter's rape of Ganymede (*Metamorphoses* X. 155 and XI. 756) and Apollo's love for Cyparissus (X. 106–142) as the only clear instances of homoeroticism in Ovid's narrative repertory. He later praises the stories of Narcissus and of Hermaphroditus as "two of the most haunting episodes of the whole poem," but he hastens to add that they "deal with abnormal sexuality of a slightly different kind."[25]

The concern of Ovid's modern interpreters to assert his dislike of homoeroticism has led to an unfortunate inflexibility towards those moments in his poetry where this subject is undeniably and significantly present. Neither Narcissus nor Hermaphroditus actually engages in homosexual love, but both are described as androgynously beautiful youths and both find the sexual advances of women repellent. And the song of Orpheus in Book X of the *Metamorphoses,* where both the Pygmalion and the Venus and Adonis stories are told, is strongly conditioned by the fact that after the loss of Eurydice Orpheus shunned all love of women ("omnemque refugerat Orpheus / femineam Venerem," X. 79–80) and set the example for the people of Thrace by giving his love to young boys ("ille etiam Thracum populis fuit auctor amorem / in teneros transferre mares," X. 83–84). The point to be made, I would suggest, is not that Ovid disapproved of homoeroticism, but that he refused to exploit it in the furtive, sensationalistic way characteristic of much Hellenistic and Roman erotic poetry. He does not use episodes involving homoeroticism, just as he does not use episodes involving bestial transformation or incest, merely as negative contrasts to an ideal of "true, normal, even conjugal love."[26] Rather, he presents homoeroticism with the same ambivalence which distinguishes his presentation of all erotic experience. Homosexual love, like heterosexual love, can be violent and grotesque as well as beautiful and attractive. Therefore, when we come to consider the presence of homoeroticism in the Elizabethan epyllion (manifested most often in the figure of the softly beautiful youth averse to heterosexual love), we shall not be talking about a kind of erotic experience which Ovid himself regarded as abominable and degrading. We shall instead be talking about a kind of experience which Ovid handles infrequently and with restraint but which is nonetheless present, in a richly evocative way, in "two of the most haunting episodes of the whole poem," those of Narcissus and Hermaphroditus. These two episodes have, as it happens, a thematic importance for the Elizabethan epyllion which far exceeds their obvious significance as the main sources for epyllia by Thomas Edwards and Francis Beaumont.

Another erotic motif of special importance for the epyllion also has its antecedents in Ovid's ambivalent approach to sexual love. This is the aggressive female wooer.[27] Otis lays considerable stress on the motif of frustrated "feminine libido" in the *Metamorphoses* and shows how this motif functions in the stories of Medea, Scylla, Deianira, Byblis, and Myrrha.[28] He has less to say about the Ovidian figures who become the aggressive female wooers of Elizabethan epyllia—Scylla (the lover of Glaucus), Venus, Oenone, Aurora, Salmacis—but many of his perceptions about Ovid's interest in what he terms the "pathology"[29] of frustrated feminine libido can be applied to these figures as well. In some respects the term "pathology" is not ill-chosen: the sexual desire of Byblis and of Myrrha, for example, is not only uncontrollable, it is also incestuous. But even in these two stories the chief emphasis falls on the savage fury of desire, a fury which Ovid presents as a kind of awesome natural phenomenon. Byblis discovers that her beloved twin brother Caunus has fled from her embraces:

Tum vero maestam tota Miletida mente
defecisse ferunt, tum vero a pectore vestem
diripuit planxitque suos furibunda lacertos;
iamque palam est demens, inconcessamque fatetur
spem veneris, . . .

(IX. 635–639)

[Then, in truth, the wretched daughter of Miletus went completely out of her
mind; then, in truth, she tore the garments from her breast and beat her arms
in mad passion. Now she was openly demented, and confessed her hope of
forbidden love. . . .]

In contrast to the sexual exploits of Jove, Neptune, or Mercury, where an
element of comedy is usually present to offset the terror and grotesqueness
of divine lust, the sexually obsessed women of the *Metamorphoses* are
rarely, if ever, comic. In the story of Biblys, for instance, the ambivalence
arises not from the coexistence of comedy and grotesqueness, but from the
way in which both the moral repugnance and the pathetic quality of her
dilemma are made to seem insignificant in comparison with the sheer
violence of her passion. In Elizabethan epyllia, on the other hand, the
aggressive female wooer is often treated comically and even satirically,
and this has to do, as we shall see, with her function as an anti-type of the
chaste, idealized, cruelly reluctant mistress so prominent in Renaissance
lyric and pastoral poetry. But the savagery and violence of frustrated
feminine libido are also present in the epyllion and indicate that Lodge,
Shakespeare, and Beaumont were responsive to Ovid's tormented and
desperate women.

To insist as I have done on the ambivalence of Ovid's attitude
towards sexual experience tends to make his poetry seem less emotionally
engaging than it really is. There is an aloof, detached, almost cruel aspect
to Ovid's writing in the *Metamorphoses,* and this aspect is one of the most
troubling things about the poem. But as the examples of feminine lust I
have cited make apparent, there is also that quality for which Ovid has
long been praised—an ability to evoke, even in the most bizarre of
mythological situations, the presence of intense, individualized emotion.
It is because Ovid's ambivalence is so often engaged with deeply emotive
experience that the modulations into cool, detached observation disturb
us as they do. At times Ovid's narrator will lead the reader into an episode
of extreme emotional intensity and then, at a climactic moment, distance
himself with refined calculation from both narrative and reader.

To understand the importance for the Elizabethan epyllion of Ovid's
approach to what, for want of a better term, we may call "the pathos of

love,"[30] we must again look back from the *Metamorphoses* to Ovid's earlier poetry. In the *Amores* erotic pathos emerges at the most surprising moments, in passages where Ovid's wit and savoir faire seem to have precluded any serious engagement with the emotional content of an encounter. In the fourth elegy of the first book, Ovid amuses us with the speaker's advice to his mistress about how the unhappy prospect of attending a banquet at which she and her husband will be present might be made less painful for him. At the end of this poem, as the speaker's mind turns from anticipations of the banquet and the frustrating presence of his mistress to the separation which will come when she returns home with her husband, the reader suddenly finds himself involved on another emotional level. The amusing irony of the first part of the poem extends into the conclusion, but it is now complicated by a deeper participation in the speaker's vacillating emotions:

> verum invita dato—potes hoc—similisque coactae;
>   blanditiae taceant, sitque maligna Venus.
> si mea vota valent, illum quoque ne iuvet, opto;
>   si minus, at certe te iuvet inde nihil.
> sed quaecumque tamen noctem fortuna sequetur,
>   cras mihi constanti voce dedisse nega!
>   (I.iv.65-70)

[But still, give against your will—this you can do—like one who is forced; let your allurements be silent, and may Venus be ill-disposed. If my vows are worth anything, I pray that she may not gratify him; if they are worth little, may she at least not give you any pleasure in it. But whatever be the fortune of the night, tomorrow tell me with a steadfast voice that you refused!]

The speaker's ironic sense of consciously willed deception—his need to have his lover be "steadfast" ("constanti") in voice, if not in deed—makes the underlying pathos of the situation all the more convincing.

In the *Heroides*, Ovid dramatizes erotic pathos within the more formal and rhetorically conventionalized requirements of the epistolary format and of *ethopoeia*, the classical tradition of conjecturing speeches appropriate to the character of a famous figure from myth or history.[31] But as the Elizabethans so fully realized, rhetorical formality and distance are not incompatible with personal expressive intensity. They could look back to the *Heroides* for such models of extravagantly impassioned artifice as Phaedra's appeal to Hippolytus:

> venit amor gravius, quo serius—urimur intus;
>   urimur, et caecum pectora vulnus habent.

> scilicet ut teneros laedunt iuga prima iuvencos,
> frenaque vix patitur de grege captus equus,
> sic male vixque subit primos rude pectus amores,
> sarcinaque haec animo non sedet apta meo.
>
> (IV. 19-24)

[Love has come all the more painfully for its coming late—I am burning inside; I am burning, and my breast has a hidden wound. Surely, as the first bearing of the yoke galls the young steer, and as the bridle is hardly endured by the colt taken from the herd, so painfully and with difficulty does my untried heart submit to love's first impulses, and this burden does not set well upon my spirit.]

The rhetorical strategies for projecting erotically obsessive or (as in the epistles of Helen, Oenone, and Hero) conflicting and contradictory states of mind, are more readily apparent in the *Heroides* than in any of Ovid's other poems. For this reason the influence of the *Heroides* is especially conspicuous.

In the extended first-person speeches of the *Metamorphoses*, Ovid is able to deploy with consummate control the dramatic skills in creating amatory pathos which he had perfected in the *Heroides* and the *Amores*. Here, even more subtly and consistently than in his earlier poetry, he demonstrates a special resourcefulness in dramatizing divided, shifting emotional states. Medea's passionate ambivalence in the opening scene of Book VII has already been mentioned in the Preface. Another example, one which brings out very forcefully the connections back to the *Heroides* epistles, is Byblis's letter to her brother in Book IX. The letter is convincingly the product of a wavering mind ("dubiam mentem," l. 517) caught between shame and bold resolution ("audacia mixta pudori," l. 527):

> iura senes norint, et quid liceatque nefasque
> fasque sit, inquirant, legumque examina servent.
> conveniens Venus est annis temeraria nostris.
> quid liceat, nescimus adhuc, et cuncta licere
> credimus, et sequimur magnorum exempla deorum.
> nec nos aut durus pater aut reverentia famae
> aut timor impediet: tamen ut sit causa timendi,
> dulci fraterno sub nomine furta tegemus.
>
> (IX. 551-558)

[Let old men examine what is lawful, and inquire into what may be proper or criminal or righteous, and preserve consideration of the law. Venus is compliant and heedless to those of our age. We are still ignorant of what is allowed, and we believe all things are allowed—we follow the gods' example. Neither a strict father nor concern for reputation nor fear hinders us. And yet, since there may be cause for fear, under the sweet name of brother and sister let us conceal our secret love.]

Outside such directly dramatic speeches, Ovid often relies upon extended metaphor and simile to express the emotional tension of erotic dilemma. Myrrha lies in her bed overcome with burning passion ("igni / carpitur indomito," X. 369–370) and yet filled with shame and despair:

> . . . utque securi
> saucia trabs ingens, ubi plaga novissima restat,
> quo cadat, in dubio est onmique a parte timetur,
> sic animus vario labefactus vulnere nutat
> huc levis atque illuc momentaque sumit utroque,
>
> (X. 372–376)

[. . . and just as a great tree struck by the axe, when only the final blow remains, is in doubt which way to fall and is feared on every side, so her mind, weakened by many wounds, leaned unsteadily this way and that, and inclined in both directions.]

The hyperbole and anticipatory symbolism of Ovid's simile (Myrrha is later transformed into a tree) both point forward to the supreme Elizabethan realization of Ovidian emotional drama in Marlowe's *Hero and Leander,* with its famous comparison of the flustered Hero to a "planet, moving several ways, / At one self instant" (I. 361–362). Hero's slips-of-the-tongue only a few lines before this image show Marlowe building upon Ovid's directly dramatic means of projecting conflicting emotional states.

If one defines "pathos" as the "sympathetic comprehension of human passion,"[32] one may well ask how Ovid is able to generate this quality in the *Metamorphoses* and at the same time to exploit the comic and grotesque possibilities of exaggerated anthropomorphism. Efforts to contend with this issue by relegating the mythological comedy and grotesqueness to one sequence of books and the "amatory pathos" to another make the experience of reading Ovid seem much simpler and more susceptible of categorization than it really is. The same may be said of attempts to draw a sharp distinction between episodes of destructive, degrading sexual passion, where the inclusion of comic and grotesque elements is presumably justified, and episodes in which the pathos of love is presented in an ideal, untroubled form.[33] Amatory pathos pervades early episodes such as those of Apollo and Daphne in Book II and Salmacis and Hermaphroditus in Book IV, where the horror of the final metamorphosis renders the pathos all the more haunting. On the other hand, in the later episode of Cephalus and Procris in Book VII, an especially poignant tale of amatory pathos is complicated by a motif of jealousy and mistrust which is ultimately realized in painfully grotesque irony.[34] And even the most obvious instances of "degrading passion," such as Myrrha's incestuous love for her father Cinyras, can be intensely moving. Contradictory attitudes and impulses are as irreducible a part of reading the *Metamorphoses* as they are of the human experiences to which Ovid's mythological fictions refer.

The erotic pathos I have been trying to describe and to relate without simplification to the other dominant strains in Ovid's poetry provides a better standard for judging the extent of genuine Ovidianism in Elizabethan epyllia than does the presence of irony, comedy, and verbal wit. All Elizabethan epyllia—not just *Hero and Leander* and *Venus and Adonis*—contain reflections of the humorous, ironic, satirical aspects of Ovid's poetry. These latter qualities are, to be sure, projected with greater imaginative resourcefulness by Marlowe and Shakespeare, but what really sets their epyllia apart is the level of erotic pathos. Only in *Hero and Leander* and *Venus and Adonis* do we experience anything approaching the sustained, complex simultaneity of irony, humor, verbal wit, grotesqueness, and erotic pathos which characterizes Ovid's poetry at its finest. Lodge, Edwards, Heywood, Marston, Weever, and Beaumont all recreate with varying degrees of success some aspects of the characteristic Ovidian poetic experience, but they are unable, except in a few isolated moments, to engage us emotionally as Ovid, Shakespeare, and Marlowe are able to do.

We come, finally, to the question of Ovid's style and to the difficulty of assessing its influence on the Elizabethan epyllion. We know that Ovid's Latin was greatly admired in the sixteenth century, even by orthodox scholars and pedagogues who insisted on a selective, moralized interpretation of the potentially objectionable content of his poetry. For the Elizabethans he was the consummate model of polished versification and rhetorical ornament. One would assume, then, that this traditional admiration for Ovid's verbal facility must have provided a positive basis for the extravagant stylistic richness of late Elizabethan Ovidian poetry, despite the fact that in every other respect the authors of this poetry were inclined to satirize and subvert the traditional ways in which Ovid was valued. But with one exception, the relation between Ovid's Latin style and the style of the Elizabethan epyllion is indirect and generalized. There are, of course, specific instances in which Ovid's metaphors and rhetorical patterns are taken over directly, virtually translated. But there is no consistent, programmatic attempt in Elizabethan epyllia to reproduce the stylistic intricacies of Ovid's Latin. The very fact that Ovid was used so assiduously as a stylistic model in Elizabethan schools probably worked against any tendency towards rigorous, extended verbal imitation. The chief importance of Ovid's stylistic virtuosity for the epyllion was that it encouraged the self-conscious verbal artifice already manifested in the "new poetry" of Sidney and Spenser, with its emphasis on what Gabriel Harvey called "excellent artificiality."[35]

The one exception to the diffuseness of Ovid's stylistic influence on the epyllion is the importance of Ovid's elegiac couplets for the heroic couplets of Marlowe's *Hero and Leander* and of subsequent epyllia inspired by Marlowe's poem. The flexibility and wit of Marlowe's *Hero and Leander* couplets represent the culmination of a process of technical mastery which began with his translation of the *Amores* during his Cambridge years. Marlowe's choice of the pentameter couplet for his translation was not fortuitous. Allowing for the obvious differences deriving from quantitative as opposed to accentual meter, unrhymed as opposed to rhymed endings, and lines of unequal as opposed to equal length, a significant parallelism of poetic effect exists between Latin elegiac couplets and English heroic couplets.[36] Marlowe's translation of the *Amores* should be seen as an important Elizabethan attempt to render the qualities of Ovid's elegiac couplets, with *Hero and Leander* as a brilliant extension into narrative verse of what Marlowe learned from this early exercise. It would be wrong, of course, to grant exclusive importance to Ovid's elegiacs and to Marlowe's version of the *Amores*. There were previous English writers—above all Chaucer—who had explored the possibilities of the pentameter couplet and would have exerted an influence on the epyllion. And it must also be said that while some Elizabethan epyllion writers followed Marlowe in choosing the couplet as the vehicle for their essays in Ovidian poetry, others did not. For just as Marlowe was establishing a model for what we might call the "couplet epyllion," an alternative model was established by Shakespeare's *Venus and Adonis* sixains, a stanza form which has come to be especially associated with Shakespeare's poem but which was already familiar in Elizabethan poetry and had already been employed by Lodge for an Ovidian narrative poem. Elizabethan epyllia divide almost exactly into "couplet" and "sixain" varieties: Edwards, Weever, and Beaumont emulate Marlowe's couplets; Heywood and Marston adopt the sixains of Shakespeare and Lodge. One must conclude, therefore, that while there is an important line of influence running from Ovid's elegiac couplets through Marlowe's *Amores* and *Hero and Leander* to subsequent "couplet epyllia," this line of influence was not pure, and it certainly did not dominate the versification of Elizabethan epyllia.

In turning from questions of versification and rhetorical detail to the larger structural and strategic aspects of Ovid's poetic technique, it is useful to reflect upon the inclination to regard Elizabethan epyllia simply as expanded, ornamented versions of episodes from the *Metamorphoses*. To begin with, not all epyllia are based on the *Metamorphoses*. Lodge, Shakespeare, Edwards, Marston, and Beaumont derive their main narratives from it, but Marlowe's comes from Musaeus and from the *Heroides*, Heywood's is adapted from epistles XV and XVI of the *Heroides*, and Weever's is largely his own invention. Even more importantly, the usual approach fails to take adequate account of the fact that Ovid's mythological episodes are small parts of an extremely long and elaborately organized poem; their length, scope, and structure are determined by their status as units in a massive "continuous narrative"— a *carmen perpetuum* (see *Met*. I. 4). Elizabethan poets, on the other hand, had to treat their mythological narratives, whether derived from the *Metamorphoses* or not, in such a way as to establish a convincing narrative and poetic self-sufficiency. It is the need for this, and not merely the Elizabethan penchant for intricate verbal ornament and "copy," which governs the larger structural features of Elizabethan epyllia.

In narrative technique and strategy as in the other areas we have been looking at, the Elizabethan epyllion reflects an amalgam of influences from many parts of Ovid's oeuvre. The digression, a feature of Elizabethan epyllia which, along with the aggressive feminine wooer, has been singled out more than any other as a generic characteristic, certainly derives in part from Ovid's use of this device in the *Metamorphoses*. The digression was a conspicuous feature of Hellenistic and Roman epyllia, and it was these poems which showed Ovid the possibilities of incorporating subsidiary tales into the major narrative line.[37] Ovid transforms the device by making much more subtle and complex use of digressions than his Hellenistic and Roman predecessors had done, and by cultivating a deliberately cryptic, elusive way of introducing subsidiary narratives. He avoids the explicit links between major and minor narrative segments common in works such as Callimachus's *Aetia* and relies instead on establishing a sense of a larger forward narrative movement.[38]

Elizabethan poets do not follow Ovid in this reluctance to provide explicit transition. They tend instead to exploit transitions playfully, often by means of a whimsically elaborated etiology. "Harken awhile," says Marlowe's narrator in *Hero and Leander* (I. 385), "and I will tell you why." Beaumont adopts a similar tone in *Salmacis and Hermaphroditus:*

> But the fayre Nymph had never seene the place,
> Where the boy was, nor his inchanting face,
> But by an uncouth accident of love
> Betwixt great *Phoebus* and the sonne of *Jove,*
> Light-headed *Bacchus:* . . .
>
> (ll. 405–409)

For Marlowe and Beaumont, the transition to a digression becomes an occasion for displaying the narrator's wit and cleverness. Elizabethan poets also depart from Ovid's approach to digressions in that they often use them to include in a single epyllion mythological episodes which Ovid treats quite separately and often with very different emphasis. Shakespeare has Venus tell Adonis of her love affair with Mars; Beaumont takes off from the story of Salmacis and Hermaphroditus on a long digression which interweaves the story of Astraea with the story of Venus, Vulcan, and Mars. In a number of instances, however, Elizabethan epyllionic digressions may have no specific Ovidian source at all. The two digressions in *Hero and Leander* are almost entirely Marlowe's own inventions. Basically, then, the digression is a device fundamental to Ovid's narrative technique, but the handling of this device in the Elizabethan epyllion differs considerably, in both form and content, from Ovid's own practice.

The extent to which the role of the narrator in Elizabethan epyllia derives from Ovid is a complicated issue, one to which we shall return many times in subsequent chapters. As a point of departure, we might simply consider the way in which the highly distanced, elusive narrator of the *Metamorphoses* distinguishes himself from the vividly present, self-mocking, constantly posing speaker of the *Amores* and from the avuncular worldliness of the speaker of the *Ars Amatoria*. Even critics like Otis who insist upon the "subjectivity of the point of view"[39] in the *Metamorphoses* acknowledge that this "subjectivity" is not the same as that of Callimachus or of Ovid himself in his elegiac poetry. "Subjectivity" in the *Metamorphoses* "is never elegiac," Otis observes; "it never sacrifices the sense of real event, of objective event, to the narrator's whim or fancy,"[40] as it does so wittily and entertainingly in the *Amores* and *Ars Amatoria*.

The terms "subjective" and "subjectivity" are inherently problematic in discussions of narrative persona or voice. If the point of view in the *Metamorphoses* is "subjective," how does one characterize the point of view in the elegiac poems? My approach will be to abandon these terms but retain the distinction which Otis and other scholars have drawn between the strategy of Ovid's elegiac poetry, where the speaker time and again calls attention to himself and makes his thoughts and feelings the explicit object of the reader's attention, and the strategy of the *Metamorphoses*, where the narrator's presence is much more indirectly and elusively felt, and where that presence never undermines the reader's sense of fictional event and action. With some adjustment, this distinction may be transferred to the Elizabethan epyllion. The virtually simultaneous appearance in 1593 of *Venus and Adonis* and *Hero and Leander* (the latter only in manuscript, of course) meant that two approaches to this kind of poem were made available as guides for the subsequent development of the genre. There was Shakespeare's unobtrusive, unselfconscious narrator—Coleridge says of the poem that "you seem to be told nothing, but to see and hear everything"[41]—and there was Marlowe's intrusive, highly self-conscious and self-dramatizing narrator who never lets the reader forget that he is being told what he sees and hears. If Shakespeare's narrative strategy comes closer to Ovid's manner in the *Metamorphoses*, Marlowe's strategy is even more deeply indebted to that of the *Amores* and the *Ars Amatoria*.

I have devoted considerable space to characterizing the distinctive features of Ovid's poetry because the kinds of assumptions often made about that poetry underlie what is most inadequate in previous evaluations of the Elizabethan epyllion. When Douglas Bush says that the epyllia of Lodge, Shakespeare, and Marlowe reflect "the growth of a more aesthetic and 'pagan' conception of mythology in general and of the *Metamorphoses* in particular,"[42] he is expressing a view which is widely held and, in its broad outlines, essentially true. But when one believes, as Professor Bush does, that Ovid is a poet of witty erotic entertainment and not much else, then Renaissance poems which eschew orthodox allegorical and moral adaptation for "a more aesthetic and 'pagan' conception" of Ovid will at best be clever and charming, and at worst frivolous and trivial. My contention is that in going to Ovid's poetry with a new freedom and openness, the authors of epyllia were looking afresh at a poetic world which was as often dark and disturbing as it was light and entertaining.

The environment in which what Bush calls "a more aesthetic and

'pagan' conception" of Ovid first flourished was not so much the court of
Elizabeth, as some critics have suggested, as the Universities and the Inns
of Court.[43] Bush may be right when he says that such an openness to Ovid
on his own terms was latent in some earlier sixteenth-century literature.
But the first really overt testimony to the "neo-pagan" Ovid is
Christopher Marlowe's translation of the *Amores*, which most scholars
now agree must be assigned to Marlowe's early years at Cambridge (1580-
1584).[44] No classical work previously translated into English could
approach the witty, urbane eroticism of the *Amores*, and Marlowe, despite
numerous awkwardnesses, manages to recreate these qualities with
impressive frequency:[45]

> I have been wanton, therefore am perplexed,
> And with mistrust of the like measure vexed.
> I and my wench oft under clothes did lurk,
> When pleasure moved us to our sweetest work.
> Do not thou so, but throw thy mantle hence,
> Lest I should think thee guilty of offence.[46]
>
> (I. iv. 44-50)

What comes across more than anything else in Marlowe's translation is
the sheer energy and excitement with which the difficult task seems to
have been performed.[47] And Marlowe's own excitement about the *Amores*
seems to have been shared by readers sufficiently in the know to put their
hands on a copy of one of the six editions published surreptitiously in the
1580s and 1590s.[48]

One imagines that it was not just Ovid's own wit and eroticism
which aroused the interest of Marlowe and his friends, but the status of
the *Amores* in the minds of conservative sixteenth-century readers. All of
Ovid's other poems, even the *Ars Amatoria*, had been sanctioned at one
time or another during the century as being of some moral or pedagogical
worth. The *Amores*, however, remained forbidden fruit. It is hardly
mentioned in Elizabethan accounts of Ovid, doubtless because those who
had read it in Latin realized the impossibility of accommodating it within
the prevailing moral-allegorical mode of interpretation. Marlowe would
have looked upon the *Amores* not only as a challenge to his skill as a poet,
but also as an opportunity to flout and subvert the established approach
to Ovid's poetry.[49] The excitement of defying orthodox opinion was
added to the excitement of translating Ovid's elegantly erotic elegiacs.
What the ecclesiastical authorities thought of Marlowe's venture is clear
enough: in the summer of 1599 the Archbishop of Canterbury and the

Bishop of London ordered Marlowe's translation, along with several other erotic and satirical works which they considered scurrilous and offensive, to be called in and burned.[50] We shall consider this event in greater detail in Part Two when we come to examine the relationship between satire and the Elizabethan epyllion.

The interest in the *Amores* signaled by Marlowe's translation had more than just a general importance for the epyllia of the 1590s—there were concrete poetic consequences of this interest as well. The Elizabethan poets we shall be dealing with go primarily to the *Metamorphoses* for their narrative material, but their handling of this material is strongly influenced by Ovid's elegiac poetry—and above all by the *Amores*. Shakespeare prefaces *Venus and Adonis* with two lines from *Amores* I.xv which indicate quite clearly the extent to which the authors of epyllia associated their poems with the urbanity and sophistication of Ovid's most notorious work:

> vilia miretur vulgus; mihi flavus Apollo
> pocula Castalia plena ministret aqua,
>
> (ll. 35-36)

[Let the crowd admire what is cheap; for me may golden Apollo provide full cups from the Castalian fountain. . . .]

We have already glanced at the significance of Marlowe's couplets in his *Amores* translation for *Hero and Leander* and other "couplet" epyllia. As numerous editors have pointed out, Marlowe actually echoes his translation at several points in *Hero and Leander*.[51] Many of the extended wooing scenes in *Hero and Leander* and in subsequent epyllia are indebted to the rhetorical gambits of Ovid's ingenious, self-concerned speaker.[52] There is also the wealth of witty mythological allusion in the *Amores*, for which Marlowe exhibits a special flair:

> By verses hornèd Io got her name,
> And she to whom in shape of swan Jove came,
> And she that on a feigned bull swam to land,
> Griping his false horns with her virgin hand.[53]
>
> (I. iii. 21-24)

Such a passage might well have come from an epyllion of the 1590s. Here we can see Marlowe working his way towards the ironic eroticism of the mythological allusions in *Hero and Leander*.

Marlowe was ultimately the most important propagator of Ovidian eroticism to emerge from the University environment of the late 1570s and 1580s, but he was certainly not the only undergraduate to display a mastery of those areas of Ovid's oeuvre obscured by the orthodox moral, allegorical, and pedagogical approaches. The most prolific "penner of Love Pamphlets" during the 1580s was Marlowe's close friend and slightly older contemporary at Cambridge, Robert Greene.[54] It was "at the Universitie of Cambridge," Greene writes in his *Repentence* (1592), that he fell "amongst wags as lewd as my selfe, with whom I consumed the flower of my youth. . . ."[55] Ovid's influence can be seen throughout Greene's writing, most conspicuously and pervasively in the *Alcida: Greene's Metamorphosis* (1588), but also in many of the poems set within his prose romances and plays. These poems, together with similar in-set pieces by Lodge and Sidney which we shall look at in later chapters, represent one of the most important antecedents of the independent epyllia of the 1590s. Only rarely do Greene's poems extend beyond a few stanzas, and their narrative content is slight. But their playful eroticism and mythological wit demonstrate an obvious kinship of spirit with Marlowe's version of the *Amores*:

> The Cnidian doves, whose white and snowy pens
> Do stain the silver-streaming ivory,
> May not compare with those two moving hills,
> Which topped with pretty teats discover down a vale,
> Wherein the god of love may deign to sleep;
> A foot like Thetis when she tripped the sands
> To steal Neptunus' favour with her steps;[56]

> ("The Description of Silvestro's Lady," from *Morando*, 1584)

> Apollo, when my mistress first was born,
> Cut off his locks, and left them on her head,
> And said, I plant these wires in nature's scorn,
> Whose beauties shall appear when time is dead.

> ("Melicertus' Eclogue," from *Menaphon*, 1587)

When Greene came to repudiate his former way of life and his "sundry wanton pamphlets" in the years just before his death, he frequently depicted himself as a repentant and reformed disciple of Ovid: "They which held *Greene* for a patron of love, and a second *Ovid*, shall now thinke him a *Timon* of such lineaments, and a *Diogines* that will barke at every amourous pen."[57] In Greene's own mind, his career as a "penner of Love Pamphlets" was rooted, as was Marlowe's, in the waggishly daring Ovidianism of his Cambridge years.

An environment perhaps even more important than the Universities for the growth of an unorthodox openness to Ovid's poetry was provided in London by the Inns of Court. A tradition of Ovidian interest within this environment can be traced back at least as early as the mid 1560s. George Turberville's translation of the *Heroides*, published as the *Heroycall Epistles* in 1567, was very likely undertaken while he was resident at one of the Inns of Court (1562–1567).[58] Philip Finkelpearl's fine study of the later sixteenth-century Inns-of-Court milieu in *John Marston of the Middle Temple* (1969) provides a richly suggestive account of an environment in which a "more aesthetic and 'pagan' conception" of Ovid flourished among law students ostensibly preparing themselves for the most conservative of professions. Finkelpearl reconstructs "an inbred milieu of young men, mostly wealthy, whose orthodox ideas and ambitions mingled easily with licentious conduct (or the pretense of it). . . ."[59] Here, as in the Universities, the informal activities of clever young men in an extremely orthodox setting led to an exploration of Ovidian eroticism and wit which must have had an aura of piquant anti-authoritarianism about it.

Almost all the authors of Elizabethan epyllia except Shakespeare were at one time or another formally connected either with one of the Universities or with the Inns of Court, or with both. Thomas Lodge was admitted to Lincoln's Inn as a student in the spring of 1578 and found the environment so congenial that he continued to have lodgings there for seventeen years as a "gentleman in chambers."[60] *Scillaes Metamorphosis* is dedicated "To His Especiall good friend Master Rafe Crane, and the rest of his most entire well willers, the Gentlemen of the Innes of Court and of Chauncerie."[61] But Lodge had already been a scholar at Trinity College, Oxford, from 1573 to 1577, and it may have been there, when he was a member of a literary circle which included John Lyly, George Peele, Abraham Fraunce, and Thomas Watson,[62] that his poetic interest in Ovid began. Marlowe's career at Cambridge has already been mentioned. Thomas Heywood had just come down to London from Cambridge when, at the age of nineteen or twenty, he wrote *Oenone and Paris* and translated the *Ars Amatoria* and the *Remedia Amores*.[63] Marston was still resident at the Middle Temple when he wrote *The Metamorphosis of Pigmalions Image*.[64] John Weever wrote *Faunus and Melliflora* soon after leaving Queens' College, Cambridge.[65] Francis Beaumont's biographer, Charles Mills Gayley, imagines Francis and his older brother John taking time off from their studies at Broadgates Hall (now Pembroke College),

Oxford, to wander by the same "Isis floud" evoked by Lodge at the
beginning of *Glaucus and Scilla*: " . . . they would have under arm or in
pocket a tattered volume of Ovid, preferably in translation,—
Turberville's *Heroical Epistles*, or Golding's rendering of the *Metamorphoses. . . .* "[66] Francis eventually followed John and the other Beaumont
brother, Henry, to the Inner Temple, and he was in residence there when
he wrote *Salmacis and Hermaphroditus*.

Some readers of Renaissance poetry have remained suspicious of the
importance, even of the existence, of "a more aesthetic and 'pagan'
conception" of Ovid in the late sixteenth century. They have insisted that
the orthodox moral, allegorical, and pedagogical approaches to Ovid
documented in such detail by twentieth-century scholarship[67] continued
to be accepted through the Elizabethan period right into the seventeenth
century of Sandys and Milton. And of course in some respects they are
correct. But among the authors of Elizabethan epyllia and what we may
take to be their immediate audience there is considerable evidence of an
ironic detachment from these older approaches. Much of this evidence can
be found in the epyllion itself. But glimpses of it also appear in the very
midst of well-known expositions of the orthodox approach to pagan
poetry by late Elizabethan writers who elsewhere, in their writings and in
their lives, exhibit a sensibility very far from that of Sir Arthur Golding.[68]
Thomas Lodge had just turned twenty and had been at Lincoln's Inn less
than a year when he wrote his *Reply to Stephen Gosson Touching Plays*
(1579), an essay often cited as an example of the moral and allegorical
defense of pagan poetry. But Lodge's comments on Ovid are informed by
a clever and insinuating argumentative pragmatism:

> . . . have you not reason to weigh that . . . whatever *Virgil* did write of his
> gnat, or *Ovid* of his flea, was all covertly to declare abuse?[69]

The unavoidable sense that Lodge is not entirely serious in his orthodox
defenses of Ovid is borne out elsewhere in the essay when he departs from
this approach altogether to appeal to his reader's tolerance and generosity
("I like not of an angry *Augustus* which will banish *Ovid* for envy . . . "[70])
or to his unguarded literary instincts ("Who liketh not the promptness of
Ovid?"[71]). There are indications in the *Reply to Gosson* that as early as
1579 the author of *Glaucus and Scilla*, a poem innovative in that "it does
not treat the myth as allegory" but develops it "without moral
purpose,"[72] was operating at an ironic distance from the traditional
approaches he would eventually give up entirely.

A similar situation arises in a slightly later and better-known essay,
Sir John Harington's "Preface" to his translation of the *Orlando Furioso*.

Harington's view of ancient poetry, and especially his four-fold allegorization of Ovid's story of Perseus and Andromeda, has often been invoked as Elizabethan orthodoxy without any notice of the facts that Harington was apparently made to translate this massive work as a fitting punishment for having entertained his friends at Court with a translation of the ribald twenty-eighth canto;[73] that the Queen herself, Harington's god-mother, handed down the punishment and was presumably the recipient of the completed version; or that Harington went on to author numerous bawdy epigrams and the Rabelaisian *Metamorphosis of Ajax*. Nor have those who have read Harington's "Preface" without a sense of irony and occasion noticed that when he eventually turns to defend the allegedly scurrilous episodes of Ariosto's epic, he slyly seizes the opportunity to convert apology into advertisement:

> . . . alas if this be a fault, pardon him this one fault, though I doubt that many of you (gentle readers) will be too exorable in this point, yea me thinks I see some of you searching already for those places of the booke, and you are halfe offended that I have not made some directions that you might finde out and reade them immediately. But I beseech you stay a while, and as the Italian sayth *Pian piano*, fayre and softly, & take this caveat with you, to read them as my author ment them, to breed detestation and not delectation.[74]

As it happens, Harington had in fact "made some directions that you might finde out and reade them immediately" by naming the erotic episodes in his "Preface" and then providing, at the end of the translation, "An Exact and Necessarie Table in Order of Alphabet, Wherein You May Readilie Finde The Names of the principall persons in this worke. . . . "

I am not arguing that writers such as Lodge and Harington placed no positive value at all in the allegorical and moral positions they expound. To make such an assumption would be as wrong-headed as to assume that medieval and Renaissance writers clearly committed to the Christian tradition of moral and allegorical exegesis had no sense of the erotic and comic appeal of the works they felt obligated to interpret. Thomas Roche has shown, in his application of the principles of Harington's "Preface" to the poetry of *The Faerie Queen*, how central those principles are to allegorical poetry of the Elizabethan period.[75] But that Lodge and Harington were both capable on occasion of viewing the traditional approaches they expound with irony and detachment is evident from the tone of their writing and from the fact that such approaches were above all expedient, particularly if one were debating with a Puritan clergyman, as in Lodge's case, or doing penance for a previous indiscretion, as in Harington's. We can no more take the statements of moral and allegorical orthodoxy in Lodge and Harington at simple face value than we can take Shakespeare's Holofernes as a serious embodiment of the pedagogical approach to using Ovid as a stylistic model in the schools.[76]

We would do well to recall at this point that a tradition of irony and skepticism towards the older ways of interpreting pagan literature existed throughout the sixteenth century on the Continent, alongside the prevailing orthodoxy inherited from the late Middle Ages. Letter twenty-eight of the *Epistolae obscurorum virorum* (1515–1517), a German work widely known in England, contains a parody of the elaborate allegorical method of reading Ovid exemplified in the anonymous fourteenth-century *Ovide moralisé* and in the *Metamorphosis Ovidiana moraliter explanata* of Petrus Berchorius.[77] And there is Rabelais' famous mockery of allegorical exegesis in the Prologue to *Gargantua* (1534), where he claims "that Homer no more dreamed of all this allegorical fustian than Ovid in his *Metamorphoses* dreamed of the Gospel."[78] This playful skepticism towards the established moral and allegorical exegesis of Ovid's poetry may have been "sporadic," as Professor Bush claims,[79] but it was nonetheless present throughout the sixteenth century. One need not deny the continuing value and importance of moral and allegorical orthodoxy to think that for Lodge and Harington, as for Shakespeare and Marlowe, such skepticism was an important aspect of a less restricted exploration of Ovid's poetry.

But if young Elizabethan writers were initially inspired to reinvestigate Ovid through a partly subversive delight in witty eroticism, what they eventually discovered was a much deeper and more disturbing range of expression. Perhaps the most important conclusion to draw from the examination of Ovid's poetry with which this chapter began is that the alternative to an orthodox "Elizabethan Ovid," an Ovid made safe for the Christian reader, is not necessarily a frivolous, indulgently decorative, decadently "Italianate Ovid." Even in Marlowe's translation of the *Amores* one can see, along with the obvious interest in Ovid's urbane sexual comedy, a sensitivity to the violent pathos and psychic torment which disrupt and complicate both the wit and the lyricism of these remarkable poems. The epyllia of the 1590s represent a further exploration of that characteristic Ovidian ambivalence which Marlowe and some of his contemporaries were beginning to probe in the 1580s. A close, uncondescending look at these explorations may reveal for the modern reader, as perhaps it would have for the late Elizabethan reader, a rather surprising awareness of the contradictions as well as the comedy and excitement inherent in human sexual experience.

Chapter II
Glaucus and Scilla

❧❦❧

Thomas Lodge's *Glaucus and Scilla* has suffered the curse of "historical significance," of having "an importance independent of intrinsic merit."[1] Except for a nineteenth-century attempt to fabricate a manuscript version of *Venus and Adonis* written in the mid-1580s from which Lodge supposedly derived his inspiration,[2] *Glaucus and Scilla* has been generally accepted as the first Elizabethan epyllion. Yet this very judgment has tended to obscure the real literary value and interest of the poem. It is usually passed over with a brief plot summary and an acknowledgment that it did after all inaugurate the "vogue" of the epyllion in the 1590s. On the few occasions when *Glaucus and Scilla* has received more detailed attention, critics have complained of Lodge's eclecticism and of the awkwardness of his writing. It is possible to acknowledge Lodge's culpability on both these counts, however, and yet to claim that he still achieves something of genuine importance through his recasting of an episode from the *Metamorphoses* which, as Charles Segal points out, is particularly illustrative of a characteristically Ovidian "juxtaposition of tones, beginning . . . as a light, amorous adventure and ending in horror."[3]

The genesis of *Glaucus and Scilla*, in both its biographical and in its strictly literary aspects, suggests a good deal about the environment which produced the epyllia of the 1590s. Lodge's epyllion bears every mark of having originally been a private piece, probably written during the period 1584–1588 and circulated among his friends at Lincoln's Inn.[4] It was apparently published in 1589 only because a pirated copy threatened to appear in print without acknowledgment of Lodge's authorship.[5] The first Elizabethan epyllion began, it would seem, as a poet's own private performance, designed to give free play to his technical virtuosity and to delight readers with a taste for witty eroticism.

The eclectic, derivative nature of *Glaucus and Scilla* has been emphasized by critics who, at the same time, grant Lodge the achievement of having inaugurated a new kind of English poem. Bush, for example, says that "Lodge has been justly credited with introducing into English a new genre," but he then goes on to describe *Glaucus and Scilla* as "not so much the first poem in a new genre as one of the last in an old one," since it is "less a minor epic than a love-complaint."[6] The only detailed attempt to extend Bush's judgment and to find a definite precedent for Lodge's epyllion in previous love-complaint literature is that of Walter F. Staton, Jr., who argues that Thomas Watson's Latin *Amyntas* (1587), or more likely the English translation of it by Abraham Fraunce (1591), provided the primary inspiration for Lodge's poem.[7] Lodge would certainly have known Watson's work: he was a friend and contemporary of both Watson and Fraunce at Oxford in the 1570s;[8] he alludes specifically to "Amyntas" in *Glaucus and Scylla* (ll. 505–506); and he seems to have been influenced by Watson's writing in some of the more preciously erotic passages of his epyllion.[9] But in structure, format, narrative emphasis, and tone, the *Amyntas* has little in common with *Glaucus and Scilla* and other Ovidian narratives—in fact it is much more closely tied to the eclogues of Virgil, Petrarch, and Sannazaro than it is to Ovid.[10] And Lodge himself provides a more direct link between the pastoral love-complaint and the Elizabethan epyllion in the couplet eclogue inserted in his prose romance *Forbonius and Prisceria* of 1584.[11]

The love-complaint most often suggested as an immediate source for *Glaucus and Scilla* is Ronsard's *Complainte de Glauque à Scylle nymphe*.[12] Lodge's imitation of the French poets has been well documented,[13] and it is quite possible that he was led to the episode which bridges Books XIII and XIV of the *Metamorphoses* by Ronsard's elegant handling of the subject. But when one compares the two poems in detail, *Glaucus and Scilla* seems more an alternative to than an imitation of Ronsard's poem. Ronsard's *Complainte* is only forty-eight lines long and takes the form of a single speech of lamentation by Glaucus,[14] whereas Lodge's poem is 780 lines long and employs Glaucus as a secondary narrator and as only one of the participants in the action. Ronsard does not even mention Scylla's final metamorphosis, and he alludes to many features of Ovid's narrative (Glaucus's former life as a fisherman and his transformation into a sea-god after having eaten a magic herb) which Lodge omits. There is some detailed correspondence in the description of Glaucus's physical appearance,[15] and both poets exploit the irony of making Glaucus's divinity a barrier rather than an aid in the pursuit of Scylla (she takes him to be a monster). But Lodge sees a comic aspect to this situation which Ronsard does not develop. Ronsard's poem is essentially lyrical, and he refracts the story through a single significant moment and point of view. Lodge, on the other hand, expands the narrative through descriptive elaboration and develops the dramatic interplay between Glaucus and the narrator. The fifty-four line poem called "Glaucus complaint," which appears just after *Glaucus and Scilla* in the 1589-1590 edition of *Scillaes Metamorphosis*, actually comes much closer to representing Lodge's imitation of Ronsard's poem than does the epyllion with which we are mainly concerned.

Simply documenting Lodge's eclecticism, as we can see from the material we have just been looking at, is relatively uninstructive: what is wanted is some indication of the larger poetic concern governing the appropriations. To see exactly what Lodge does with the conventions of the love-complaint, and indeed with many of the other features he adapts from previous kinds of amatory poetry, we need to look closely at what C. S. Lewis called the "medieval frame" of *Glaucus and Scilla*.[16] The situation Lodge employs in his epyllion—that of the love-sick narrator who attempts to console another unfortunate lover and, in the process, is himself not only consoled but taught a lesson in love and inspired to write a poem—is medieval in that it goes back to the genre of dream-poems to which Chaucer's *The Book of the Duchess* belongs. In the sixteenth century the situation was adapted to the love-complaint and used to frame an Ovidian tale (Chaucer, of course, had incorporated the story of Ceyx and Alcyone into his poem) in George Gascoigne's *Complaynt of Philomene* (1576). Gascoigne's despairing narrator hears the "waymenting" of the nightingale and is consoled by her story[17] much as Lodge's narrator is consoled when he learns of Glaucus's plight (ll. 46–48). What distinguishes Lodge's narrator from Chaucer's and Gascoigne's, however, is the degree of comic exaggeration in the way he is presented. Both Chaucer and Gascoigne had seen certain ironic and comic possibilities in this narrative situation—Chaucer in particular exploits the naive gullibility of his speaker in a manner which is at times comic. But Lodge goes beyond Chaucer and Gascoigne in this respect and gives his narrator a more obviously exaggerated posture:

> Walking alone (all onely full of griefe)
> Within a thicket nere to Isis floud,
> Weeping my wants, and wailing scant reliefe,
> Wringing mine armes (as one with sorrowe wood);
>   The piteous streames relenting at my mone
>   Withdrew their tides, and staid to hear me grone.
>
> (ll. 1-6)

Although an element of comic exaggeration seems quite unmistakable in the language of this first stanza, only one commentator, as far as I know, has suggested that the tone of Lodge's epyllion is anything other than straightforwardly serious.[18]

Any doubts about the intended comedy in the opening stanza of

Glaucus and Scilla should be laid to rest immediately in the exchange which follows between the narrator and Glaucus himself. A certain comic monstrosity seems to have been part of the traditional sixteenth-century conception of Glaucus [Fig. 1], and Lodge develops this with considerable resourcefulness. The appearance and behavior of Lodge's Glaucus are related to the exaggerated anthropomorphism I described in Chapter I as a major feature of Ovid's handling of myth. But in Lodge's epyllion this comically exaggerated anthropomorphism is projected through a narrator whose straight-faced gullibility is closer to Chaucer's manner in *The Book of the Duchess* than to the sophisticatedly detached tone of the *Metamorphoses*. The narrator tells how Glaucus

> Reposd his head upon my faintfull knee:
> And when my teares had ceast their stormie shower
> He dried my cheekes, . . .
>
> (ll. 15-17)

Glaucus punctuates his opening lamentations with gestures which cannot but seem risible when we think of them being performed by the hairy, moss-covered sea-god:

> Here gan he pause and shake his heavie head,
> And fould his armes, and then unfold them straight:
>
> (ll. 43-44)

The narrator's naively earnest response to Glaucus heightens the humor of this kind of behavior:

> Whil'st I that sawe what woes did him awaight,
> Comparing his mishaps and moane with mine,
> Gan smile for joy and drie his drooping eyne.
>
> (ll. 46-48)

Part of what Lodge is doing here and in later stanzas of his epyllion is satirizing the self-pitying pose so fashionable in the love poetry of the 1570s by carrying it to ridiculous extremes. At times the narrator actually seems confused as to whether his or Glaucus's state is the more pitiable.

> Alas woes me, how oft have I bewept
> So faire, so yong, so lovely, and so kinde,
> And whilst the God upon my bosome slept,
> Behelde the scarres of his afflicted minde,
>
> (ll. 427-430)

The narrator and Glaucus together enact what comes close to being a parody of the conventional love-complaint.

A similar process of comic exaggeration and transformation characterizes Lodge's handling of the pastoral features of *Glaucus and Scilla*. Lodge's indebtedness to pastoral poetry and prose is undeniable: the relationship of his epyllion to Thomas Watson's pastoral complaint in Latin, the *Amyntas*, has already been mentioned.[19] Bush even sees in the poem "'the fundamental theme of the Italian pastoral'"—"' the idea of a Nemesis overtaking the disdainful nymph or shepherd. . . .'"[20] But what Lodge does with the pastoral conventions is anything but straightforward. To begin with, the setting of *Glaucus and Scilla* is not merely pastoral—it is located in England, "nere to Isis floud." The point of this localized setting is not the development of any "myth of locality" in the tradition of the Italian pastoral,[21] but the witty exploitation of allusions to life at Oxford, allusions obviously intended for the enjoyment of the ex-University men in Lodge's Inns-of-Court audience. "Thy books have schoold thee from this fond repent," Glaucus tells the narrator, "And thou canst talke by proofe of wavering pelfe" (ll. 21-22). Of course the narrator's implied experience at Oxford is of no use at all to him in his present situation. Glaucus even tries to remind the narrator of one of the most basic of all scholastic sententia, but in so doing demonstrates its irrelevance:

> In searching then the schoolemens cunning noates, . . .
> Conclude and knowe times change by course of fate,
> Then mourne no more, but moane my hapless state.
> (ll. 37-42)

These allusions to the University background of Lodge's epyllion are related to the more explicit references near the end of the poem to Lodge's audience and to the contemporary literary scene. This kind of articulated consciousness of the immediate historical context will become a recurring feature in later epyllia. What should be emphasized here is the comic and even satiric way Lodge has exploited the range of local allusions in his pastoral setting.

A poetic device often associated with the pastoral—the so-called "pathetic fallacy," the sympathetic participation by the natural world in the emotional states of the main figures—appears recurrently in the early stanzas of *Glaucus and Scilla* and indeed throughout the poem. But Lodge rarely uses the device without a certain exaggerated artificiality. The first stanza ends with the image of the Isis withdrawing its tides to listen to the narrator's laments. Several stanzas later, when Thetis and her

1. Nicholas Reusner, "De Glauco" (woodcut). *Picta Poesis Ovidiana*, Frankfurt, 1580, p. 146[R].

Impudentia.

Pube tenus mulier, succincta latrantibus infra
Monstrorum catulis, Scylla biformis erat.
Monstra putantur auarities, audacia, raptus.
At Scylla est nullus cui sit in ore pudor.

2. Andrea Alciati, "Impudentia" (woodcut). *Emblemata*, Lyon, 1550, p. 76.

nymphs have appeared on the scene, the river demonstrates its sensitivity
in a rather different manner:

> . . . all the Nimphs that waight on Neptunes realme
> Attended from the hollow of the rocks.
>   In briefe, while these rare paragons assemble,
>   The watrie world to touch their teates doo tremble.
>   (ll. 57–60)

The erotic wit and artificiality of these lines recall Sidney's account in the
New Arcadia (Chapter 11, Book II) of Pamela and Philoclea bathing in
the river Ladon[22] and suggest that Lodge may have had access to Sidney's
sophisticated pastoralism in manuscript during the early 1580s. Even the
less obviously exaggerated instances of the "pathetic fallacy" later in the
poem are executed with a degree of self-conscious wit which brings them
to the verge of parody. Take, for example, the following lines describing
Scylla's swoon:

> And when through inward griefe the lasse did sound,
> The softned grasse like billowes did arise
>   To woe her brests, and wed her limmes so daintie.
>   (ll. 645–647)

Muriel Bradbrook has pointed out how Lodge allows the grass in this
passage to suggest both the sea where Scylla lives and the lover, Glaucus,
whom she now desires.[23] But what also strikes one about this way of using
the "pathetic fallacy" is its overt, unabashed artificiality. The self-
conscious playfulness and extravagance of Lodge's conceits represent an
important anticipation of the tone with which such figurative language is
celebrated in subsequent epyllia.

   One other aspect of the framing situation in *Glaucus and Scilla* can
help us see more clearly Lodge's attitude towards the features he adopts
from previous poetry. The catalogue of feminine charms appears in so
many different kinds of sixteenth-century poems that one tends to forget
about its existence as a genre of its own in the French *blason*. The most
famous Elizabethan example of the *blason* appears in the episode from
Book II of the *New Arcadia* we have already mentioned, where Sidney has
Pyrocles (disguised as Zelmane) take up the lute and voice his excitement
at seeing Pamela and Philoclea bathing in a song which, as one editor has
pointed out, "anticipates the erotic spirit of *Hero and Leander*. . . . "[24]
Lodge's seven-stanza description of Scylla's charms recalls Sidney's poem
in several details, including the speaker's lament that his descriptive

powers are not fully adequate to the task at hand. But whereas Pyrocles only says that Ovid could do greater justice to Philoclea's beauty ("Yet never shall my song omitte   Those thighs, for Ovid's song more fitte," ll. 87–88),[25] Glaucus finds that he must leave off describing Scylla's beauty altogether:

> Confounded with descriptions, I must leave them;
> Lovers must thinke, and Poets must report them:
> (ll. 319–320)

To imagine Glaucus uttering these words is even more amusing than to imagine Pyrocles, in female disguise, giving vent to his desire by singing a tantalizing *blason*. Lodge has given a special comic twist to the catalogue of feminine charms, much as Shakespeare will do when he has Venus enumerate her own physical charms in *Venus and Adonis*.

Lodge is not, then, merely eclectic—he builds up the frame of his epyllion with features taken over from previous types of amatory poetry and adapted to a pervasively comic and ironic situation. He extends the comic irony of the frame throughout the entire poem—and at the same time clearly distances himself from his narrator—by means of humorous reflexive references to the process of writing itself. "Lovers must thinke, and Poets must report them," Glaucus says: the line is amusing not simply because we realize that Glaucus's words are in fact being "reported" by a poet, but because his disclaimer of being able to describe Scylla's beauty and his deference to "Poets" wittily draw attention to the entire rhetorical fiction Lodge has created. This humorous poetic self-consciousness is extended later through the narrator's exhortations to himself as he "composes" his "tragick tale":

> My wandring lines, bewitch not so my sences:
> But gentle Muse direct their course aright,
> Delayes in tragicke tales procure offences:
> Yeeld me such feeling words, that whilst I wright
>   My working lines may fill mine eyes with languish,
>   And they to note my mones may melt with anguish.
> (ll. 433–438)

The narrator's insistence upon the tragedy and anguish of the poetic effect he intends ironically heightens the humor of the poem's actual effect.

Lodge is extremely clever in extending the comic poetic self-consciousness of the frame into the Ovidian narrative itself. Throughout most of the poem a certain distance is maintained between the narrator's present sphere of consciousness and the pastoral-mythological world of his past experiences on the banks of the Isis, where, we are told, he met Glaucus and heard him recount the first stage of his affair with Scylla. This distance is greatly reduced when Scylla herself appears on the scene and the narrator becomes a witness to the last stage of the Ovidian myth, including the metamorphosis (ll. 565 ff.). And near the end of the poem the distance between the poet-narrator's present consciousness and his recollected experiences breaks down altogether. When Scylla swims off to the Sicilian coast in a fit of despair, Glaucus hoists the narrator on a dolphin's back,[26] and the two set off "To see what would ensue" (l. 666). The narrator's comment at this point exposes the fiction of the entire narrative situation in a moment of remarkable self-irony:

> What need I talke the order of my way,
> Discourse was steersman while my bark did saile,
> My ship conceit, and fancie was my bay:
> (If these faile me, then faint my Muse and faile,)
> (ll. 685-688)

None of the authors of later epyllia, not even Marlowe, quite matches this degree of poetic self-consciousness. But they all follow Lodge in playfully dramatizing an awareness of the rhetorical fiction and process of their poems.

The narrator's naive comprehension of his own situation and of what he sees and reports, together with his and Glaucus's exaggerated and often ludicrous appropriation of the conventions and postures of sixteenth-century love poetry, turn the so-called "medieval frame" of *Glaucus and Scilla* into a humorously entertaining vignette. But this frame surrounds and infuses a tale of metamorphosis which, as Segal says, begins "as a light, amorous adventure and end[s] in horror." The most interesting critical problems posed by *Glaucus and Scilla* arise when one examines the relationship of the frame of Lodge's epyllion to the Ovidian narrative it encloses.

The freedom and inventiveness with which Lodge reworks Ovid's Glaucus and Scylla episode establish yet another important precedent for subsequent epyllia. In Ovid's tale Glaucus, having been spurned by Scylla, visits Circe in hope of some recourse. But Circe herself falls in love with Glaucus and, when she in turn is rejected, poisons the peaceful little pool ("parvus . . . gurges, . . . grata quies Scyllae," XIV. 51-52) which is Scylla's favorite haunt. Segal sees in this part of the episode a recurrent symbolic pattern of the *Metamorphoses*—the intrusion of violence and horror into a pristinely beautiful pastoral landscape. The pollution of Scylla's clear, secluded pool (ambivalently suggestive of an innocent but potentially corruptible sensuality—"curvos sinuatus in arcus," XIV. 51) symbolizes the sexual violation which Scylla wants so much to avoid when she first confronts the enamoured but monstrous Glaucus in a deep, secluded pool ("seductos nacta recessus / gurgitis," XIII. 902-903).[27] Circe's poison and her elaborate curse produce a hideous double metamorphosis—Scylla is first turned into a monster whose waist is encircled with the heads of vicious barking dogs (XIV. 59-67), then into the notorious rock dreaded by all sailors (XIV. 68-74). Segal interprets the first metamorphosis as "a horrible mock-pregnancy, a cruelly ironic inversion of her previous maidenhood."[28] And with the second transformation into the dreaded rock, Scylla ironically gains the isolation from men which she previously desired ("scopulum quoque navita vitat," XIV. 74).

The changes Lodge makes in Ovid's story seem at first glance to mute the violence and grotesqueness of the episode. In *Glaucus and Scilla* there is no visit by Glaucus to Circe's monstrous abode. Instead, Thetis (Glaucus's mother) and her nymphs take pity on Glaucus and appeal directly to Venus and Cupid, who in turn heal Glaucus of his lovesickness and inflict an identical wound in Scylla's heart (ll. 475-594). One effect of this change is the introduction in the first Elizabethan epyllion of the aggressive feminine wooer:

> The tender Nimph attainted unawares,
> Fares like the Libian Lionesse that flies
> The Hunters Launce that wounds her in his snares:
> Now gins shee love and straight on Glaucus cries;
> (ll. 595-598)

The image of the "Libian Lionesse" prepares quite beautifully for the shift from Scylla the pursued victim of the hunt of love to Scylla the aggressive seductress. Lodge's Scylla is more coy and flirtatious than Ovid's even before she is struck by Cupid's arrow, so this reversal of roles is made to seem like just punishment. The word "attainted" in line 595 suggests that Lodge was remembering Circe's poison in Ovid's account, even as he transformed that poison into the arrow from Cupid's bow which "cleft [Scylla's] heart."

There is another, even more important result stemming from Lodge's change in Ovid's episode. By eliminating the visit to Circe and instead having Venus and Cupid intervene directly to reverse the course of the action, Lodge places the major emphasis of the poem on love itself as a contradictory, all-powerful, ultimately ambivalent force. The theme of the story, as Lodge reconceives it, turns upon the idea of love as an indomitably self-perpetuating and paradoxically self-frustrating power. This idea is playfully articulated early in the poem in the song of the nymph Nais:

> Of love (God wot) the lovelie Nimph complained:
> But so of love as forced Love to love her;
> And even in love such furious love remained,
> As searching out his powerfull shaft to prove her,
> He found his quiver emptied of the best,
> And felt the arrowe sticking in his breast.
>
> (ll. 73–78)

Though these lines, with their exaggerated *traductio*, at first seem merely entertaining, they in fact anticipate through ironic reversal Scylla's fate. No sooner has Cupid healed Glaucus's love-wound than Scylla appears, coyly displaying her beauty before the assembled company (ll. 565–570). Cupid initially appears to have been struck once again by his own arrow and "desires to touch the wantons thie" (l. 579). But instead he assents to Thetis' request and inflicts the wound on Scylla which will bring about her downfall. The crisis of the poem thus depends on the ability of Cupid's arrows both to cure from and to enflame with lovesickness, both to frustrate and to perpetuate sexual desire. Lodge's changes in the myth have the effect of focusing even more directly than Ovid had done in this episode of the *Metamorphoses* on the fickleness and ambivalence of love.

Lodge's way of intensifying the direct mythological presentation of love in *Glaucus and Scilla* becomes clearer when we look at the two most often-quoted passages in the poem. The first of these passages, the three-stanza allusion to the story of Venus and Adonis in Glaucus's first lament, functions in a way parallel to the stanza from Nais' song quoted above. These stanzas show that while in the case of Glaucus and Scylla Venus's power works ambivalently on others, it can also be turned against the Queen of Love herself, with tragic results:

> He that hath seene the sweete Arcadian boy
> Wiping the purple from his forced wound . . .
>
> And Venus starting at her love-mates crie,
> Forcing hir birds to hast her chariot on;
> And full of griefe at last with piteous eie
> Seene where all pale with death he lay alone, . . .

> How on his senseless corpes she lay a crying,
> As if the boy were then but new a dying.
> (ll. 121–138)

These lines display Lodge's sixain style at its best. We may assume that they attracted and influenced Shakespeare, who makes the tragic self-frustration of love a central part of the subject of his epyllion.[29]

The three-stanza hymn to Venus later in the poem (ll. 481–498) seems at first to provide the contrasting complement to Glaucus's allusion to the tragedy of Venus and Adonis. These strikingly elegant stanzas with their couplet refrain could easily stand by themselves as an independent lyric. But in the context of Lodge's reconstructed fable they also have an important thematic function, one which is closely related to their rhetorical sonority. They present an ideal of the Goddess of Love against which we can judge the eventual outcome of the doubly thwarted and unrequited attraction between Glaucus and Scylla:

> Borne of the Sea, thou Paphian Queene of love,
> Mistris of sweete conspiring harmonie:
> (ll. 481–482)

The nymphs go on to sing of the ideal of *Venus genetrix*, of love as joyful, fruitful, fulfilling. But the pun on "conspiring" in the first two lines of the hymn is Lodge's way of indicating that the actions of Venus and her son in this story do not fully correspond to the hymn's glorious ideal. While these actions lead in a sense to "sweete harmonie" for Glaucus, they lead to pain and suffering for Scylla. Venus and Cupid have actually "conspired" with Thetis in a cruel, sadistic way. What they eventually effect in the poem is not fulfilled love at all, but revenge and torture.

Lodge's second major alteration of Ovid's narrative results in additional focusing on the theme of love as cruelly ambivalent and indirectly links the final metamorphosis with the exaggerated language of love poetry given to Glaucus and the narrator. Lodge omits Scylla's first metamorphosis into a monster whose waist is encircled with hounds. Instead she is transformed directly into the notorious rock:

> . . . hir locks
> Are chang'd with wonder into hideous sands,
> And hard as flint become her snow-white hands.
> (ll. 736–738)

Lodge sees Scylla's metamorphosis as an ironically literal enactment of the metaphors of Scylla's hard-heartedness used earlier by Glaucus and the narrator:

> Aies me my moanings are like water drops
> That neede an age to pearce her marble heart,
> (ll. 355–356)

This strategy of adapting Ovidian transformations so that they become part of an ironic and satirical treatment of the conventional conceits of love poetry will be taken up in later epyllia—by Marston in *The Metamorphosis of Pigmalions Image*, by Beaumont in *Salmacis and Hermaphroditus*. But while Lodge has eliminated some of the explicit grotesqueness of the double transformation in the *Metamorphoses* in order to extend his own special interests in the episode, he still presents the reader with an experience which is genuinely Ovidian in its coolly clever juxtaposition of verbal wit and violence. Scylla's coy hard-heartedness has ended in a metamorphosis which is cruelly as well as ironically appropriate in the way that Ovid's own metamorphoses often are.[30]

The horror of the myth haunts the conclusion of *Glaucus and Scilla*, even though Lodge does nothing to keep this horror before his readers. Emphasis falls rather on the narrator's delight in being able to warn the "ladies" in his fictional audience against proud, disdainful resistance to their lovers' advances, a warning which Lodge's actual Inns-of-Court audience would certainly have enjoyed. In the seven stanzas which follow the metamorphosis the narrator seems himself to be transformed, from a lugubrious, wasted lover into a confident, triumphantly clever man of experience. In stanza 125 he picks up the irony of Scylla's petrification and makes an obvious, and rather cruel, joke of it:

> Ah Nimphes thought I, if everie coy one felt
> The like misshappes, their *flintie hearts* would melt.
> (ll. 749–750; my italics)

The narrator seems as shallow and inadequate in his obtuseness to Scylla's suffering here as he was in his pity for himself and Glaucus in the early stages of the poem. And his account of the joyful celebration in Neptune's palace (ll. 751–774) shows that he is not alone in his insensitivity.

Is Lodge exposing the superficiality of his narrative pose even as he uses it to entertain his Inns-of-Court friends? To a certain extent I think he is—the ironic distance between Lodge and his narrator is particularly apparent in the last stanza before the Envoy, as the narrator tells how Glaucus returned him to the banks of the Isis:

> At last he left me, where at first he found me,
> Willing me let the world and ladies knowe
> Of Scillas pride, and then by oath he bound me
> To write no more, of that whence shame dooth grow:
>   Or tie my pen to Pennie-knaves delight,
>   But live with fame, and so for fame to wright.
>
> (ll . 775–780)

Lodge allows his audience their joke at the expense of the narrator's newly discovered wisdom and then twits them for indulging in such frivolity by calling them "Pennie-knaves," possibly a slang term for the lowest kind of theatre-goer and thus a satirical reference to the special fondness for plays exhibited by young men at the Inns of Court.[31] This is all very clever and witty—and yet the reader is left with the disturbing, unresolved tension between violent, painful metamorphosis and sophisticated poetic joking. The tension at the end of *Glaucus and Scilla* is essentially Ovidian, although Ovid controls this tension more directly and yet more subtly through the urbane sensibility of his narrator. Lodge's narrator seems totally unaware of the tension, and were his pretentiousness and obtuseness not so obviously exposed, one might think Lodge unaware of it as well. As it is, however, one may be inclined to grant Lodge the benefit of the doubt.

In the Envoy the narrator draws the "moral" of his story for his readers and gives us the first instance of what will become a recurring feature in later epyllia—a parody of the orthodox moralizing commentary on the *Metamorphoses*. In Alciati's *Emblemata* the metamorphosed Scylla appears as an image of shameless feminine pride [Fig. 2].[32] Lodge's envoy contains a playfully witty variant of this moralization:

> Ladies he left me, trust me I missay not,
> But so he left me as he wild me tell you:
> That Nimphs must yeeld, when faithfull lovers straie not,
> Least through contempt, almightie love compell you
>   With Scilla in the rockes to make your biding
>   A cursed plague, for womens proud back-sliding.
>
> (ll. 781–786)

With this address to the "ladies" Lodge's narrator ends by fulfilling the claim made on the title-page of the first edition, where *Scillaes*

Metamorphosis is advertised as "verie fit for young Courtiers to peruse, and coy Dames to remember."

I have consciously emphasized the virtues of *Glaucus and Scilla* and avoided detailed commentary on the weaknesses. Lodge's faults have been fully documented in previous accounts, but his achievement has not been adequately described or evaluated. If I have overestimated Lodge's control of the multiple ironies in his poem, this may in part represent a reaction against readings which have allowed Lodge no irony at all. *Glaucus and Scilla* clearly distinguishes itself from the poetic forms to which it is indebted and establishes many features which will recur in later epyllia: the freedom to alter Ovid's narrative in pursuit of a refocused theme; the ironically handled narrator; the humorously anthropomorphic deity; the aggressive feminine wooer; the indirect appeals to a sophisticated audience; the satirical enactment of love-poetry clichés; the final parody of Ovidian moralized commentary. Lodge is less profoundly Ovidian than Shakespeare in his presentation of the simultaneously comic and tragic ambivalence of love, but *Glaucus and Scilla* does anticipate *Venus and Adonis* in its central theme, as it does also in its elaborately rhetorical sixains (which, interestingly enough, are at their best in the passage on Venus and Adonis). Lodge's epyllion is important not just because it is the first, but because it indicates so many of the possibilities explored in the epyllia which follow it.

Chapter III

Venus and Adonis

Shakespeare's first published work as a poet was an epyllion. With the London theatres closed in 1592-1593 by the plague, Shakespeare was temporarily prevented from writing for "Pennie-knaves delight" (to borrow Lodge's phrase from *Glaucus and Scilla*), so he took the opportunity to write and publish *Venus and Adonis* and thus to put himself before the public as a "serious" author.[1] This "first heir of my invention," as he calls *Venus and Adonis*, is dedicated to the Earl of Southampton, whose sybaritic taste it was presumably meant to flatter.[2] Shakespeare's strategy for the occasion, we might speculate, was this: he would treat one of the most familiar of mythological subjects,[3] but he would elaborate the subject into the new kind of poem introduced by Lodge three or four years earlier. Whether or not the striking stanzas on Venus and Adonis in *Glaucus and Scilla* actually suggested the subject of Shakespeare's epyllion it is impossible to say. But it does seem probable that without Lodge's epyllion, Shakespeare's career as a professional poet would not have begun as it did.

The poem which marks this auspicious moment has proved especially troubling to modern readers and critics. Coleridge's praise of the style of *Venus and Adonis* is well known, but even he complained of "the unpleasing nature of the subject."[4] Later nineteenth- and early twentieth-century critics tended to agree about the subject, and many of them found the style "unpleasing" as well, although allowances were always made for passages of beautiful natural description, such as the lines on "poor Wat" (ll. 697–708). This tradition of disparaging criticism culminates in Douglas Bush's attack on *Venus and Adonis*. The poem is, for Bush, a not-very-original indulgence in literary fashion which fails both as "an orgy of the senses" and as "a decorative pseudo-classic picture."[5] A rather daunting number of critics since Bush have tried to rescue the poem from his judgment by emphasizing the deliberate humor and satire, by reading the poem as a traditional moral and even religious allegory, or by proposing rather more pluralistic readings intended to accommodate the poem's many contradictory aspects.[6]

This last approach has come closest to doing justice to Shakespeare's epyllion, not just because it allows one to avoid a restrictive commitment either to a comic or to a conventionally moral interpretation, but because

Shakespeare's handling of the mythological material is so deeply, at times even confusingly, ambivalent. Working with a myth that already carried a number of established philosophical and allegorical significances, Shakespeare evokes, plays with, even parodies many of these significances, and in the process develops a version of the story to which all the previously established interpretations are inadequate. It is not surprising, really, that we have had such trouble reading *Venus and Adonis*. As for imagining the effect of the poem's complexity and difficulty on Southampton and the sophisticated audience it was originally meant to please, we are in no better, and no worse, a position than when we speculate about contemporary understanding of *Twelfth Night*, *Hamlet*, or *Measure for Measure*.

With Shakespeare, as with Lodge, alterations made in adapting Ovid's episode are a key indication of the main thematic concerns. Shakespeare's major change was to make Venus more aggressively lustful than she is in the *Metamorphoses* and to have Adonis actively resist her advances. The effect of this change is the creation of a sexual conflict which is not present at all in the *Metamorphoses*. Ovid's Venus is comparatively restrained and decorous in her approaches. Having been accidentally grazed by one of Cupid's arrows (X. 526) and for the first time made to fall in love with a mortal (X. 529), she tucks her garments up about her knees like Diana (an irony which Shakespeare eliminates) and accompanies Adonis for an unspecified length of time as his hunting companion (X. 533-541). When they stop to rest Venus begins her wooing with kisses and with the tale of Atalanta and Hippomenes, the latter ostensibly meant to persuade Adonis to give up hunting savage animals. There is no suggestion that Adonis is either bashful or that he finds Venus's solicitations unpleasant:

> Sed labor insolitus iam me lassavit, et, ecce,
> opportuna sua blanditur populus umbra,
> datque torum caespes: libet hac requiescere tecum'
> (et requievit) 'humo' pressitque et gramen et ipsum
> inque sinu iuvenis posita cervice reclinis
> sic ait ac mediis interserit oscula verbis:
>
> (X. 554–559)

["But now this unaccustomed toil has tired me out, and look!—a poplar beckons us with its welcome shade, and the turf provides a couch: I would like to rest here with you" (and she reclined) "on the ground." She lay down on the grass and on him, and leaning backwards, with her head resting in the curve of the youth's neck, she spoke, interspersing her words with kisses.]

This cool, shady, secluded spot, as Segal has shown, is one of Ovid's characteristic settings for violent sexual aggression[7]—but Ovid's Venus is not aggressive or threatening at all. She is seen leaning back and resting her head on Adonis's neck ("inque sinu iuvenis posita cervice reclinis," I. 558)—the gesture is almost demurely submissive.

Ovid says nothing about Adonis's response to Venus, but the reader is led to suppose that he submits to her advances since there is no indication to the contrary. Ovid's Adonis is certainly old enough to understand what Venus is about: although he is referred to in line 558 as "iuvenis," we are given a clear statement of his development into young manhood earlier in the episode:

> nuper erat genitus, modo formosissimus infans,
> iam iuvenis, iam vir, iam se formosior ipso est
>
> (X. 522-523)

[. . . only lately born, he was soon a most beautiful child, then a youth, then a man, now more beautiful than his former self. . . .]

In the *Metamorphoses* Adonis is not averse to love, nor is he too young to respond to Venus's blandishments. He simply refuses to heed Venus's warnings against hunting savage beasts and is subsequently killed by a boar.

Shakespeare could have found many suggestions in previous Renaissance poetry for making Venus more aggressively lustful. In Abraham Fraunce's *Amintas Dale* (1592), to name just one extraordinary English example which appeared a year before *Venus and Adonis*, Venus makes love to Adonis with greedy abandon:

> Adonis lipps with her owne lipps kindely she kisseth,
> Rolling tongue, moyst mouth with her owne mouth all
>   to be sucking,
> Mouth and tong and lipps, with *Joves* drinck Nectar
>   abounding.[8]

There are almost no previous examples, however, of a chaste, petulant Adonis repelled by Venus's advances. In fact most of the evidence suggests that the Elizabethans tended to view Adonis, as Fraunce clearly does in the lines just quoted, as amorous and willing to be seduced. The arras of Spenser's Castle Joyous in Book III of *The Faerie Queene* depicts Adonis giving in to Venus and becoming her "Paramoure." Five cantos later Spenser tells how Venus would visit the Garden of Adonis to "reape sweet pleasure of the wanton boy" (*FQ* III.vi.46.3).[9] A four-stanza lyric in Robert Greene's *Perimedes the Blacke-Smithe* (1588) presents "Wanton Adonis" as a playful "wag" who "waxt bold" and was "fierd by fond desire" when Venus kissed him.[10]

Were there no precedents at all for Shakespeare's reversal of the traditional Elizabethan conception of Adonis? Erwin Panofsky has proposed that the version of Titian's *Venus and Adonis* now in the Prado, Madrid [Frontispiece], inspired Shakespeare's actively resistant Adonis.[11] This painting was commissioned for Philip II and sent to him in London in 1554, where it may have remained well into the seventeenth century.[12] Shakespeare could conceivably have seen the painting itself, then, although it is more likely that he would have known one of the sixteenth-century engravings done after it. Titian depicts Venus in an extremely awkward pose—she twists around and clutches at Adonis as he strides away with his spear and his hunting dogs. Adonis appears rather pleased with himself, and perhaps slightly embarrassed at the goddess's pathetically undignified behavior. The first four lines of the stanza which Coleridge has made one of the most famous in the poem could serve as a poetic "title" for Titian's painting. Adonis has just delivered his long speech on love and lust:

> With this he breaketh from the sweet embrace
> Of those fair arms which bound him to her breast,
> And homeward through the dark laund runs apace;
> Leaves love upon her back deeply distress'd.
>   Look how a bright star shooteth from the sky,
>   So glides he in the night from Venus' eye;
>   (ll. 811–816)

Earlier criticism of Shakespeare's poetry is full of vague, impressionistic adjectives like "Titianesque" and "Rubenesque," as a glance through the Variorum edition of the *Poems* will show. One would like to be able to follow Panofsky in thinking that for once we have a concrete instance of Shakespeare's being inspired by a great Renaissance painting.

Certain aspects of Panofsky's argument are open to question. Although Titian's decision to treat the "leave-taking of Adonis" represents a departure from the usual Renaissance approach to the myth, his treatment is not unprecedented, as Panofsky claims. There are antique representations of this moment, such as that in the relief scene from a sarcophagus of the second century, A.D., in the Lateran Museum [Fig. 3]. Titian does appear to have been the first sixteenth-century artist to revive the subject, however, and he was clearly the most prominent: the numerous treatments of this subject in late sixteenth- and early seventeenth-century Italian and northern painting all look back more or less directly to Titian's painting. More important for our purposes are the differences between Titian's painting and Shakespeare's epyllion, differences which Panofsky does not mention. Titian's Adonis looks somewhat older and considerably larger and stronger than Shakespeare's—Titian's Venus could not possibly "pluck" this Adonis from his horse, as Shakespeare's does (l. 30). And although Titian's Adonis is shown resisting Venus, there is nothing in the painting which proves that Titian thought of Adonis as having resisted Venus throughout the encounter (unless it is the fact that Cupid is shown asleep without his arrows, suggesting that perhaps, having mischievously caused Venus to fall in love with Adonis, Cupid has failed to inflict the "wound" upon Adonis which would satisfy his mother's desire).[13] But the striking correspondences between Titian's painting and the pivotal stanza of Shakespeare's narrative remain, and once we have acknowledged these qualifications, we may go on to conclude that Shakespeare's handling of the myth was quite possibly influenced by Titian's *Venus and Adonis* or by a sixteenth-century print after it.

But if Titian's painting gave Shakespeare the hint for a chaste, resistant Adonis, Ovid himself provided the models for developing this conception in the tales of Hermaphroditus *(Metamorphoses* IV. 285-388), Narcissus *(Metamorphoses* III. 342-510), and Hippolytus *(Metamorphoses* XV. 492-546). Like Shakespeare's Adonis, all of these figures are supremely beautiful young men full of self-love and self-ignorance who come to tragic ends when they refuse to acknowledge the power of sexual love.

The structural and thematic consequences which follow from Shakespeare's alteration of the behavior of Ovid's Venus and Adonis are profound. The antithetical, bipartite structure of *Venus and Adonis,* the vaguest outline of which Shakespeare found in the *Metamorphoses,* is made much more prominent and is charged with significance. Several structural patterns have been proposed for *Venus and Adonis,*[14] but the fundamental one is that of the wooing and the hunt,[15] or as Don Cameron Allen sees it, of the "soft hunt" of love and the "hard hunt" after the boar.[16] On the narrative level the division between the two parts comes after Venus finally forces Adonis to yield a kiss and asks for a meeting on the next day:

> He tells her no, tomorrow he intends
> To hunt the boar with certain of his friends.
>
> (ll. 587–588)

3. Relief scene from a Roman sarcophagus (2nd cent. A.D., Antonine) showing the "leave-taking of Adonis" (Rome, Museo Profano Lateranense, No. 769).

Photo Alinari.

4. Bartholomeus Spranger, *Venus and Adonis* (Amsterdam, Rijksmuseum; ca. 1595).

These lines, with their peculiar note of colloquial bathos (it is one of the few times in the poem when indirect speech is used), function as the hinge in the "pattern set up between the two parts" of the poem, through which Shakespeare "explores the nature of Venus' love, of Adonis' refusal, and of the significance of the Boar."[17]

Shakespeare's way of handling Venus and Adonis sets them in absolute opposition to one another and throws into relief a whole set of conflicts inherent in their relationship and in their own separate identities. On the most literal level their relationship is based upon the polarities of female/male and goddess/mortal, and Shakespeare disrupts the normal condition of both these polarities. Much more emphatically than Lodge, he reverses the conventional sexual roles of "wooer" and "wooed": Venus is the "bold-fac'd suitor" (l. 6); Adonis is the shy, reluctant beauty, "stain to all nymphs, more lovely than a man" (l. 9). In addition, this reversal of sexual roles is yoked to an inversion of the normal relation between divinity and mortal. Venus, as a goddess, should work her will upon the mortal Adonis, but she does not. On the contrary, passion makes her totally dependent upon him.

> Poor queen of love, in thine own law forlorn,
> To love a cheek that smiles at thee in scorn!
> (ll. 251-252)

Shakespeare exploits to the full the fact that in this myth the "sexual order" and what we might for want of a better term call the "cosmological order" are inseparable. Disorder in the sexual sphere (female wooing male) means disorder in the "cosmological" sphere (a divinity dependent upon the affection and fancy of a mortal).[18] Underlying this double conflict is an acute perception about sexual love which Shakespeare develops with ambivalent irony: the wooer, although he (or she) initiates and takes the lead in a relationship, is actually more dependent than the person being wooed, since it is the wooer who offers his (or her) affection and risks being rejected.

Shakespeare expands the thematic resonance of the sexual and "cosmological" conflicts in his epyllion in terms of the traditional association of Venus with love and Adonis with beauty. The theme of the poem may be crudely described as a tragic parody of the Platonic doctrine that love is the desire for beauty. The controlling idea has been succinctly stated in a fine essay on the poem by Eugene Cantelupe: "Adonis-Beauty and Venus-Love should be complementary and sequential, but they are opposed and contradictory."[19] This theme is most familiar to us, perhaps, through its repeated appearance in the sonnets. And in *Venus and Adonis*, as in the sonnets, Shakespeare is concerned not just with the conflict and incompatibility between love and beauty, but also with the contradictions inherent in love and beauty which bring this incompatibility about. So we can describe the theme of the epyllion somewhat more concretely as the opposition between sexual love so intense and aggressive that it becomes self-frustrating and beauty so selfish and inaccessible that it becomes self-destructive.

Let us now bring this abstract thematic introduction into line with the dramatic and verbal details of what Shakespeare actually wrote. To talk of *Venus and Adonis* as I have done in the preceding paragraph is to make the poem seem a very serious work indeed. But in addition to offering his poetry for the first time to the reading public, Shakespeare, like Lodge before him, was out to entertain a small sophisticated audience. The comedy, satire, and witty eroticism of *Venus and Adonis* must have succeeded marvelously in diverting Southampton and his coterie. The extraordinary thing about the poem, however, is that its seriousness—its insight into the turbulence and frustration of sexual love—is inseparable from its comedy and its entertaining eroticism. Whereas in *Glaucus and Scilla* one felt that Ovid's narrative had been changed into a clever, richly ornamented joke about Elizabethan love poetry, with the darker side of the myth present only in an implicit and unresolved way, in *Venus and Adonis* Shakespeare manages to intensify the potentially disturbing conflicts in Ovid's narrative and at the same time to exploit, as no one before him had done, the comic, satirical, and erotic possibilities of the myth.

The fundamental ambivalence of *Venus and Adonis* is nowhere more conspicuous than in Shakespeare's handling of Venus. He wastes no time in capitalizing on the comic and satirical potential of making her more aggressively lustful. In the opening stanzas Ovidian comic anthropomorphism is inflated and extended far beyond its range in the *Metamorphoses* as Shakespeare plays with the idea of a Venus human enough to make use of conventional poetic hyperbole and superhuman enough to tuck a young man under her arm:

> With this she seizeth on his sweating palm,
> The precedent of pith and livelihood,
> And trembling in her passion, calls it balm,
> Earth's sovereign salve to do a goddess good;
>   Being so enrag'd, desire doth lend her force
>   Courageously to pluck him from his horse.
>
>   (ll. 25-30)

Venus's attempt to convert the sweat of Adonis's hand into a "sovereign salve" fit for the gods is comically undermined by that superb colloquialism—"to do a goddess good"—which exposes the real earthiness of this goddess's desires. Throughout these early stanzas Venus's sheer physical grossness deflates her efforts to place her wooing of Adonis on a properly divine and transcendent level:

> Panting he lies and breatheth in her face.
> She feedeth on the steam as on a prey,
> And calls it heavenly moisture, air of grace,
>
> (ll. 62-64)

Here the very sound of the words—the repeated *p, h, th, sh, st*—evokes the rudimentary physical reality which Venus tries to elevate verbally to a "heavenly" sphere. Never was a goddess more earthbound than Venus, or more human in her desire to etherealize the essential physicality of sensual experience.

The satiric dimension of Venus's behavior derives primarily from the way in which her speeches often parody the conventions of Renaissance love poetry.[20] What takes Shakespeare's exploitation of such parody so far beyond that of Lodge is not merely his superior verbal imagination, but the way in which the parody is related to and becomes expressive of the poem's deepest thematic concerns. Venus's extravagant hyperboles are interesting not just as humorous exaggerations of poetic convention, but also as expressions of the overbearing, suffocating love she offers Adonis:

> If thou wilt deign this favour, for thy meed
> A thousand honey secrets shalt thou know.
> Here come and sit, where never serpent hisses,
> And being set, I'll smother thee with kisses.
>
> (ll. 15-18)

Shakespeare adds to the subtlety of these expressive parodies by having Venus herself become aware on occasion that her verbal wooing has gotten out of control. Here she realizes that Adonis might not enjoy being smothered with kisses and "A thousand honey secrets," and she quickly tries to reverse her rhetorical strategy:

> "And yet not cloy thy lips with loath'd satiety,
> But rather famish them amid their plenty,
> Making them red, and pale, with fresh variety:
>
> (ll. 19-21)

Venus cannot get away from the imagery of feeding, however much she varies that imagery. Nor can she avoid hyperbole for very long—in the very next line she is back promising Adonis "Ten kisses short as one, one long as twenty" (l. 22). She ends the stanza on a very clever note, however, appealing subversively to Adonis's fondness for "sport":

> A summer's day will seem an hour but short,
> Being wasted in such time-beguiling sport."
> (ll. 23-24)

The puns on "sport" (common Elizabethan usage for "womanizing" or "whoring"[21]) throughout *Venus and Adonis* expose the relationship—the difference and the similarity—between Adonis's love of hunting and Venus's "soft hunt" of love.

Shakespeare grants Venus a great deal of wit and resourcefulness in her wooing. We often laugh sympathetically with her as well as critically at her. Take, for example, her three-stanza allusion to her love affair with Mars (ll. 97-114). Robert P. Miller has shown how Shakespeare turns this allusion into "a piece of delightful dramatic self-revelation" by having Venus tell it not as a story of adultery and shameful exposure, as it is in Homer (*Odyssey* VII. 266 ff.) and in Ovid (*Ars Amatoria* II. 561 ff. and *Metamorphoses* IV. 171 ff.), but as the ultimate proof of the power of her attractiveness.[22] One need not invoke the Christian allegorical interpretation of the story of Mars, Venus, and Vulcan as Miller does to establish the dramatic function of the allusion—the classical version itself is completely altered by Venus's failure to mention Vulcan and his net.

But ironic self-exposure is not the only effect of this speech. Venus is trying here to shame Adonis into compliance, and she is extremely skillful in her efforts. The masculine sexual imagery she employs, for example, has the desired effect of placing Mars in critical opposition to Adonis:

> "I have been woo'd as I entreat thee now,
> Even by the stern and direful god of war,
> Whose sinewy neck in battle ne'er did bow,
> (ll. 97-99)

> "Over my altars hath he hung his lance,
> His batter'd shield, his uncontrolled crest.
> (ll. 103-104)

Venus may have overlooked the fact that the phrase "as I entreat thee now" results in a partial transference of Mars's masculinity to herself, but never mind. Without a moment's hesitation she goes on to give a very convincing and triumphantly ironic picture of her domination over Mars:

> And for my sake hath learn'd to sport and dance,
> To toy, to wanton, dally, smile and jest,
>   Scorning his churlish drum and ensign red,
>   Making my arms his field, his tent my bed.
>   (ll. 105-108)

One has to admire that final chiasmus. Marlowe clearly did, for he reinforces the joke about Hero's tantalizing attempt to "evade" Leander with a line which recalls Venus's victory over Mars: "And as her silver body downward went / With both her hands she made the bed a tent" (II. 263-264). In the next stanza Venus delivers what remains one of the great lines in the poem, however many sources for it may be culled from previous literature.[23]

> "Thus he that overrul'd I oversway'd,
>   Leading him prisoner in a red rose chain:
>   (ll. 109-110)

Shakespeare wants the reader to be aware of the distortion involved in Venus's allusion to her affair with Mars, but he also wants us to admire the verbal resourcefulness of her performance.

A few stanzas after the allusion to Mars, Venus extols her own beauty in what several critics have shown to be a parody of the convention which Lodge also treated ironically in Glaucus and Scilla—the blason, or catalogue of feminine charms. Normally the supplicating wooer enumerates the physical delights of the lady to whom he is appealing; here the lady is wooer, and she enumerates her own charms. First, however, she catalogues the physical defects she does not possess:

> Were I hard-favour'd, foul, or wrinkled old,
> Ill-nurtur'd, crooked, churlish, harsh in voice,
> O'erworn, despised, rheumatic, and cold,
> Thick-sighted, barren, lean, and lacking juice,
>   Then mightst thou pause, for then I were not for thee;
>   (ll. 133-137)

This stanza may work ironically against Venus by suggesting that she is sensitive about her age. But it also works for her, in that it sets up an image of ugly, unappealing femininity against which any woman would look good. It also makes the catalogue of self-praise which follows less ridiculous than it would be otherwise. The reader is drawn into Venus's rhetorical world and made to see things from her point of view, even as he is made to laugh at her over-heated, self-defeating wooing.

Shakespeare never allows the reader's attitude towards Venus to settle into an established position. We find ourselves sympathizing with her when she seems most grotesque and ludicrous; we also find ourselves critically distanced from her just when she seems to be enjoying her strongest moments. Consider, for instance, Venus's comment on the episode of the courser and the jennet (ll. 259–324). The argument over this episode has been between those who view the behavior of Adonis's courser towards the jennet as an emblem of animal lust which Shakespeare wants the reader to condemn and which he uses to dramatize the bestial nature of Venus's love,[24] and those who see the behavior of the horses as lending "force to Venus's argument that physical love is natural and inevitable."[25] The latter view is more nearly correct, but it needs considerable adjustment.

It has been argued that the episode reflects Venus's and not the poem's ideal of healthy sexual energy, but this view overlooks the fact that the sequence is related by the narrator, not by Venus. The episode is placed so as to bring about a welcome release from the tension built up over the first 250 lines of confrontation and impasse, and this release of tension draws the reader sympathetically into what has justly been called an "anti-type to the main action."[26] Adonis's courser is described in language betokening power, freedom, and masculine dignity. "Strong-neck'd steed" (l. 263) recalls the "sinewy neck" of Mars (l. 99) which "in battle ne'er did bow," and like Mars's "uncontrolled crest," the courser's "braided hanging mane / Upon his compass'd crest now stand on end" (ll. 271–272). He moves towards the jennet "with gentle majesty and modest pride" (l. 278). The behavior of the horses is presented as admirable and natural, and in this sense it does support Venus's earlier argument that "By law of nature thou art bound to breed" (l. 171—Venus's use of "breed" in this line is important). The majestic sexual energy of the courser also reflects contemptuously on Adonis's coy petulance. Shakespeare sums up the relationship in an ambiguous couplet:

> Look what a horse should have he did not lack,
> Save a proud rider on so proud a back.
>
> (ll. 299–300)

We may first take this to mean that Adonis's horse ought to be under the control of a rider, that his freedom is somehow not right. But the pressure on the repeated word "proud" makes us see that while Adonis is "proud" in the sense of having an inordinate self-esteem, he lacks "pride" in the sense of "sexual desire."[27] Adonis's courser deserves a master equal to himself in "pride"—a master who combines lofty self-esteem with masculine sexual drive.

Given the verbal details just noted, the episode of the courser and the jennet would appear to place Venus in an extremely favorable position. Yet Venus's over-eagerness to turn the episode to her own benefit (ll. 385–408) reminds us that horses are, after all, animals, and that any attempt to look to the behavior of animals, however full of dignified natural energy and freedom they might be, as a model for human or divine behavior will have to confront the limiting implications of such an analogy. Venus's superficial inferences make us aware of the limitations of all comparisons between animal and human behavior. At the same time, Venus's insistence on such comparison forces us to realize that her own animal lust is less worthy of respect than that of the horses. She possesses little of the physical grace and majesty of the horses, however fervently she proclaims these virtues for herself. Even the parallels with the Mars allusion show that Venus's behavior towards Adonis is not in accord with the natural sexual behavior of the horses. What Venus emphasized in that allusion was that Mars "hath . . . been my captive and my slave" (l. 101), that he "was . . . servile to my coy disdain" (l. 112). Venus wants to control and dominate powerful masculine sexuality, not revel in it as the jennet does (ll. 307–318); her overt aggressiveness is the very opposite of the jennet's cunningly provocative behavior. So when Venus comes to comment on the horses, her conclusions are partly undermined by her own failure to act with the natural beauty, dignity, and freedom of the animals she praises.

The conflicts in Venus's sexual nature become clear when we compare these stanzas where animal sexuality is presented in human terms with the more prevalent examples of the reverse, of Venus's own sexuality presented in animal terms. The narrator sees Venus not as an embodiment of healthy animal sexuality, but as a savage bird of prey:

> Even as an empty eagle, sharp by fast,
> Tires with her beak on feathers, flesh and bone,
> Shaking her wings, devouring all in haste,
> Till either gorge be stuff'd or prey be gone:
>> (ll. 55–58)

This view of Venus as a ravaging animal culminates in the moment when Adonis finally agrees to grant Venus a kiss as a reward for permission to go home. His kiss turns Venus from an eagle into a vulture:

> He with her plenty press'd, she faint with dearth,
> Their lips together glued, fall to the earth.
>
> Now quick desire hath caught the yielding prey,
> And glutton-like she feeds, yet never filleth.
> Her lips are conquerers, his lips obey,
> Paying what ransom the insulter willeth;
>   Whose vulture thought doth pitch the price so high
>   That she will draw his lips' rich treasure dry.
>
> (ll. 545-552)

It is significant that Venus is seen at her worst when Adonis momentarily submits to her lust and together they "fall to the earth." Beauty is complicit in Love's degradation. Nevertheless, this imagery of savage bestiality,[28] joined as it is here and elsewhere with imagery of voracious appetite, works against any tendency to treat Venus merely comically, as "a forty-year-old countess with a taste for Chapel Royal altos,"[29] or merely pathetically, as "Poor queen of love, in thine own law forlorn." Venus is at times both comic and pathetic, but at other times her lust is repellent and grotesque. Our attitude towards her—like our attitude towards sexual experience itself—must somehow incorporate all these conflicting responses.

The first epithet used of Venus is "Sick-thoughted"—to remember the term now is to see it reverberate with a more disturbing range of meanings than it might have at first, when one could accept the usual gloss of "love-sick." The full implications of Adonis's first epithet, "rose-cheek'd," are not realized until the final metamorphosis at the end of the poem. But we can begin to examine Shakespeare's handling of Adonis, which has received much less attention than his handling of Venus, by looking at the emphasis on his soft, effeminate beauty suggested in the poem's opening stanza.

The context in which the Venus and Adonis episode appears in the *Metamorphoses* is important to the way in which Shakespeare conceives of Adonis and thus to the establishment of a type which appears in a number of later epyllia—the ideally beautiful young man who appeals to both sexes but who is himself uninterested in love. In the *Metamorphoses* the story of Venus and Adonis is told by Orpheus as part of his long lamenting discourse to the assembly of wild animals after the final loss of Eurydice. Orpheus's song begins with two tales of homosexual love, the reason being that after the loss of Eurydice he shunned all love of women and set the example for the people of Thrace by giving his love to young boys (X. 79-85). Orpheus's song is attended by the cypress (X. 106), the metamorphosed form of the youth Cyparissus, beloved of Phoebus. And Orpheus begins by singing of Jove's love for Ganymede (X. 155-161) and of Phoebus's love for Hyacinthus (X. 162-219). There then follow three tales involving aberrant feminine sexuality: prostitution in the case of the Propoetides, who also play a part in the tale of Pygmalion which follows; incest in the case of Myrrha, mother of Adonis. These three tales relate obviously, if indirectly, to Orpheus's homoerotic theme and may have influenced Shakespeare's handling of Venus. Finally, Orpheus concludes his song with the story of Venus and Adonis. There is nothing explicitly suggestive of homoeroticism in Orpheus's presentation of Adonis, but the fact that the Venus and Adonis episode comes as the conclusion to a discourse which begins with a strong emphasis on homoeroticism may have influenced the homoerotic overtones of Shakespeare's presentation of Adonis—his soft beauty, his petulant self-concern, his excessive aversion to feminine sexual advances.[30]

The androgyny of Adonis's beauty is announced by Venus in the very first lines she speaks:

> "Thrice fairer than myself," thus she began,
> "The field's chief flower, sweet above compare;
> Stain to all nymphs, more lovely than a man,
>
> (ll. 7-9)

Language of this sort, and subsequent references to the "maiden burning" of Adonis's cheek (l. 50) and to his "mermaid voice" (l. 429), suggest Adonis's kinship to Hermaphroditus. But the phrase "more lovely than a man" is ambiguous: Adonis is more beautiful than a "man" understood sexually, and hence demands comparison with the fairest of women; he is also more beautiful than "man" understood generically, more beautiful than a mortal. This ambiguity is richly expressive of the way in which the soft, effeminate male became for the Renaissance an ideal type of human beauty. Shakespeare's attitude towards this ideal, however, is deeply ambivalent. He goes on to develop the two principal aspects of Adonis's beauty—its effeminacy and its ideality—in a way which elicits responses as shifting and as contradictory as those elicited by Venus.

Part of the difficulty in evaluating Adonis stems from the fact that much of what we learn about him comes from Venus.[31] The most explicit comments about the feminine quality of his beauty come from her, as do the imputations of an unmasculine self-love. There is, for example, the stanza in which Venus links Adonis with Narcissus. Ovid's emphasis on

Narcissus's androgynous beauty (he appeals to both sexes) and on his aversion to the erotic interest others show in him suggests that Shakespeare was thinking of him throughout his presentation of Adonis [see Fig. 5].[32] But the avidity with which Venus uses the story of Narcissus to charge Adonis with unnatural self-love challenges the reader's sense of objectivity:

> "Is thine own heart to thine own face affected?
> Can thy right hand seize love upon thy left?
> Then woo thyself, be of thyself rejected;
> Steal thine own freedom, and complain on theft.
>   Narcissus so himself himself forsook,
>   And died to kiss his shadow in the brook.
>   (ll. 157–162)

On the verbal level Venus's warning is extremely effective—notice how the imagery and repeating syntax evoke the idea of Narcissus longing after his own reflection. And in some respects Adonis's pouting self-concern does seem to bear out Venus's charge. "The sun doth burn my face," he complains, "I must remove" (l. 186). But there is nothing in the poem to indicate that Adonis is actively narcissistic about his own beauty, that his "own heart" is in fact to his "own face affected." The point is— and here we can agree with Venus—that a potential or latent narcissism certainly does exist in Adonis.

The ambivalence with which Shakespeare treats the ideality of Adonis's beauty poses similar interpretive problems. Critics have complained of the superficiality of Adonis's character, calling him "an incomplete sketch of what might, in a less confusing poem, have been a characterization,"[33] or "'a man of wax,' a beautiful but self-centered and baffling creature."[34] What these critics are responding to, I think, is the extreme externality with which Shakespeare treats Adonis in order to bring out his thematic significance as an embodiment of ideal but unresponsive beauty. Adonis sometimes seems to us, as he does to Venus, a work of art rather than a human being:

> "Fie, lifeless picture, cold and senseless stone,
> Well-painted idol, image dull and dead,
> Statue contenting but the eye alone,
> Thing like a man, but of no woman bred!
>   Thou art no man, though of a man's complexion,
>   For men will kiss even by their own direction."
>   (ll. 211–226)

5. Jaspar de Isaac, "Narcissus" (engraving). *Images ou Tableaux de Platte Peinture des deux Philostrates Sophistes Grecs*. Paris, 1614-1615, p. 191.

As Geoffrey Bullough has pointed out, Venus's lines recall another of the tales from Orpheus's song in Book X of the *Metamorphoses,* the tale of Pygmalion.[35] Adonis seems to Venus like Pygmalion's statue before it was given life—ideally beautiful and erotically arousing but cold, inanimate, unresponsive. The allusion, and the language Venus employs here ("Thou art no man . . . "), extend the connection between the ideality and the effeminacy of Adonis's beauty. But as with the allusion to Narcissus, one must be wary of accepting Venus's charges at face value. The constant emphasis in the poem on the way Adonis looks, rather than on what he thinks or feels, makes us want to agree with Venus. On the other hand, the descriptive details we are given about Adonis show him to be anything but an "image dull and dead." His "sweating palm," as Venus herself points out, is a "precedent of pith and livelihood" (ll. 25-26), as is his panting breath (ll. 62-64). Even his excessive blushing, though it is often described in the stylized contrasting imagery of red and white, shows Adonis to be full of physical and emotional intensity. The paradox for Venus, and to a certain extent for the reader, is that this remarkably beautiful and vibrantly alive creature refuses to interest himself in the love he arouses and seems so well suited for.

I say the reader sympathizes with Venus's frustration to a certain extent: there is something mean and perverse in Adonis's aversion to love as such ("Hunting he lov'd, but love he laugh'd to scorn," l. 4), but there is also something very understandable about his aversion to the domineering, suffocating, oppressive love Venus offers him. Shakespeare allows the reader to sympathize both with Venus's frustration and with Adonis's reluctance; he also forces the reader to recognize the excessive lust which makes Venus's frustration inevitable and the priggish dislike of sexual love which makes Adonis's reluctance so unappealing.

The demands upon the reader's capacity to be simultaneously sympathetic and critical are perhaps at their greatest at the end of the first "movement" of the poem, when Venus argues the "infirmities" of beauty and the consequent need to procreate with at least some of the force these arguments generate in the sonnets (ll. 733-768).[36] Adonis follows with his surprisingly eloquent discourse on the difference between love and lust. The reader's initial tendency is to be suspicious of this discourse, since it comes from one so lacking in experience and so primly confident of his moral purity:

> For know, my heart stands armed in mine ear,
> And will not let a false sound enter there; . . .

> "Lest the deceiving harmony should run
> Into the quiet closure of my breast,
> And then my little heart were quite undone,
> (ll. 779-783)

Yet Adonis's speech contains a distinction which Shakespeare wants us to apply to the poem, if only to demonstrate that the distinction between love and lust cannot be held absolutely. He therefore partly undermines our misgivings about Adonis's lack of experience by having Adonis himself anticipate this objection:

> "More I could tell, but more I dare not say:
> The text is old, the orator too green.
>
> (ll. 805–806)

Adonis also directly contradicts the narrator's introductory statement about his aversion to love ("love he laugh'd to scorn") by distinguishing between the love that "is all truth" (l. 804) and Venus's "sweating lust":

> I hate not love, but your device in love
> That lends embracements unto every stranger.
> You do it for increase: O strange excuse
> When reason is the bawd to lust's abuse!
>
> (ll. 789–792)

Adonis's conception of love is inadequate, since it makes no allowance at all for the power and importance of sexual experience. But the rhetorical effectiveness with which he articulates his view of love and his repugnance for "sweating lust" prevent the reader from "bracketing" this speech as easily and as clearly as he might wish.

The narrator's role in presenting the ambivalent confrontation between Venus and Adonis in the first half of the epyllion is extremely important. Coleridge, Dowden, and other early commentators noted the objectivity and detachment of Shakespeare's narrator.[37] Unlike Lodge's narrator in *Glaucus and Scilla*, whose past experiences and present reactions figure centrally in the poem's drama, Shakespeare's narrator rarely intrudes his own interests or sympathies. When he does, it is primarily to direct the reader's attention to the action he describes rather than to divulge anything about his own emotional state and sensibility:

> O what a sight it was, wistly to view
> How she came stealing to the wayward boy!
> To note the fighting conflict of her hue,
> How white and red each other did destroy!
>
> (ll. 343–346)

The narrator's exclamations here encourage the reader "to view," "to note." Coleridge slightly overstates the narrator's detachment, I think, when he describes him as "unparticipating in the passions" of the main figures and talks of his "alienation" and "utter aloofness."[38] On one or two occasions the narrator does address the main figures directly and manifests a sensitivity to their feelings, as in the epitomic couplet beginning "Poor queen of love, in thine own law forlorn" (ll. 251–252), or in the following comment after Venus in desperation has pulled Adonis down on top of her:

> But all in vain; good queen, it will not be.
> She hath assay'd as much as may be prov'd:
> (ll. 607–608)

Even here the narrator moves immediately after the first line from direct address to indirect commentary. All the narrator's exclamations and apostrophes are directed towards the event or situation he is describing. Shakespeare's narrator has no persona, in the sense that Lodge's narrator or Marlowe's narrator has a persona.

It is partly the neutrality and transparency of Shakespeare's narrator that give the style of *Venus and Adonis* its special effectiveness. The extreme artificiality of the style, particularly the elaborate use of syntactic and metaphorical antithesis, has come in for considerable censure from critics who have seen Shakespeare's writing in this poem as his sacrifice to the Elizabethan taste for extravagant verbal ornament and decoration.[39] And it is true that *Venus and Adonis*, like *Glaucus and Scilla*, reveals an "intoxicated delight in words,"[40] a "conscious, self-delighting artistry."[41] But Lodge's elaborately rhetorical sixains, however locally effective and cleverly parodic they sometimes are, never give one the sense that verbal structure is reflecting the structure of the narrative itself. Shakespeare's sixains constantly do this. Antithesis is the key verbal figure in the poem, as Bush points out;[42] antithesis is also the key to Shakespeare's conception of his myth, particularly in the first half of the poem. The intricate antithetical imagery and syntax with which the narrator presents the action reveal, on the most fundamental stylistic level, the ambivalent conflict between and within the protagonists.

Rhythm and syntax are often as important as metaphor to the narrator's antithetical description of the action:

> Backward she push'd him, as she would be thrust,
> And govern'd him in strength, though not in lust.
> (ll. 41–42)

The powerful caesuras in this couplet, intensified in the first line by the aural similarity of "push'd" and "thrust" and in the second line by the syntactic turn with "though," give one an almost physical sense of the struggle—not between Venus and Adonis, for she is doing all the pushing—but within Venus, between her actual physical aggression and her passionate desire that this aggression be returned. The "thrust" /"lust" rhyme points up the conflict between what she wants ("as she *would be* thrust") and what she gets (*"though not* in lust").

The most elaborately antithetical passages use syntax and line-endings to accentuate metaphorical antitheses:

> He burns with bashful shame, she with her tears
> Doth quench the maiden burning of his cheeks;
> (ll. 49–50)

Pausing at the end of line 49, we think that both Adonis and Venus are burning—he "with bashful shame," she "with her tears" (the repeated preposition is largely responsible for initiating this line of thought, plus the fact that "burning tears" is as common a notion as "burning shame"). But we read on to discover that Venus's tears actually "quench" (perhaps in the sense of "to satisfy" as well as "to extinguish") "the maiden burning of his cheeks." The underlying antithesis of fire and water is first disguised, then revealed in full.

Shakespeare sometimes heightens the ultimate effect of verbal antithesis by presenting it within a context of ostensible sameness or similarity:

> Full gently now she takes him by the hand,
> A lily prison'd in a gaol of snow,
> Or ivory in an alabaster band:
> So white a friend engirts so white a foe.
>   This beauteous combat, wilful and unwilling,
>   Show'd like two silver doves that sit a-billing.
> (ll. 361–366)

Coleridge quoted the first four lines as an example of "fancy . . . the faculty of bringing together images dissimilar in the main by some one point or more of likeness distinguished."[43] The "fancy" in this stanza, however, is permeated with an extraordinary degree of imaginative power. The "point of likeness," of course, is the whiteness of "lily," "snow," "ivory," "alabaster," and, as Muriel Bradbrook has pointed out, all these entities possess symbolic as well as physical characteristics ostensibly opposed to the heated attempt at seduction actually taking place:

The lily, the snow, the ivory, and the alabaster are all chosen for their chilly whiteness, which has nothing in common with that of flesh. They are all symbols of chastity: alabaster was used for the effigies on tombs and hence was opposed to blood, the symbol of life . . . lilies were the emblem of virginity: snow was an ancient symbol of chastity and its coldness suggests death. . . . Again there is a direct contrast to the warm flexuous restraint of Venus's melting palm in the *hardness* of the ivory and alabaster which *binds* it, in the idea of *imprisonment* in a gaol, and the besieging force *engirting* the enemy. This passage is built on sensuous opposites. . . .[44]

Miss Bradbrook does not notice, however, that the images in the stanza may turn out to be ironically appropriate when one looks at the full range of their connections with Venus and Adonis. The lily's connection with chastity *is* appropriate to Adonis—and so is the fact that it is a flower (Adonis is "the field's chief flower"). Ivory picks up the idea Venus has established of Adonis as "cold and senseless stone / . . . Statue contenting but the eye alone" (ll. 211-213). The connections of snow and alabaster with death are ironically prophetic of Adonis's death. The complex similarity and contrast in the stanza is even more complicatedly ambivalent than Miss Bradbrook allows.

One must see this stanza in its dramatic context, however, to become fully aware of its stylistic effectiveness. Having failed in her opening aggressive maneuvers, Venus has now changed her tactics and is trying to deal more delicately with Adonis. This shift in strategy, anticipated in the preceding stanzas and in the phrase "Full gently now" (l. 361), is the basis for the shift in imagery: instead of the alternating red and white of warm, moist, soft flesh, we have flesh presented entirely in terms of whiteness, coldness, and hardness. The imagery of the first four lines is as "unnatural" as is this kind of soft approach for Venus. The underlying conflict is present throughout, however, in the idea of imprisonment, in the paradox of a *friend* "engirting" a foe (not *foe* "engirting" foe), and in the "beauteous combat" of the "two silver doves," "wilful and unwilling," a combat which is ironic not only because doves are associated with peace, but also because doves are associated with Venus and love.[45] The imagery of the stanza reflects a moment of superficial, contrived harmony in a relationship which is fundamentally one of strife and conflict.

I have dealt at length with the first part of Shakespeare's epyllion, with the "soft hunt" of love, because it is here that he establishes, dramatically and stylistically, the ambivalent conflict so central to the meaning of *Venus and Adonis*. Adonis disappears from the poem in lines 811-816 and only reappears at the very end, when Venus comes upon his dead body. Adonis's departure brings to an end the confrontation upon which the first part of the poem is based; the second part belongs entirely to Venus, at least as far as dramatic interest is concerned. The hunt after the boar and the death of Adonis are presented either through Venus's own words or through the narrator's account of her reactions to these events.

With Adonis gone and with the entire focus of the epyllion on her, Venus becomes an even more ambivalent figure than she had been previously. Her vulnerability at the moment of Adonis's departure is conveyed in a couplet which shows how Shakespeare's antithetical style will be accommodated to the new situation:

> So did the merciless and pitchy night
> Fold in the object that did feed her sight.
> (ll. 821-822)

These lines are every bit as characteristic of the poem's stylistic virtues as the couplet of the preceding stanza which Coleridge praised at such length. The contrasting vowels of the alliterated "fold" and "feed" point up very powerfully the ominous way in which nature has deprived Venus of Adonis. The heightened sense of vulnerability which comes in at this point does not mean an end to the ironic treatment of Venus's love-sickness. The narrator tells us that the echoing lament she sings when Adonis has gone "was tedious, and outwore the night" (l. 841). And the next day, as Venus struggles through the underbrush towards the frothing boar and Adonis's baying hounds, she is met with this response from one of the wounded dogs:

> And here she meets another sadly scowling,
> To whom she speaks, and he replies with howling.
> (ll. 917-918)

The irony at Venus's expense continues through this section, but at the same time our sympathy for her is deepened. The image of the forlorn, anxious goddess begins to replace the image of the sweating, sexually ravenous amazon of the first 800 lines.

The most puzzling motif which emerges in the stanzas between the departure of Adonis and the discovery of his corpse is the idea of a maternal-filial relationship between Venus and Adonis. Venus breaks free from the brambles which hinder her rush towards Adonis

> Like a milch doe, whose swelling dugs do ache,
> Hasting to feed her fawn, hid in some brake.
> (ll. 875-876)

Miss Bradbrook reads these lines as a supreme expression of Venus being driven towards Adonis "by purely animal instinct,"[46] but the maternal overtones of the passage are stronger than the animalistic. These lines certainly work towards balancing our previous image of Venus as a savage bird of prey, with Adonis as her victim. Venus herself anticipates the image two stanzas earlier in her apostrophe to the rising sun:

> There lives a son that suck'd an earthly mother,
> May lend thee light, as thou dost lend to other."
>
> (ll. 863–864)

The way in which these lines remind us of the mortal/divine aspect of Adonis's relationship to Venus is clear, but the maternal imagery again strikes one as curious.

Looking back through the poem for some indication of how the reader is to respond to the maternal-filial imagery, one finds Venus speaking of Adonis's mother and anticipating the later passages as early as lines 201-204:

> Art thou a woman's son and canst not feel
> What 'tis to love, how want of love tormenteth?
> O had thy mother borne so hard a mind,
> She had not brought forth thee, but died unkind.

These lines work ironically against both Venus and Adonis. Adonis's mother, Myrrha, was indeed "unkind": she was possessed by an incestuous passion for her father Cinyras and conceived Adonis by him (*Metamorphoses* X. 311–519). But Myrrha did not die "unkind"—she was metamorphosed into a tree and as such gave birth to Adonis. Adonis has a turbulent sexual heritage of which both he and Venus seem to be unaware. Yet the idea of Adonis's mother comes to Venus on several occasions throughout the poem. What meaning are we to give to this recurring motif?

The critics who have noticed this maternal-filial imagery offer little help. D. C. Allen sees the relationship from a reverse perspective. Adonis "fusses over Venus as a boy might fuss over his mother," he says, while Venus merely "takes advantage of this filial-maternal relationship which is really all Adonis wants."[47] A. C. Hamilton speaks of Venus as "at times . . . the bustling mother caring for that petulant boy who weeps when the wind blows his hat off. . . ."[48] These comments get at some of the surface irony of the imagery, but they never really penetrate to the deeper level of suggestiveness. In addition to the obvious irony—Venus is old enough to be Adonis's mother—there is a submerged suggestion of incest, a suggestion which glances at the story of Adonis's mother Myrrha and, possibly, at Golding's comment on Book X in the "Epistle to Leicester":

> The tenth books cheefly dooth containe one kynd of argument
> Reproving most prodigious lusts of such as have bene bent
> To incest most unnaturall.
>
> (ll. 213–215)

What Shakespeare suggests with the implicitly incestuous maternal-filial imagery applied to Venus and Adonis is not a scandalous unnaturalness, but a connection between the erotic and the maternal aspects of the feminine psyche. Venus lusts after Adonis, but she is also maternally protective of him, especially in the second part of the poem.

The final scene of Shakespeare's epyllion, Venus weeping over the dead Adonis, was a favorite Renaissance set piece.[49] The way in which Shakespeare prepares for and conducts this scene transforms its usual significance and confronts one with the poem's most difficult interpretive problem. The crux of the problem is the relationship between Venus and the boar. Shakespeare begins to develop this relationship at the very first mention of the boar by showing Venus to be obsessively preoccupied with this particular beast:

> He tells her no, tomorrow he intends
> To hunt the boar with certain of his friends.
>
> "The boar," quoth she: whereat a sudden pale,
> Like lawn being spread upon the blushing rose,
> Usurps her cheek; . . .
>
> (ll. 587–591)

Venus's reaction to the boar here is, admittedly, occasioned by Adonis's own words, but the force of her reaction, intensified by the shift from indirect to direct speech, is suggestive of what we come to see as an obsession. And it is an obsession which Shakespeare did not find in Ovid's version of the story. In the *Metamorphoses* Venus warns Adonis about the savagery of boars, but she also warns him about lions and other savage beasts he might encounter in his hunt (*Metamorphoses* X. 547–552).

What Shakespeare does with the boar in *Venus and Adonis*, as A. T. Hatto has shown, is in part based on the medieval and Renaissance tradition of the boar as a symbol of "overbearing masculinity in love and war."[50] Chaucer develops both aspects of this tradition when he describes Troilus's dream of Criseyde after she has gone to the Greeks with Diomede:

> He mette he saugh a boor with tuskes grete,
> That sleep ayein the brighte soones hete.
> And by this boor, faste in his armes folde,
> Lay kissing ay his lady bright Criseyde.[51]
>
> (V. 1238-1241)

Shakespeare adapts the dream of the boar in *Richard III* (V.ii.7) and, more relevant to its appearance in *Venus and Adonis*, in *Cymbeline*, where Posthumus Leontes imagines Iachimo as "a full-acorned boar" who has "mounted" his wife (II.v.6). In *Cymbeline* and in Chaucer's *Troilus* the boar appears in the dreams or imaginations of jealous men who fear the unfaithfulness of their lovers. In *Venus and Adonis*, the vision of a boar torments a love-starved goddess who fears the loss of the young man to whom she is so powerfully attracted.

Adonis's first casual mention of the boar hunt moves Venus to put aside all restraint and to pull Adonis down on top of her (ll. 591-606). Then, when Adonis finally struggles free, Venus launches into a seventeen-stanza warning about the danger of the boar, a warning which includes two stanzas on the subject of jealousy. Venus had earlier mentioned jealousy in the process of telling how Adonis excited each of the five senses:

> "But oh what banquet wert thou to the taste,
> Being nurse and feeder of the other four!
> Would they not wish the feast might ever last,
> And bid suspicion double-lock the door,
> Lest jealousy, that sour unwelcome guest,
> Should by his stealing in disturb the feast?
>
> (ll. 445-450)

This first rather curiously motivated reference to jealousy is the prelude to the stanzas in the warning to Adonis. One notices the repeated imagery of locked doors and sentinels and of feasting and eating, and the similarity of "sour unwelcome guest" and "sour informer":

> "For where love reigns, disturbing jealousy
> Doth call himself affection's sentinel; . . .

> "This sour informer, this bate-breeding spy,
> This canker that eats up love's tender spring . . .

> Knocks at my heart, and whispers in mine ear,
> That if I love thee, I thy death should fear.
> (ll. 649–660)

Venus's jealousy here is based in part upon her identification of the boar with death and destruction, with the force that will deprive her of Adonis. But her jealousy also has an unmistakable sexual dimension.[52] Venus goes on to envision Adonis's death:

> "And more than so, presenteth to mine eye,
> The picture of an angry chafing boar,
> Under whose sharp fangs on his back doth lie
> An image like thyself, all stain'd with gore.
> (ll. 661–664)

This image of Adonis on his back having been gored by the boar is the reverse of the posture which Venus herself assumes when, upon first hearing of the boar,

> She sinketh down, still hanging by his neck;
> He on her belly falls, she on her back.
> (ll. 593–594)

Venus, as aggressive feminine sexuality, lies on her back and forces Adonis down on top of her. Her vision of the boar reverses the image into one of destructive masculine sexual aggressiveness, with Adonis in the usual feminine position. This idea of the boar enacting the destructive potential of Venus's lust is, as we shall see, carried out in Venus's account of Adonis's death.

Through a bitterly ironic translation of imagery, Shakespeare envisions the boar as the sexual rival of Venus who literally destroys the beauty which Venus has figuratively destroyed throughout the poem. The following lines early in the poem seem, upon first reading, a harmless hyperbole:

> He saith she is immodest, blames her miss;
> What follows more, she murders with a kiss.
> (ll. 53–54)

Only in retrospect do we see that Venus's kiss here prophesies the boar's kiss which kills Adonis:

> He thought to kiss him, and hath kill'd him so.
>
> 'Tis true, 'tis true, thus was Adonis slain:

> He ran upon the boar with his sharp spear,
> Who did not whet his teeth at him again,
> But by a kiss thought to persuade him there.
> And nuzzling in his flank, the loving swine
> Sheath'd unaware the tusk in his soft groin.

> "Had I been tooth'd like him, I must confess,
> With kissing him I should have kill'd him first.
> (ll. 1110-1118)

F. T. Prince and Douglas Bush both insist that no special significance be attributed to this passage. Prince merely notes that the "conceit goes back to Theocritus' Id., XXX. 26-31" (actually this poem has been shown on the basis of style and meter to be the work of a later poet and not by Theocritus at all), and that it "had already been reproduced in several 16th.-cent. poems, such as Minturno's epigram *De Adoni ab apro interempte,* and Tarchagnota's *L'Adone.*"[53] But when we compare Shakespeare's handling of the boar's kiss with that of these earlier poems, we see that he infuses the "conceit" with special ironic significance. Shakespeare's lines function as a grotesque parallel to all the previous occasions when Venus's embraces were described as the attack of a wild beast. Instead of an amorous embrace depicted as a savage attack, we have just the reverse. Furthermore, in the Greek poem long attributed to Theocritus and in Tarchagnota's Italian adaptation, the boar himself tells Venus how he gored Adonis while trying to kiss him.[54] By transferring the passage to Venus, Shakespeare heightens the irony (especially in lines 1117-1118, which have no equivalent in the Greek or Italian) and makes the conceit part of Venus's attempt to console herself and come to grips with Adonis's death.

Yet the fact that this passage is spoken by Venus means that one must hesitate in interpreting the boar's deadly kiss as the ironic literal fulfillment of the destructiveness of Venus's lust. What the reader gets is *Venus's* view of Adonis's death, although the irony of this view has been prepared for by the narrator as well as by Venus. Has Venus imposed her sexually-oriented vision of experience upon a more general force of unthinking evil and destruction? Perhaps she has, but the traditional symbolism of the boar lends support to her vision. So does the way in which Adonis himself had articulated his desire to hunt the boar:

> "I know not love," quoth he, "nor will not know it,
> Unless it be a boar, and then I chase it.
> (ll. 409-410)

Adonis, like Hippolytus, has committed himself to chastity and redirected all his repressed erotic energies to the hunt. Both Hippolytus and Adonis are ultimately destroyed through their life-denying pursuits. And Adonis's destruction as Shakespeare treats it is directly linked, metaphorically and symbolically, to the sexual experience he tries to avoid. Restated in terms of the abstract thematic scheme suggested earlier in this chapter, beauty's destruction is made inevitable by its own death-seeking efforts to avoid involvement with possessive, threatening sexual love.

The final ten stanzas of Shakespeare's epyllion begin with Venus acting more like a goddess than she has at any other time in the poem and issuing a "prophecy" which in fact comes closer to being an accurate description of past and present reality than anything she has said heretofore:

> "Since thou art dead, lo here I prophesy,
> Sorrow on love hereafter shall attend:
> It shall be waited on with jealousy,
> Find sweet beginning, but unsavoury end;
> (ll. 1135–1138)

> Sith in his prime death doth my love destroy,
> They that love best, their loves shall not enjoy.
> (ll. 1163–1164)

Venus is here making herself responsible for the "chaos" which before she had presented as a necessary and inevitable consequence of the death of Adonis:

> For he being dead, with him is beauty slain,
> And beauty dead, black Chaos comes again.[55]
> (ll. 1019–1020)

The deeper irony of Venus's "curse" on love, however, is that throughout the poem love has been what Venus prophesies it will be in the future. Venus's erotic illusions have blinded her to the disorder and conflict inherent in the love of which she is the goddess—she is indeed in her "own law forlorn" (l. 251). Yet these erotic illusions are themselves an essential aspect of the view of love enacted in the poem. As for the beauty which love seeks, its existence rather than its death has intensified the disorder and "sickness" of love and has acted as the bait for love's illusions. Shakespeare's epyllion is not about the fall from the perfection of beauty and the subsequent usurpation of the place of love by lust.[56] It is about the inherent limitations and imperfections of love and beauty and of love's relationship to beauty.

Shakespeare extends his theme through the stanzas describing Adonis's metamorphosis in a manner which is both disturbingly and playfully subversive. He is guided here by the details of Ovid's own extraordinary conclusion, although he exploits these details in a new way. By the time Venus has completed her prophecy, a purple flower has sprung up from Adonis's blood. In the *Metamorphoses* Adonis does not seem to be transformed into a flower. Rather, a flower is made to grow from Adonis's blood by the magic of Venus:[57]

> sic fata cruorem
> nectare odorato sparsit, qui tactus ab illo
> intumuit sic, ut fulvo perlucida caeno
> surgere bulla solet, nec plena longior hora
> facta mora est, cum flos de sanguine concolor ortus,
> qualem, quae lento celant sub cortice granum,
> punica ferre solent; brevis est tamen usus in illo;
> namque male haerentem et nimia levitate caducum
> excutient idem, qui praestant nomina, venti."
>
> (X. 731-739)

[So saying, with fragrant nectar she sprinkled the blood which, touched by it, swelled as when clear bubbles rise up from yellow mud; and no longer than an hour's time had passed when a flower sprang up of blood-red color, like that borne by pomegranates, which hide their seed under a resistant skin. But brief is the enjoyment of this flower, for so weakly and lightly attached is it, and destined to fall, that the very winds which give it its name (Anemone, "the wind flower") shake it off."]

Unlike Ovid's Venus, Shakespeare's Venus does nothing to make the flower appear. Adonis simply melts "like a vapour from her sight" (l. 1166) and a flower, purple and white to recall the red and white of Adonis's complexion, springs from his blood.

Shakespeare, even more than Ovid, makes it clear that Adonis is not reincarnated in the flower, although the flower resembles him (ll. 1169-1170). And Venus herself realizes this—she initially allows the flower a separate, fully natural existence. She begins by bending down to smell the flower and by "Comparing" (l. 1172) its odor to the breath of Adonis. She then "crops the stalk" and "compares" (the word is repeated for emphasis) the drops of sap to the tears which came to Adonis's eyes with "every little grief" (ll. 1175-1176).[58] At the beginning of the poem Venus had called Adonis "'the field's chief flower, sweet *above compare*'" (l. 8;

italics mine). Now she has found a flower comparable to Adonis—or rather, she has been forced by Adonis's death to imagine a flower comparable to him.

Venus's realization that the flower is not Adonis contributes to the pathos of her comparisons and, in a sense, mitigates the shock of her "cropping" the flower. At the same time the language does recall the imagery used earlier to describe her relation to Adonis: "cropping" is what animals do to plants they eat, and of course Adonis—"rose-cheek'd," "the field's chief flower"—has been the beautiful virgin flower throughout. Shakespeare's handling of this final scene is extraordinarily deft. A shockingly ironic reenactment of Venus's relationship to Adonis is suggested but sufficiently distanced by being placed at the level of simile.

Venus's final words reaffirm the attitude towards experience she has manifested all along. Shakespeare significantly transforms the idea expressed in the final lines of Book X of the *Metamorphoses*: whereas Orpheus laments the inevitable natural withering of the short-lived anemone, Venus is unwilling to allow the flower to grow and wither naturally:

> To grow unto himself was his desire,
> And so 'tis thine; but know, it is as good
> To wither in my breast as in his blood.
> (ll. 1180-1182)

Venus offers the flower the same kind of overbearing, suffocating love she offered Adonis. As she continues, the maternal imagery returns one last time along with the hyperbole which has characterized her speech from the beginning:

> "Here was thy father'd bed, here in my breast;
> Thou art the next of blood, and 'tis thy right.
> So in this hollow cradle take thy rest;
> My throbbing heart shall rock thee day and night;
> There shall not be one minute in an hour
> Wherein I will not kiss my sweet love's flower.
> (ll. 1183-1188)

Despite her "prophecy" that "Sorrow on love hereafter shall attend" (l. 1136), Venus seems totally unchanged by Adonis's death. Her way of talking about the flower which has sprung up so miraculously embodies the same deluded idealizing ("Here was thy father'd bed, here in my breast") and the same gross attachment to physical immediacy ("Thou art the next of blood") which have permeated her language throughout the poem. Were she to meet another beautiful young man, one imagines, she would conduct herself very much as she has done with Adonis. For Venus a flower exists to be picked, an attractive youth to be seduced.

One of the aspects of *Venus and Adonis* which I have had to slight in this chapter is the vital relationship between Shakespeare's epyllion and his sonnets:

> A woman's face with Nature's own hand painted
> Hast thou, the master-mistress of my passion;
> (Sonnet 20, ll. 1-2)

In this and a number of the other sonnets Shakespeare explores the same frustrations and limitations inherent in sexual love's imperfect access to human beauty which he dramatizes in the mythological fiction of *Venus and Adonis*. Sonnet 53 makes explicit the connection between Adonis and the young man addressed in the early sonnets; the account in Sonnet 129 of lust "in action" and lust "till action" recalls in a striking way Venus's savage, thwarted desire. And there is also an even more fundamental artistic similarity between *Venus and Adonis* and the sonnets, a similarity deriving from what Stephen Booth has described as Shakespeare's ability to cope "with the problem of the conflicting obligations of a work of art"—the obligation to satisfy the mind's need for order, and the obligation to remain true to "the experience of disorderly natural phenomena" by transcending the mind's capacity to exhaust that order conceptually.[59]

Venus and Adonis presents the reader with an extraordinarily dense artificial order. As I have tried to show, this order grows out of and embodies Shakespeare's response to Ovid's tragedy of love's self-provoked passion for a mortal beauty inevitably doomed to destruction. On the one hand this order is conceptually satisfying: it provokes and rewards a remarkable range of aesthetic attention. On the other hand, the elusive complexity of the poem's formal order defeats all our attempts to reduce the poem's meaning to complete conceptual clarity even as it guides, teases, and compels us to think coherently about the ambivalence of sexual experience. The antithetical style of *Venus and Adonis*, with its intricate artificiality and its disturbingly persistent wit, both clarifies and complicates the closely-entwined, conflicting relationship of the two main figures. Shakespeare intensifies every aspect of Ovid's episode, but he does so in a manner which remains deeply Ovidian. As so often in Ovid's own poetry, the sexual drama in *Venus and Adonis* oscillates between the extremes of savage grotesqueness and broad comedy and yet generates, finally, a surprisingly powerful sense of erotic pathos.

Chapter IV

Hero and Leander

❧

Hero and Leander seems to have been written at the same time as *Venus and Adonis*. Although Marlowe's epyllion was not entered in the Stationers' Register until 28 September 1593, almost five and a half months after Shakespeare's (18 April), and of course not published until 1598, it must have been written by the spring of 1593, since Marlowe was killed at Deptford on 30 May of that year.[1] The plague of 1592-1593 had interrupted Marlowe's career as a dramatist much as it had Shakespeare's; he probably worked on *Hero and Leander* during his stay at Sir Thomas Walsingham's house at Scadbury, near Chislehurst in Kent, where he had gone to wait for the plague to subside in London and the theatres to reopen.[2] He may well have contemplated a poem like *Hero and Leander* during his Cambridge days, when he was translating Ovid's *Amores*. But the confident virtuosity of the couplets of his epyllion suggests that the stylistic development manifested in the plays intervened between *All Ovids Elegies* and *Hero and Leander*.

Marlowe, like Shakespeare, set himself the challenge of treating a familiar myth with distinctive originality. The story of Hero and Leander was, if anything, even more familiar in the sixteenth century than the story of Venus and Adonis. As Abraham Fraunce observed in 1592, "Leander and Heroes love is in every mans mouth."[3] Fraunce was probably thinking of the numerous Continental versions of the Alexandrian epyllion attributed to the writer known as Musaeus (fifth century A.D.):[4] Clément Marot's French translation (1541), Bernardo Tasso's Italian version (c. 1540), or possibly the Spanish *Leandro y Ero* of Juan Boscán (1543), based mainly on the elder Tasso's Italian version and quoted by Fraunce in his *Arcadian Rhetoric* (1586). English readers were even more likely to have known the Latin translation of Marcus Musurus, which from 1518 on was widely available in *Aesopi Phrygis, Fabellae Graece et Latine*.[5] The story had been told or alluded to in other sources,[6] but its remarkable popularity in the sixteenth century centered around Musaeus's poem, in its various versions.

It is impossible to know for certain whether Marlowe used the Greek text of Musaeus, the Latin translation of Musurus, or one of the sixteenth-century Continental translations. He may very well have used a combination of these. If, for example, he employed the Musurus translation included in the collection of Aesop's fables, he would have had parallel Greek and Latin texts before him and could have consulted the original in key passages.[7] What needs to be emphasized at this point, however, is Marlowe's response to those aspects of the overall structure and theme of Musaeus's epyllion which would have been apparent either in the Greek original or in the translations.

With "Leander and Heroes love...in every mans mouth," the last thing one would expect from Marlowe is a conventional, straightforward rendering of the story. And in fact Marlowe's approach transforms Musaeus' poem—or at any rate a large part of it. The Greek text is 343 lines long, not counting a one- or two-line lacuna at line 331.[8] Structurally the poem divides into a rising, triumphant movement narrating and celebrating the love of Hero and Leander (ll. 1-282) and a much shorter, falling, tragic movement which tells of the drowning of Leander and of Hero's suicide (ll. 283-343). Marlowe's poem, or "fragment" as it is sometimes called, does not end at just any point in the story as Musaeus tells it, but at the crucial point where triumphant love turns into tragedy, with a marked shift in pace and tone. This is the most important point established by C. S. Lewis in his well-known discussion of Marlowe's "fragment" and of Chapman's "continuation."[9] Where Lewis goes wrong, I would argue, is in his claim that we can read Marlowe and Chapman together to obtain uniquely effective renderings of the two movements of Musaeus. Chapman expands only an eighth of Musaeus' poem, 61 lines, into 1544 lines; nothing could differ more from the swift, plummeting ending of Musaeus than the extraordinarily intricate moral and philosophical transformations of Chapman's "continuation."[10] More important for our immediate purposes, however, is Marlowe's transformation of Musaeus's first movement. Despite his deep and generally underestimated indebtedness to Musaeus, Marlowe does not give us the "unclouded celebration of youthful passion"[11] which Bush and many other readers have found in the poem. He gives us a poetic experience much more disturbing and ambivalent than that presented by Musaeus or by any other previous writer, including Ovid in epistles XVIII and XIX of the *Heroides*.

It is clear from the first line of his epyllion—"On Hellespont, guilty of true love's blood"—that Marlowe wanted to make his readers aware of the tragic ending of the story which they all knew so well. Critics like Clifford Leech and Brian Morris, who have argued, in opposition to the prevailing "romantic" readings of the poem, that *Hero and Leander* dramatizes the comedy and absurdity of young love, have disregarded the way in which Marlowe preserves in muted form an awareness of the final tragedy.[12] At the same time, however, it is clear that Marlowe's interest in the story is not focused on, does not emphasize, its familiar tragic dimension. He is much more concerned with the living relationship of Hero and Leander than with their eventual tragic fate. What he depicts in this relationship includes both the comedy and the pathos of youthful romance—and it also includes more. Marlowe's recasting of the story includes a remarkably perceptive sense of the risks, limitations, and disappointments of romantic love. If Marlowe shows his young lovers, once stripped of their amusing postures and poses, to be admirable in their uncompromising passion, he also shows them to be vulnerable and unstable when confronted with the reality of actual sexual experience.[13]

The key to Marlowe's approach to Musaeus lies partly in his heightening of the Ovidian aspects of the Greek poem. Musaeus himself may have known Ovid's Hero and Leander epistles in the *Heroides*,[14] and in one or two passages he adopts strategies which remind us of Ovid's other elegiac amatory poems. But on the whole his more distanced and elevated narrative manner is quite unlike the intensely dramatic *ethopoeia* of the *Heroides* or the self-conscious wit of the *Ars Amatoria* and *Amores*. Marlowe's own use of the *Heroides* is, with one exception, restricted to a few descriptive details, primarily because Ovid imagines his exchange of letters taking place after Hero and Leander have consummated their love, just before the final attempted meeting. The *Heroides* epistles could offer Marlowe little direct guidance for presenting the phase of the relationship he was most interested in. But the *Ars Amatoria* and the *Amores* are a different matter altogether. Marlowe draws extensively on these poems: directly, as commentators have noted, in Leander's arguments against virginity;[15] indirectly, and even more importantly, in establishing his narrative persona.

Marlowe's narrator is not exactly the urbane, witty *praeceptor* of the *Ars Amatoria*, nor is he the clever, tormented speaker of the *Amores*. But he partakes at times of both these voices. He sounds most like the speaker of the *Ars Amatoria* when he comments knowingly on the effect of Leander's *Amores* arguments:

> These arguments he us'd, and many more,
> Wherewith she yielded, that was won before.
> Hero's looks yielded, but her words made war;
> Women are won when they begin to jar.[16]
>
> (I. 329-332)

He sounds most like the speaker of the *Amores* when he describes, with obvious delight, Hero's efforts to escape from Leander's embrace:

But as her naked feet were whipping out,
He on the sudden cling'd her so about
That mermaid-like unto the floor she slid;
One half appear'd, the other half was hid.[17]

(II. 313-316)

The narrator of *Hero and Leander* is as distanced from Marlowe as the speaker of the *Amores* is from Ovid; he is usually as distanced from the story he tells as the speaker of the *Ars Amatoria* is from his subject. He shares with both Ovidian voices a sophisticated, often cynical erotic expertise. Above all, he calls attention to his own presence in a way which constantly reminds us that a cunningly created and projected persona is guiding our experience of the narrative. It is this conspicuous, intrusive, self-dramatizing persona, as I have already suggested, which most clearly differentiates Marlowe's epyllionic technique from Shakespeare's.

The skill with which Marlowe uses his narrator to control the reader's experience of the narrative is nowhere more apparent than in the two opening portraits. Structurally the Hero portrait (II. 5-50) parallels the Leander portrait (II. 51-90) quite closely: both intertwine descriptions of Hero's and Leander's beauty with mythological conceits, often in the form of etiologies, telling of the effect their beauty has upon all who see them, including the gods. In verbal detail and tone, however, the two portraits are strikingly different.

The attitude of Marlowe's narrator towards Hero evolves throughout the poem into a subtle ambivalence as profoundly Ovidian as anything in the Elizabethan epyllion. Yet Marlowe's handling of Hero is also more deeply indebted to Musaeus than is generally recognized. It is from Musaeus that Marlowe derives that curious, apparently paradoxical epithet which, coming as it does in the extravagant cosmic hyperbole at the end of the opening portrait, sums up the irony of the portrait and provides the basis for much of Hero's subsequent development:

So lovely fair was Hero, *Venus' nun,*
As Nature wept, thinking she was undone;

(ll. 45-46; my italics)

The phrase "Venus' nun" derives from Musaeus's reference to Hero as "κύπριδος ἱέρεια" —priestess of the Cyprian goddess (Aphrodite).[18] Cedric Whitman's modern English translation shows how close the relevant passage in Musaeus is to Marlowe's line:

Ἡρὼ μὲν χαρίεσσα Διοτρεφὲς αἷμα λαχοῦσα
Κύπριδος ἦν ἱέρεια· ...

(ll. 30–31)

Hero the beautiful, heiress of Zeus-engendered blood
Was priestess of Aphrodite. . . .[19]

The juxtaposition here of praise for Hero's beauty with the description of her relationship to Venus is significant—Musaeus goes on to develop this juxtaposition ironically, and Marlowe follows him. But the most important and most puzzling aspect of Hero's role as "κύπριδος ἱέρεια" is that she has chosen to serve Aphrodite by dedicating herself to a life of chaste solitude (ll. 31–32). Musaeus is more specific than Marlowe in explaining why Hero has made a vow of chastity to, of all goddesses, Aphrodite:

> Yet ever as she appeased Aphrodite the Cytherean
> Often she would assuage Love too with sacrifices
> Together with his Heavenly mother, fearing his quiver of flame.[20]

(ll. 38–40)

Musaeus's Hero has pledged herself to the service of Aphrodite in order to avoid the dangers and risks of love. This is a motive which Marlowe implies but never makes explicit. He leaves the motives for Hero's seemingly contradictory commitment to Venus vague, and we are never entirely sure why she has vowed chastity to Venus.

The derivation of Marlowe's "Venus' nun" from Musaeus has been noted by several previous critics and editors,[21] but none of them has pointed out the importance of this phrase for either the Greek or the English poem. One of these critics even tries to dismiss the irony by arguing that Marlowe misinterpreted the passage in Musaeus: "The reference in the original story of Musaeus is probably not to the 'vulgar Venus,' daughter of Jupiter and Dione, but to the daughter of Coelus, celestial Venus, a Syrian goddess renowned for her purity. It is quite in order that Hero should make a vow of chastity to such a goddess."[22] This interpretation distorts Musaeus's poem. Not only does he use the Homeric title κύπριδος which always designated Cyprian Aphrodite, the Greek goddess of earthly love, but he has Leander point out to Hero the contradiction of vowing chastity to this goddess:

> Since you are Cypris' priestess, attend to the works of Cypris.
> Come, conduct the mystery, the marriage laws of the goddess;
> It is not fitting a virgin attend on Aphrodite.[23]

(ll. 141–143)

There can be no doubt that Musaeus was exploiting the irony of "κύπριδος ἱέρεια" or that Marlowe was guided by Musaeus in his own development of the idea of Hero as "Venus' nun."

The phrase "Venus' nun" would have represented a literal translation of Musaeus's "κύπριδος ἱέρεια" in the sixteenth century: "nun" was commonly used by the Elizabethans to refer to a priestess or votaress of a pagan deity as well as to a member of one of the female orders of the Christian church.[24] But as every reader of *Hamlet* knows, "nun" and "nunnery" were also slang terms for "prostitute" and "brothel."[25] And in fact Stephen Gosson had already exploited the irony of "Venus' nun" in *The School of Abuse* (1579), where he tells how prostitutes who have become too well-known often hide out for a time "like Venus nunnes" in the friaries or cloisters of London suburbs until they are ready to "renue their acquaintance" by visiting the London theatres.[26] "Venus' nun" may actually represent a corruption or perversion of the idea of vestal virgins; in *The Choise of Valentines* (1594) Thomas Nash refers to prostitutes as "Venus bounzing vestalls."[27] In any case, even a literal translation of Musaeus's "κύπριδος ἱέρεια" would probably have carried an additional ironic significance for Marlowe's readers. They would have seen Hero's eventual capitulation to Leander as a doubly ironic fulfillment of her role as "Venus' nun."[28]

Before examining further the way in which Marlowe builds towards the irony of "Venus' nun" in the Hero portrait, we ought to remind ourselves that classical deities, and especially Venus, had a way of transforming themselves in the Renaissance until they stood for qualities or virtues quite opposed to their original pagan significance. There was, for example, a tradition in Renaissance emblem books of using a classical figure of the celestial Venus—veiled, gowned, and surrounded by symbols of purity and chastity—as an image of *pudicitia*, or chastity [Fig. 6].[29] And there was the Neoplatonic tradition of the "Venus-Virgo," of Venus disguised as Diana, goddess of chastity, and regarded as a synthesis of the two apparently contradictory forces of sexual passion and chastity [Fig. 7].[30] A number of interesting questions might be asked about the relevance of these allegorical traditions to Marlowe's presentation of Hero. Was he exploiting the potential ambiguity in the dual tradition of the celestial and the earthly Venus? Are we perhaps meant to see Hero as dedicating herself in Christian chastity to the celestial Venus only to be conquered by the power of the pagan earthly Venus? Or is Hero conceived as a "Venus-Virgo" who somehow combines sexual voluptuousness and chastity?

It is impossible to answer any of these questions affirmatively from

6. Cesare Ripa, "Pudicitia" (woodcut). *Iconologia*, Siena, 1613, p. 171.

7. Medal of Giovanna degli Albizzi (Giovanna
Tornabuoni), "Venus-Virgo," from George
Francis Hill, *A Corpus of Italian Medals of the
Renaissance before Cellini*, London, 1930, vol. II,
plate 169, no. 1022.

the point of view of Hero's conscious motives, since Marlowe tells us nothing directly about her own conception of the goddess she serves. From the point of view of Hero's actual behavior, one can only say that if Marlowe was drawing upon Renaissance allegories of Venus, he was doing so ironically. He makes it perfectly clear from the beginning that the Venus in his poem is neither the celestial Venus nor the Venus-Virgo. And if Hero herself is seen in the image of the Venus-Virgo, it is because her vaunted chastity turns out to be a weapon of Venus that arouses the very passions it purports to discourage.[31]

Marlowe begins preparing for the irony of "Venus' nun" by alluding early in Hero's portrait to the story of Venus and Adonis, a scene from which is embroidered on Hero's sleeve:

> Her wide sleeves green, and border'd with a grove,
> Where Venus in her naked glory strove
> To please the careless and disdainful eyes
> Of proud Adonis that before her lies.
>
> (I. 11–14)

Venus's appearance in this passage suggests that Leech is right when he comments, "Shakespeare's Venus is Hero's tyrannical goddess . . . ."[32] Venus's nakedness stands in direct contrast to Hero's elaborately contrived costume; her behavior stands in direct contradiction to Hero's vows of chastity. At the same time the passage anticipates, even to the extent of verbal repetition, the narrator's account at the end of the poem of how Hero "trembling strove" in Leander's arms (II. 291) and of how Leander lay in bed looking at the naked Hero much as Adonis looks at Venus in this passage.

Marlowe's narrator takes advantage of every device used in Musaeus to point up the irony of "Venus' nun." He gives us a wittier and more indirect version of Musaeus's identification of Hero and Aphrodite:

> Some say, for her the fairest Cupid pin'd,
> And looking in her face, was strooken blind.
> But this is true, so like was one the other,
> As he imagin'd Hero was his mother.[33]
>
> (I. 37–40)

Marlowe goes far beyond Musaeus, however, in describing Hero's extraordinary costume, the primary function of which is not, as has been suggested, to ridicule feminine fashions and vanity,[34] but to point up the superficiality and falseness of her pose as a chaste nun of Venus. The ridiculously ornate costume suggests alienation from the body and from immediate sensual experience. Yet the costume includes "a myrtle wreath" (I. 17) and "sparrows" (I. 33), attributes of Venus specifically associated with her erotic power.[35] Hero has surrounded herself with all the outward vestiges and symbols of sexual love while remaining oblivious to, or at any rate unresponsible for (again, Marlowe leaves this point ambiguous) their consequences. Her worship of Venus will be shown to be an illusion, a way of avoiding genuine participation in and understanding of what Venus represents.

While the narrator's ironic portrait of Hero is extravagantly and hyperbolically artificial and gives us only a vague, generalized sense of her physical beauty, his account of Leander is concretely sensual and erotic, full of an almost unqualified sexual admiration. The narrator's own comment later in the First Sestiad on the inevitability of human favoritism and partiality applies more tellingly to him than to Hero and Leander:

> When two are stripp'd long ere the course begin,
> We wish that one should lose, the other win;
> And one especially do we affect
> Of two gold ingots like in each respect.
> The reason no man knows: let it suffice,
> What we behold is censur'd by our eyes.
> (I. 169–174)

Leander's portrait makes it quite clear that, from a sexual point of view, he is the favored gold ingot in the narrator's eye, much as Hero is in Leander's eye at the end of the poem (II. 325–326). Harry Levin has pointed out that whereas in Hero's portrait the dominant visual details are filled in by an appeal to smell ("the sweet smell as she pass'd") and sound (the chirruping sparrows), in Leander's portrait the appeal is to touch and taste:[36]

> Even as delicious meat is to the taste,
> So was his neck in touching, and surpass'd
> The white of Pelops' shoulder.
> (I. 63–65)

The way in which Marlowe shifts in mid-sentence here from the imagery of tasting and eating meat to the imagery of touching and seeing ivory has the effect of mitigating (without entirely dispelling) the morbidly visceral associations of the Pelops' myth (Pelops' shoulder was literally eaten by the goddess Demeter) while preserving a sense of the powerful sensual appeal Leander holds for the narrator. The narrator continues his description of Leander's body with an extremely clever, self-confessing *occupatio:*

> I could tell ye
> How smooth his breast was, and how white his belly,
> And whose immortal fingers did imprint
> That heavenly path with many a curious dint,
> That runs along his back, but my rude pen
> Can hardly blazon forth the loves of men,
> Much less of powerful gods: . . .[37]
>
> (I. 65–71)

The fact that Leander elicits Marlowe's best erotic writing is not in itself as important as the way in which Marlowe projects a homoerotic fascination with Leander as part of the narrator's persona. The narrator is as aware as we are that Leander draws from him a different kind of response than Hero does.

Virtually all the mythological conceits in Leander's portrait dramatize his homoerotic appeal. But they are all put in the conditional mode, a strategy which enables Marlowe to acknowledge the freedom with which he is handling traditional mythological material and, at the same time, to distance Leander from actual homoerotic experience:

> His dangling tresses that were never shorn,
> *Had they been cut,* and unto Colchos borne,
> *Would have allur'd* the vent'rous youth of Greece
> To hazard more than for the Golden Fleece.
>
> (I. 55–58; my italics)

> *Had wild Hippolytus Leander seen,*
> Enamour'd of his beauty *had he been,*
>
> (I. 77–78; my italics)

This latter point is overlooked by Morris, one of the few critics who has addressed himself directly to the homoerotic aspect of *Hero and Leander.* Morris sums up his remarks on Leander's homoerotic appeal by commenting: "Leander's sexuality is, to say the least, peculiar."[38] It is not Leander's sexuality that is "peculiar," however, but that of the various masculine figures who are attracted to him.

There are one or two details about Leander's appearance, such as his "dangling tresses" (I. 55), which might suggest that he is conceived in the tradition of the soft effeminate youth to which Narcissus, Hermaphroditus, and Adonis belong. But Leander's behaviour is never effeminate in the way Adonis's behavior is. In the one passage where Leander's beauty is compared to a maiden's, the reference is to his countenance rather than to his body, and the emphasis is on what the narrator says "some" other men see in him:

> Some swore he was a maid in man's attire,
> For in his looks were all that men desire.
>   (I. 83–84)

These lines, like the allusion to Ganymede in line 26, look forward to the Neptune episode, where Leander is forced to respond to Neptune's wooing by declaring "'You are deceiv'd, I am no woman, I'" (II. 192). Leander is wooed by men as if he were a woman, but he is not himself womanish or effeminate. Bush has charged Marlowe with being inconsistent in giving effeminate traits to a young man who is supposed to be able to swim the Hellespont,[39] but it is apparent from the narrator's praise of Leander's back that there is nothing weak or unmasculine about his musculature. The narrator makes all this quite clear at the end of the portrait:

> And such as knew he was a man would say,
> Leander, thou art made for amorous play.
>   (I. 87–88)

The full significance of the homoerotic motif in the Leander portrait does not become apparent until the Neptune episode in the Second Sestiad. But in anticipation of a detailed examination of that episode, let us observe that its meaning is prepared for by another striking line in the Leander portrait:

> His body was as straight as Circe's wand
>   (I. 61)

Morris quotes Sandys' commentary on the *Metamorphoses* in arguing that "Circe's wand" would have suggested "sinister pleasure to any alert Renaissance reader."[40] A more important implication of the line is that for all its captivating charm, Leander's beauty, like Circe's wand, has the power to turn men (and gods) into beasts. One is taken back momentarily to the Pelops allusion, with its hint of savage aggression. The narrator's attitude towards Leander is already becoming more ambivalent than is at first apparent in this opening portrait.

Let us move on now to the first scene following the introductory portraits and see how Marlowe extends his conceptions of Hero as "Venus' nun" and of Leander as "made for amorous play." The citizens of Sestos are celebrating the Feast of Adonis, and Hero goes to perform rites in the Temple of Venus, where she will meet and fall in love with Leander. Venus' temple is decorated with images of "the gods in sundry shapes / Committing heady riots, incest, rapes" (I. 143-144).[41] The goddess to whom Hero has pledged herself in virginity stands, it seems, for riotous sexual license. Yet Hero's ritual sacrifice in the Temple of Venus extends the religious connotations of "Venus' nun" in a grotesque parody of what real sacrifice to Venus will come to mean. In the midst of the lusts of the gods depicted on the walls (I. 145-156) "a silver altar stood," and before this altar we see "Hero sacrificing turtles' blood . . ." (I. 157-158). It is here that we discover the cause of those curious stains on Hero's "kirtle blue" described in the opening portrait as having been "Made with the blood of wretched lovers slain" (I. 15-16). The difficulties commentators have had with this earlier passage are understandable.[42] I think Marlowe wants us to find both passages disturbing—the initial impression of human sacrifice, followed by the discovery of what the bloodstains are, makes us uncomfortably aware of the rather silly way in which Hero worships her goddess. The muted tragic overtones mentioned previously are certainly present in these lines—one cannot but recall the "true love's blood" of the first line in the poem. But these tragic overtones only make more apparent the silliness of what Hero is actually doing. In her present role as "Venus' nun" she is sacrificing the blood of turtle doves, but true allegiance to Venus will lead to sacrifice of a far different kind—the loss of virginity, and ultimately the loss of her and Leander's lives. As Nigel Alexander observes, "the rites of the goddess Venus may be rather different from the ones that Hero appears to be practising."[43]

It is immediately upon rising from this sacrifice on Venus' altar that Hero looks at Leander and both are struck by "Love's arrow with the golden head" (I. 161). Leander's response to this exchange of looks picks up and extends the religious imagery:

He kneel'd, but unto her devoutly pray'd;
Chaste Hero to herself thus softly said:
'Were I the saint he worships, I would hear him,'
And as she spake those words, came somewhat near him.
(I. 177-180)

Marlowe's couplets often deliver their ironies so quickly that the reader barely has time to savor one line, or even one phrase, before discovering that it has become the basis for another irony, made possible by the nimblest shift in perspective. First, Hero's line is itself ambiguous: she *is* the "saint" Leander worships, although she does not yet realize that she will enter into Venus' rites with him. Or does she?—her initial words, "Were I the saint he worships," may at first seem like a confession that she is not the chaste priestess she pretends to be. In any case, her action in coming nearer Leander undercuts the reluctance apparently expressed in the line as a whole. Marlowe achieves the irony here through ordinary sequential syntax, but at the same time he makes one sense the simultaneity of conflicting thoughts and more deeply expressive gestures.

Marlowe is indebted to Musaeus for a number of details in his presentation of Hero's conflicting motivations. In his own way Musaeus dramatizes the simultaneous fear and desire, uncertainty and curiosity, naiveté and sophistication, of an intelligent young woman entering into her first love affair. His Hero, like Marlowe's, only gradually becomes conscious of her seductive power and of the strategy of playing the coquette. At first she is unintentionally coy:

> But she, when she recognized Leander's ensnaring desire,
> Rejoiced in his splendid charms; and quietly she also
> Once and again bent on him her own love-quickening gaze,
> With furtive gestures sending her message to Leander,
> And turned away again.[44]
>
> (ll. 103-107)

Yet Marlowe develops Hero's fluctuating emotions far beyond Musaeus. Hero's initial response to Leander's questioning of her vows of chastity suggests that she is shocked at having been forced to realize the falseness of her previous devotion to Venus:

> Tell me, to whom mad'st thou that heedless oath?'
> 'To Venus,' answer'd she, and as she spake,
> Forth from those two tralucent cisterns brake
> A stream of liquid pearl, . . .
>
> (I. 294-297)

Hero quickly recovers, however, and her subsequent reaction to Leander's argument that true worship of Venus demands the very opposite of chastity indicates a remarkable coolness and poise:

> Thereat she smil'd, and did deny him so,
> As put thereby, yet might he hope for mo.
>   (I. 311-312)

Hero now appears to be in full control of the "Venus-Virgo" strategy—
she is using her chastity to encourage the desire she pretends to oppose.
But as Leander continues his arguments, under Hero's own subtle
encouragement, Hero is made an all but helpless victim:

> Thus having swallow'd Cupid's golden hook,
> The more she striv'd, the deeper was she strook.
>   (I. 333-334)

Despite the narrator's almost callous detachment, the reader becomes
involved in Hero's struggle. Dominated by love and yet capable of
exerting a certain degree of control over the situation, she "strives"
(Marlowe repeats the word) to retain her security and at the same time to
insure the continued ardor of her suitor.

The skill with which Marlowe presents Hero's tenuous success in
determining the course of the affair and, at the same time, exposes her
vulnerability is perhaps best seen in her indirect invitation to Leander to
visit her tower. Hero is telling of her guardian, the "dwarfish beldam,"

> That hops about the chamber where I lie,
> And spends the night (that might be better spent)
> In vain discourse and apish merriment.
> Come thither.' As she spake this, her tongue tripp'd,
> For unawares 'Come thither' from her slipp'd,
> And suddenly her former colour chang'd,
>   (I. 354-359)

The two asides here are psychologically contrasted. The first, "that might
be better spent," is a deliberately flirtatious remark, indirect enough to be
safe. The second, "Come thither," is an unintentional slip of the tongue
which embarrassingly exposes Hero's curiosity and desire. These lines
dramatize in miniature Hero's fundamental emotional conflict.

The narrator's attitude towards Hero during this first meeting is a
natural extension of the satire of the opening portrait: he clearly delights
in seeing her superficial pose as "Venus' nun" exposed and used against
her and in showing how her newly discovered strategies of flirtation elude
her full control. As for Leander, the narrator observes him fulfilling the
counsel offered in the final line of the opening portrait: "Though thou be

fair, yet be not thine own thrall" (I. 90). Leander in this first meeting is the "bold sharp Sophister" who marshals argument after argument from Ovid's *Amores* in attacking every defense Hero presents—and some that she does not. But already there are hints that Leander himself is not going to be spared the narrator's satiric irony. A "sophister," Leech tells us, was a special Cambridge term for second- or third-year undergraduates,[45] and in addition to the Ovidian echoes, Marlowe laces Leander's speech with Aristotelian definition and dicta:

> One is no number; maids are nothing then,
> Without the sweet society of men.[46]
>
> (I. 255-256)

The point of the Aristotelian and the Ovidian echoes is to suggest indirectly what will be comically demonstrated in the second meeting, that Leander's rhetoric of love has been learned from books and has no grounding in previous experience. It may be, as Miss Tuve has shown in great detail, that much of the interest of Leander's speech stems from our simultaneous admiration for Leander's "display" of "Love's holy fire, with words" (I. 192-193) and our ability to see the speciousness of his arguments.[47] But the fact that the arguments are specious is ultimately less important than the fact that they mask a raw and unsophisticated erotic imagination, and that they have little effect on Hero compared to Leander's sheer physical energy and attractiveness.

Miss Tuve describes Leander's arguments as "curt, acute, denuded of sensuous appeal." But in fact Leander's language is often sexually suggestive in a way which will be turned ironically against him:

> My words shall be as spotless as my youth,
> Full of simplicity and naked truth.
>
> (I. 207-208)

The irony here works more against Leander than against Hero, since we discover later on that Leander's youth has indeed been "spotless"—so spotless that he falters when presented with the sexual opportunity he seems to desire. Scattered throughout the rest of his speech are words which would have carried strong sexual connotations for Elizabethan readers:[48]

> Dutiful *service* may thy love *procure*.
>
> (I. 220; my italics)

> Honour is purchas'd by the *deeds* we do.
> Believe me, Hero, honour is not won,
> Until some honourable *deed* be done.
>   (I. 280–282; my italics)

On first reading we may think Leander a confident master of sexual pun and innuendo. But all this verbal craftiness merely sets the stage for the exposure of Leander's sexual inexperience.

Critics have been needlessly puzzled by what they have seen as a contradiction between Leander's sophisticated persuasion to love and his actual naiveté and inexperience. Marlowe gives us a quite believable portrait of a young man thoroughly versed in the rhetoric of love but as unacquainted with love's reality as Hero herself. Hero and Leander are in fact contrasted in terms of innocence and experience: Hero's pose as a chaste nun of Venus disguises her awakening sexual curiosity and sophistication; Leander's pose as an experienced rhetorician of love disguises his "spotless youth." Both will be forced out of their poses by the pressures of immediate erotic desire and made to confront the problematic realities of sexual love.

Marlowe ends the first meeting between Hero and Leander with the first of two major digressions. The episode of Mercury and the country maid may have been very freely adapted from Ovid's story of Mercury and Herse in Book II of the *Metamorphoses*,[49] a story of which Marlowe might have been reminded by Leander's reference to Mercury's amorous adventures in Musaeus' poem (ll. 150–153). But Marlowe's digression is more interestingly Ovidian in manner than in subject. Marlowe deliberately cultivates, as Ovid so often does in his digressions, a simultaneous sense of relevance and irrelevance, of parallelism and non-parallelism, to the main story. We must read right through the Sestiad break (inserted by Chapman in the 1598 edition, we should remember, and not a feature of Marlowe's original narrative) to see how the episode is playfully woven into the primary narrative. Hero, embarrassed and shaken at having made a direct invitation to Leander to visit her in her tower, prays to Venus and renews her vows of chastity. But "Cupid beats down her prayers with his wings" (I. 369) and shoots Hero with another burning shaft of love. We do not learn of the effect of Cupid's arrow until the beginning of the Second Sestiad:

> By this, sad Hero, with love unacquainted,
> Viewing Leander's face, fell down and fainted.
>   (II. 1–2)

While Cupid's arrow is taking effect, Marlowe tells how Cupid took pity on the stricken Hero and flew off to the palace of the Destinies. His request is not that Hero's prayer and vow of chastity to Venus be granted (how could Cupid support such a prayer!), but that Hero and Leander "might enjoy each other, and be blest" (I. 380). The digression which follows is an elaborate etiology explaining why the Destinies hate Love and why they therefore refuse to assent to Cupid's wish.

The digression itself seems at first glance to offer a series of entertaining parallels to the Hero and Leander affair and to give Marlowe an opportunity to comment with self-conscious irony on the present state of poetry and poets.[50] Mercury's initial verbal wooing of the country maid is obviously meant to recall Leander's display of "Love's holy fire, with words, with sighs and tears, / Which like sweet music enter'd Hero's ears" (I. 193-194):

> And sweetly on his pipe began to play,
> And with smooth speech her fancy to assay,
>   (I. 401-402)

Mercury follows up his "smooth speech" too quickly with aggressive physical gestures (I. 403-410) and is forced to retreat and resort again to verbal wooing; similarly Leander, after his long discourse, was repulsed when he tried to embrace Hero and was forced to draw out his suit and prove himself further (I. 341 ff.). But Mercury's embrace is much more sexually aggressive than Leander's; it is the embrace of "an insolent commanding lover" who "often stray'd / Beyond the bounds of shame, in being bold / To eye those parts, which no eye should behold." Mercury's behavior thus sets up the irony of Leander's fumbling naiveté in his next encounter with Hero.

As for the country maid, she is like Hero in her pretended innocence, but her freshness and naturalness serve as critical foils to Hero's artificiality:

>   . . . a country maid,
> Whose careless hair, instead of pearl t' adorn it,
> Glister'd with dew, as one that seem'd to scorn it.
> Her breath as fragrant as the morning rose,
>   (I. 388-391)

The parallels with Hero's hair which so charmed Apollo (I. 6) and with Hero's breath (I. 21-22) are precise. In terms of behavior, the country maid dramatizes many of the motives at work in Hero, but without the apparent idealism and insecurity which complicate Hero's attitudes. Like Hero she values her virginity, but for more overtly practical reasons—her "only dower was her chastity" (I. 412). The country maid's coyness in putting Mercury through his rhetorical paces matches Hero's, but she is more straightforwardly ambitious and self-centered in her demands. Her behavior both clarifies and brings out the subtle emotional gradations and complications in Hero's behavior.

The country maid decides to take advantage of being courted by a god and, "thirsting after immortality," requests from Mercury "A draught of flowing nectar" (I. 426–431). Mercury has to steal the nectar from Hebe, and his theft leads both to the etiological resolution of the digression and to Marlowe's comment on poets and poetry. Mercury is cast out of heaven by Jove for his theft. In revenge, Mercury persuades Cupid to make the Destinies fall in love with him so he can bring about the fall of Jove and the reign of Saturn. But because Mercury spurns the love of the Destinies, they come to hate both him and Cupid. Thus Cupid's intercession on behalf of Hero and Leander is denied (the etiology is finally completed), Jove is reinstated along with the "Murder, rape, war, lust and treachery" which characterize his reign (I. 457), and Mercury is eternally linked to poverty, with the result that the clever, learned scholar-poets associated with Mercury (and with the Elizabethan epyllion, one might add) are condemned to be poor and unknown, while fame and wealth go to "Midas' brood."[51]

The Mercury episode is a witty *tour de force* in Ovidian digression: we are led wilfully and playfully astray by the narrator, who begins by asking us to "Harken awhile" if we want to hear why Love and Fate are enemies; at the same time, we are given just enough parallelism and relevance to the main narrative to satisfy our expectations of unity. Marlowe deliberately mutes the somber import of the episode, just as he has muted the foreshadowings of eventual tragedy all along. The enmity of Love and Fate means that Cupid's desire that the relationship of the two lovers "be bless'd" will not be fulfilled, both in the sense that their love will be tragically terminated and in the sense that under the "Stygian empery" of Jove love is inevitably and inherently troubled and tormented, much as it is in *Venus and Adonis* both before and after Venus' curse on love.[52] The central irony of the episode is that the Destinies hate Love and oppose its fulfillment because they themselves have been wounded and frustrated by Cupid. Fate and Love are mutually frustrating in Marlowe's poem. And for Marlowe, as for Shakespeare, Love is responsible for its own lack of fulfillment and completion.

The first meeting ends with Hero coyly delaying her departure and yet afraid "In offering parley, to be counted light" (II. 5-9). But she has overestimated Leander's sophistication; the transition to the second meeting (II. 17-102) begins with a line which forecasts the exposure of Leander's lack of experience and indicates how this exposure will be related to the development of Hero's status as "Venus' nun." Hero drops her fan to give Leander a concrete excuse to visit her, but "He being a *novice*, knew not what she meant" (II. 13; my italics). This sets the stage for the comedy to follow. Hero receives Leander warmly and openly, though she is more torn than ever by her conflicting desires to yield to Leander and to protect "her name and honour" (II. 35). She begins to fear that her own misgivings will make her less appealing, however, and finally, "like light Salmacis," she throws herself upon him. In so doing she reverses her previous ritualistic offering to Venus and "offers up herself a sacrifice" (II. 44-48).[53] But as a "novice" Leander fails to understand this kind of sacrifice—one can sense the narrator's delight in drawing out the comic irony of Leander's response:

> Like Aesop's cock, this jewel he enjoyed,
> And as a brother with his sister toyed,
> Supposing nothing else was to be done,
> Now he her favour and good will had won.
>   (II. 51-54)

But finally Leander begins to suspect that "Some amorous rites or other were neglected" (II. 64) and embraces Hero passionately.

Having encouraged Leander's aggressiveness, Hero must now go on the defensive again. But her resistance only excites Leander more. She finds herself in the ironic position of unwittingly instructing Leander in the real rites of Venus, of teaching "him all that elder lovers know":

> . . . in plain terms (yet cunningly) he crav'd it;
> Love always makes those eloquent that have it.
> She, with a kind of granting, put him by it,
> And ever as he thought himself most nigh it,
> Like to the tree of Tantalus she fled,
>   (II. 71-75)

Hero's strategy during this second encounter is, from her point of view, eventually successful: she has aroused Leander's passionate love and yet "sav'd her maidenhead" (II. 76). The narrator's comment on her struggle to save her virginity combines cynical sophistication with an element of genuine sympathy and understanding for the first time in the poem:

> No marvel, then, though Hero would not yield
> So soon to part from that she dearly held.
> Jewels being lost are found again, this never,
> 'Tis lost but once, and once lost, lost for ever.
>
> (II. 83–86)

As the narrator has dealt more satirically with Leander in this encounter than in the first, he has begun to deal somewhat more sympathetically with Hero. He shows himself to be sensitive to the emotional tensions and conflicts he so knowingly exposes.

Marlowe separates the second and third meetings of Hero and Leander with a brief account of Leander's return to Abydos (II. 99–154) and with the episode of Neptune's wooing of Leander. In narrative technique the Neptune episode is less like Ovid's digressions than is the episode of Mercury and the country maid—there is less of the carefully cultivated aura of a "shaggy dog story" about it. Yet Neptune's behavior in this episode provides one of the most remarkable instances in the Elizabethan epyllion of Ovidian comic anthropomorphism. The idea for the episode may very well have come from the second of the two Hero and Leander epistles in the *Heroides*.[54] In epistle XIX Hero petitions Neptune to calm the raging waters of the Hellespont and recalls his own amorous exploits with Anymone, Tyro, Alcyone, Calyce, and others: "Yet, Neptune, wert thou mindful of thine own heart's flames, thou oughtst let no love be hindered by the winds . . ." (XIX. 129–130).[55] But Neptune refuses to calm the stormy sea which separates the lovers now and which will eventually cause their deaths. Marlowe's episode may therefore be read as an etiology implying, if not actually explaining, the cause of Neptune's cruelty. While the Destinies in Marlowe's first digression refuse to bless Hero and Leander because of their frustrated love for Mercury, Neptune will refuse to assist the lovers because of his frustrated love for Leander himself.

The narrator has prepared us for the Neptune episode with his account of Leander's homoerotic appeal and with his descriptions of the lechery of the gods, particularly of Jove's dallying with Ganymede (I. 148) and of Sylvanus's love for Cyparissus (I. 154–155). As Leander dives naked into the Hellespont, Neptune grows "proud" and at first imagines that Ganymede has abandoned Jove and fallen into his own realm.[56] I have already commented on the verbal skill with which Marlowe evokes Neptune's wooing, on what Leech describes as "the double sense of the movement of the water and of the god's amorous pranks":[57]

> He clapp'd his plump cheeks, with his tresses play'd,
> And smiling wantonly, his love bewray'd.
> He watch'd his arms, and as they open'd wide,
> At every stroke, betwixt them would he slide,
> And steal a kiss, and then run out and dance.
>
> (II. 181–185)

What I want to emphasize here, however, is the way in which the comedy and eroticism of Neptune's love-making constantly verge on, and occasionally become, grotesque and threatening.

J. B. Steane sees in the Neptune episode "a presentation in mythological terms and pantomime style of the nightmare intrusion of the homosexual into a normal man's life."[58] There is indeed something dream-like, if not actually "nightmarish," in the account of Leander being pulled down to the bottom of the sea by the "saphire visag'd god" and shown the "low coral groves" where mermaids "sported with their loves / On heaps of heavy gold . . . " (II. 160–163). And dream does threaten to turn into nightmarish sick-joke when we are told that Leander "was almost dead" before Neptune realized that he was not after all the immortal Ganymede. There is also something nightmarish and grotesque in the "cartoon-like comedy"[59] of Neptune's angry behavior later in the episode when he hears Leander cry out for the light reflected from Hero's tower:

> He flung at him his mace, but as it went,
> He call'd it in, for love made him repent.
> The mace returning back, his own hand hit,
> As meaning to be veng'd for darting it.
> When this fresh bleeding wound Leander view'd,
> His colour went and came, . . .
>
> (II. 209–214)

This mixing of comedy, eroticism, and sentiment with violence and grotesqueness may remind one of Ovid's technique in the *Metamorphoses* in episodes such as Jove's wooing of Europa in the form of a bull. But Marlowe's playfully detailed account exaggerates even Ovid's contrasting mixture of tones.

Brian Morris is far too optimistically single-minded, I think, in seeing in the Neptune episode a positive alternative to the "hard, jewelled, and cold" heterosexual love of Hero and Leander, in characterizing the episode as a "physical and overtly erotic description" which "enforces the peculiar power of homosexual love. . . ."[60] Morris draws a number of apt parallels with *Edward II,* but he fails to bring out the degree of ambivalence in Marlowe's presentation of homoerotic love in both works. He notes, with insufficient emphasis, that the situation in *Edward II,* where a crafty and ambitious young man plots his appeal to a man he knows to be homosexual, is in many respects the reverse of the situation in *Hero and Leander,* where an old pederast tries to persuade a naive young man to submit to his lechery.[61] In the former situation Marlowe shows us the exploitation and hopeless fantasy that can spring from homoerotic love; in the latter, he shows us the comic and grotesque consequences of an older lover's deluded passion for an attractive but uninterested youth.

Despite his obvious sexual interest in Leander, Marlowe's narrator is as aware of the ambivalence of homosexual as of heterosexual love. Steane gets closer to the truth about the episode when he says that it "implies . . . a sympathy with the homosexual's frustrated, hopeful, importunate, and often ludicrous state. . . ."[62] The narrator is as aware of Neptune's ludicrousness and grotesqueness as he is sympathetic to Neptune's passion for the masculine beauty which he himself had praised so passionately in the opening portrait. It is only by seeing the homoeroticism of the Neptune episode as part of the entire vision of erotic experience which Marlowe articulates through his narrator that one becomes fully aware of its internal meaning and of its place in the poem.

As an expression of the grotesquely comic, disturbing, potentially destructive aspects of homoerotic lust, Neptune's wooing serves as a complement to the narrator's exuberant but self-ironic praise of Leander in the opening portrait. And what of Leander's role in all this? "His body was as straight as Circe's wand" (I. 61), the narrator has told us, and its effect on Neptune is in some respects like the bestializing effect of Circe's charm. Leander himself may be innocent of any Circean evil—his sympathy for Neptune's self-inflicted wound does suggest, as Steane says, the kindness a decent man will show towards non-mutual sexual solicitation. But at the same time Leander's beauty arouses a degrading, destructive lust beyond his control. This destructive aspect is played down at the very end of the episode: Neptune mistakes sympathy for love and swims off to search the ocean for gifts with which to renew his suit (II. 219-224). But what will Neptune do when he returns and finds that Leander has swum on to consummate his love with Hero? The answer, at least in Ovid's *Heroides,* comes when Hero's prayer that Neptune calm the deadly storm on the Hellespont goes unanswered.

Once again Marlowe has simultaneously and unobtrusively suggested a violent, threatening force inherent in love itself and planted the seeds for future tragedy.[63] It is only by attending with extreme care to the mythological details of Marlowe's epyllion that one becomes conscious of the threat which often seems so remote from Marlowe's poetic concerns. Take, for instance, the one gift which Neptune has already given Leander. Helle's bracelet may at first appear to be the very opposite to a premonition of tragedy, just the thing Leander needs to insure his safety:

> The god put Helle's bracelet on his arm,
> And swore the sea should never do him harm.
>
> (II. 179-180)

Helle was the maiden who escaped with her brother Phrixus from their evil parents on the back of a golden ram, only to fall into a part of the sea thereafter called the "Hellespont."[64] Neptune has thus given Leander a token of the maiden who lost her life in the Hellespont, where Leander will lose his. The very fact that Neptune presents Helle's bracelet as a guarantee of safety from the sea ironically prophesies the form Neptune's jealous revenge will take when he sees his love for Leander frustrated.

Marlowe devotes just over a hundred lines to the final meeting of Hero and Leander, a rather extraordinary feat of poetic efficiency when one considers the way in which he is able here both to sum up and to continue to develop the complexities generated in the previous seven hundred lines. The meeting begins comically, as Hero receives Leander for the first time without the contrived, artificial costume in which she was first presented:

> She stay'd not for her robes, but straight arose,
> And drunk with gladness to the door she goes.
> Where seeing a naked man, she screech'd for fear,
> Such sights as this to tender maids are rare,
>
> (II. 235-238)

With this newly discovered openness and naturalness Hero may appear more admirable and attractive in the eyes of the narrator and reader, but she also appears more vulnerable. Every move she makes now will encourage Leander's sexual aggressiveness and increase her own vulnerability:

> The nearer that he came, the more she fled,
> And seeking refuge, slipp'd into her bed.
>
> (II. 243-244)

Hero clearly wants Leander to make love to her, but at the same time she is anxious and frightened. She has finally been drawn by Leander and by her own awakening sexual awareness out of her illusory role as a chaste nun of Venus, where she had taken on all the external manifestations of feminine sexuality but none of its actual experience, with its risks and responsibilities, into a situation where she is torn between fear of sex and sexual curiosity, between the desire to use her attractiveness to keep the upper hand and the desire to yield to an attractive and passionate lover.

Leander uses words, as before, to win Hero's consent, but it is only when words break down and his own physical exhaustion and vulnerability mingle with his passion that Hero finally surrenders:

> . . . Leander on her quivering breast,
> Breathless spoke something, and sigh'd out the rest;
> Which so prevail'd, as he with small ado,
> Enclos'd her in his arms and kiss'd her too.
> And every kiss to her was as a charm,
> And to Leander as a fresh alarm,
> So that the truce was broke, and she alas
> (Poor silly maiden) at his mercy was.
>
> (II. 279-285)

With Hero at Leander's mercy, the narrator begins to shift his emphasis more and more to the violence and turbulence of physical love:[65]

> Love is not full of pity (as men say)
> But deaf and cruel, where he means to prey.
>
> (II. 287-288)

This is the key to Marlowe's approach to the consummation, and we can best understand his treatment by contrasting it with Musaeus's elegantly sensuous yet mystical account:

> [She] purified all his skin, and anointed his body with oil
> Sweetly scented with rose, and quenched the smell of the sea.
> And while he still breathed hard on the bed of deep coverlets
> Closely embracing her bridegroom she cried these loving words:
> "Bridegroom, heavy toiler, as no other bridegroom has ever suffered,
> Bridegroom, heavy toiler, enough now of briny water
> And the smell of fish from the sea with its heavy thunderings,
> Here on my breasts repose the sweat of your labouring."
> Thus she spoke these words, and forthwith he loosed her girdle,
> And they entered into the rites of most wise Cythereia.[66]
>
> (II. 264-273)

Musaeus's Hero is calmly assured as she finally performs the rites which are properly due the Cyprian goddess; there is not a hint of uneasiness, fear, or guilt. Marlowe's Hero is, by contrast, victimized:

> Even as a bird, which in our hands we wring,
> Forth plungeth, and oft flutters with her wing,
> She trembling strove; . . .
> (II. 289-291)

Hero is far from being passively vulnerable, however—as this passage continues, the reader cannot be entirely sure that Hero's trembling is due to fear alone:

> . . . this strife of hers (like that
> Which made the world) another world begat
> Of unknown joy. Treason was in her thought,
> And cunningly to yield herself she sought.
> (II. 291-294)

The "unknown joy" of sexual passion finally converts Hero's fears into a desire to be an adept and cunning lover. But her moment of joy has been attained only after an internal emotional struggle more turbulent than the external physical struggle with Leander.

After the consummation insecurity and shame severely qualify Hero's sense of joy and fulfillment. She dreads the coming of day, at first because it will mean an end to their night of love (II. 301-302), then because the sun's light will shamefully display them "like Mars and Ericine" (II. 305) and will mean that she must confront Leander:

> Again she knew not how to frame her look,
> Or speak to him who in a moment took
> That which so long, so charily she kept,
> And fain by stealth away she would have crept,
> And to some corner secretly have gone,
> Leaving Leander in the bed alone.
> (II. 307-312)

But Leander will not allow Hero the security of privacy. He grabs her as she leaves the bed, causing her to slide to the floor and exposing her nakedness. At the end of the poem Hero is thus left standing beside the bed, naked and blushing, as Leander looks on her with the admiration of Dis contemplating a heap of gold (II. 317-326). In a sense Hero herself has finally come to realize what was ironically suggested in the phrase

"Venus' nun." The allusion to Venus' shameful exposure in the arms of Mars in line 305 anticipates Hero's final predicament. To become a true "nun" of Venus she must experience the turbulence and insecurity of love as well as the joyful erotic rapture promised by Leander. And she must run the risk of becoming a sexual object—a heap of sexual gold, as it were—treated with little more sensitivity than Elizabethan playgoers would have shown towards Gosson's "Venus nunnes." The fate of the prostitute exists for Hero as only an implied and momentary threat, but it is present, along with the recollection of ecstasy, as part of the experience of love which Hero has finally come to know.

Once again Marlowe's handling of Hero may be seen as a specifically Ovidian transformation of Musaeus's narrative. Notice the parallels between Hero's behavior and that of Corinna in Marlowe's own rendering of *Amores* I.v:

> Then came Corinna in a long loose gown,
> Her white neck hid with tresses hanging down,
> Resembling fair Semiramis going to bed,
> Or Lais of a thousand wooers sped.
> I snatch'd her gown; being thin, the harm was small,
> Yet striv'd she to be cover'd therewithal,
> And striving thus as one that would be cast,
> Betray'd herself, and yielded at the last.
> Stark naked as she stood before mine eye,
> Not one wen in her body could I spy.
>
> (ll. 9-18)
>
> I cling'd her naked body, down she fell.
> Judge you the rest: . . .
>
> (ll. 24-25)

In looking at Musaeus through this Ovidian perspective, Marlowe has transformed Ovid as well. Corinna is an experienced courtesan, so she feels none of the threatening vulnerability and shame which beset Hero. Corinna's coy pretensions of reluctance have a very different meaning for her than they do for Hero when "cunningly to yield herself she sought" (II. 293-294). And the exposure of Corinna's beauty is described by her own lover, the "I" of the *Amores,* not by a detached narrator. The separation between actual participating observer (Leander) and fictional non-participating observer (narrator) allows Marlowe a flexibility unavailable to Ovid in this particular instance.

I have referred to the narrator as "detached" and "non-participating" to distinguish him from Leander and from Ovid's speaker. But I do not mean that he is insensitive to the emotional dynamics of the situation he describes. The sympathy which the narrator began to show for Hero at the end of the second meeting is much more openly displayed in this final meeting. He is clearly more interested in Hero's internal emotional state than in Leander's. In a sense the narrator's capacity for projecting himself into the feminine psyche balances and complements his capacity for responding to masculine sexual beauty. Yet there is not a trace of softness in the narrator's attitude towards Hero. In fact his ability to understand her emotional turmoil allows him to expose her vulnerability all the more thoroughly.

At the moment of consummation the narrator presents Leander as the conquering sexual hero now able to back up those clever arguments culled from the *Amores* with actual experience:

> Leander now, like Theban Hercules
> Enter'd the orchard of th'Hesperides,
> Whose fruit none rightly can describe but he
> That pulls or shakes it from the golden tree:
> (II. 297–300)

His final view of Leander, however, is less admiring. The comparison with "Dis, on heaps of gold fixing his look" makes clear how inferior Leander's consciousness of Hero is to the narrator's own. Sexual passion and conquest have in effect blinded Leander to Hero's internal experience. Yet there is no indication that the narrator blames Leander for his insensitivity. This, perhaps, is the ultimate expression of the narrator's cynicism, that he expects nothing more from someone "made for amorous play."

The unity of Marlowe's epyllion derives primarily from the complex but coherent evolution of the narrator's attitude towards the story he tells. He began with a cleverly critical exposure of the artificiality and superficiality of Hero's pose as "Venus' nun" and with almost unqualified praise of Leander's "spotless" masculine beauty. In working out the ironic implications of these initial attitudes, the narrator has become increasingly sympathetic to Hero's dilemma and increasingly aware of Leander's limitations. The disturbingly perceptive ambivalence with which he views the two lovers at the end represents a fully coherent extension of his view of erotic experience as it has been revealed to us in the course of the narrative.

There are also other unifying features more directly grounded in the poem's formal structure. Marlowe ends with a culminating articulation of the day-night imagery which he has deployed at key points all along. Night has been presented ambivalently throughout: although it is the time when love's joys are realized, its coming signals terror and fear, as in the first meeting of Hero and Leander:

> Thus while dumb signs their yielding hearts entangled,
> The air with sparks of living fire was spangled,
> And Night, deep drench'd in misty Acheron,
> Heav'd up her head, and half the world upon
> Breath'd darkness forth (dark night is Cupid's day)
>
> (I. 187–191)

Night serves as Cupid's day by concealing lovers, from the world and from themselves. Day itself is seen as cooperating with this function of night when, at the end of the second meeting, it delays its coming:

> And now the sun that through th' horizon peeps,
> As pitying these lovers, downward creeps,
> So that in silence of the cloudy night,
> Though it was morning, did he take his flight.
>
> (II. 99–102)

Romantic love thrives on the concealing darkness of "the secret trusty night" (II. 103). But day finally intrudes upon the two lovers at the end of Marlowe's epyllion, and the imagery of these two earlier passages is reversed. First Hero's blushing reverses the sun's earlier delaying action by creating a "false morn" which "Brought forth the day before the day was born" (II. 321–322). Then the actual day comes to chase away night, and the images of night heaving up her head (I. 190) and of the "silence of the cloudy night" (II. 101) are reversed:

> By this Apollo's golden harp began
> To sound forth music to the Ocean,
> Which watchful Hesperus no sooner heard,
> But he the day's bright-bearing car prepar'd,
> And ran before, as harbinger of light,
> And with his flaring beams mock'd ugly Night,
> Till she, o'ercome with anguish, shame, and rage,
> Dang'd down to hell her loathsome carriage.
>
> (II. 327–334)

The "flaring beams" of day may make night and the experiences it allows seem ugly and shameful. The final association here of night with hell confirms the previously established connections of night with love as it exists on earth under the "Stygian empery" of Jove, where "Murder, rape, war, lust and treachery" constitute the disorder of the day. The question we are left with at the end of *Hero and Leander* is not whether their love will survive the jealous anger of Neptune and the dangers of the Hellespont. We already know the answer to that. But will their love survive the abrasively revealing light of day which forces them—or at least Hero—to look realistically at the problems and tensions of sexual love?

In making the case for *Hero and Leander* as a seriously perceptive as well as an entertaining poem about erotic experience, I have had to give less emphasis than I would have wished to certain more generally recognized features of Marlowe's writing, particularly to the sheer fun of his extraordinary verbal wit. In an effort to redress the balance somewhat, let us see how Marlowe's more extravagant conceits might be accommodated within the view of the poem I have been arguing for. One critic has found Marlowe's conceits so extravagant that he urges us not to take them seriously: Marlowe conceives of his narrator, he says, as a "hack poet . . . with an over-active awareness of his literary heritage and almost no ability to master it poetically."[67] While this view seems to me entirely misdirected, it does point to the way in which the carefully distanced narrative persona allows Marlowe to indulge in flights of stylistic fancy which otherwise would have been impossible. Two striking conceits involving Hero's tears, for example, may seem less gratuitously far-fetched if we think of them as extensions of the narrator's preoccupation with Hero's artificiality. The first occurs in the crucial passage already quoted where Leander asks Hero to whom she has sworn chastity:

> 'To Venus,' answer'd she, and as she spake,
> Forth from those two tralucent cisterns brake
> A stream of liquid pearl, whereon the gods might trace
> To Jove's high court.
>
> (I. 295-299)

One senses in the exaggeration of this conceit a certain humorous awareness appropriate to the irony with which the narrator has treated Hero's pose as "Venus' nun" all along. The notion of the gods playfully exploiting Hero's jewel-like tears is repeated when Hero begins weeping after Cupid has struck her with his second arrow of love:

> And as she wept, her tears to pearl he turn'd,
> And wound them on his arm, and for her mourn'd.
>
> (I. 375-376)

There is no question of one taking a conceit like this seriously; even more than in the previous passage, one is aware of a playful stylistic self-consciousness.[68] Cupid's gesture mocks the metaphor of Hero's tears as pearls by subjecting it to a comically literal extension. Yet the image does convey the way in which Love toys with Hero even as he takes pity on her.

Marlowe's style is most playfully extravagant at moments when the narrator shows Hero under the greatest erotic pressure. It is partly this self-delighting verbal performance that insures us of the narrator's detachment from and control over the most passionate moments of his story. Leander is embracing Hero in the final scene:

> For though the rising iv'ry mount he scal'd,
> Which is with azure circling lines empal'd,
> Much like a globe (a globe may I term this,
> By which love sails to regions full of bliss),
> Yet there with Sisyphus he toil'd in vain,
>
> (II. 273–277)

The narrator is working his way here towards the metaphor he finally elaborates fully a few lines later as the "world . . . of unknown joy" generated by Hero's passionate striving. The explicit stylistic self-consciousness of the parenthesis ("a globe may I term this . . .") is Marlowe's way of assuring us, through the narrator, that he is aware of the extremity of his conceit. The narrator is capable of turning the most intense erotic moments into occasions for whimsical verbal display, without obliterating the human intensity and pathos of such moments. It is in this use of an actively self-dramatizing narrative persona to project a fundamentally ambivalent attitude towards the action of the poem that Marlowe's Ovidianism is most creative, and most unlike Shakespeare's technique in *Venus and Adonis*.

I have dealt with Marlowe's *Hero and Leander* as a self-sufficient poem throughout this chapter because I am convinced that it can and should be read in this way. Marlowe narrates only a "fragment" (proportionately a very large "fragment") of the entire story, but he treats this "fragment" with a remarkable unity of conception and execution. It is impossible to know exactly what Marlowe thought of the state of his poem when he died. It is hard to imagine how he would have made good on his muted but unmistakable forebodings of tragedy had he wanted to and had he lived to be able to. The irony with which he explores both the comic and the serious imperfections in the love of Hero and Leander would have made the tragedy of their deaths very difficult to realize artistically, if not emotionally and intellectually. For a long time it was believed that in his dying moments Marlowe had charged Chapman with the task of "completing" the poem. But neither Chapman's obscure allusion to Marlowe in the Third Sestiad of the 1598 edition (ll. 183-198) nor the circumstances of Marlowe's death as we now know them warrant such a belief.[69] Chapman was Marlowe's friend, and it is possible that for various reasons he felt a responsibility to continue the story of Hero and Leander to its tragic conclusion. But it is difficult to say exactly what Chapman means when he tells us "how much his late desires I tender" (III. 195). A careful reading of Chapman's four Sestiads reveals that he understood Marlowe's epyllion very well indeed, for he addresses himself directly to the problems inherent in erotic experience as Marlowe presents it and develops his own complex responses to these problems.[70] But Chapman's poetic responses could not differ more, stylistically and conceptually, from Marlowe's. "New light gives new directions"—the opening line of Chapman's "continuation" makes the alteration of basic terms quite clear. Chapman gives us not only a different moment of Musaeus's narrative, but an entirely different vision of the human experience that narrative embodies.

PART TWO

The Epyllion
and Late Elizabethan Satire

Chapter V

Mythological Parodies and Satirical Attacks on Lust and Erotic Poetry

There might you see one sigh, another rage,
And some (their violent passions to assuage)
Compile sharp satires, but alas too late,
For faithful love will never turn to hate.

(Hero and Leander I. 125–128)

It has become part of the traditional view of the epyllion to say that with the arrival of the seventeenth century the Elizabethan delight in languid eroticism and extravagant artificiality gave way to an increasingly satirical and parodic approach to Ovidian fable, and to point to Marston's *The Metamorphosis of Pigmalions Image* (1598) and to Beaumont's *Salmacis and Hermaphroditus* (1602) as indicators of the new direction in which Ovidian poetry was tending.[1] But as Marlowe's ironic description of Hero's scorned suitors makes apparent, and as I hope my previous chapters have already suggested, satire impinges on the epyllion from the beginning. The central argument of this chapter and of the three which follow is that the overtly satirical dimension of certain Ovidian poems written around the turn of the century represents an intensification of the tendency towards satire present in the epyllion all along. This process of intensification may be attributed in part to the Elizabethan epyllion's inherent ironic self-consciousness.[2] It was also encouraged, however, by certain satirical tendencies in drama, prose, and epigram during the 1590s, and by the volatile, contradictory development during this same period of formal verse satire.

In the fullest and most recent study of Elizabethan satire, Louis Lecocq touches briefly on the main point at issue here when he observes that "criticism of Ovidian poetry places the satirists in a much more difficult situation than does criticism of Petrarchan poetry."[3] The epyllion did not provide the satirists of the 1590s with the sort of complacent indulgence in idealizing love rhetoric which they could find

in many of the sonneteers. When such rhetoric appears in the epyllion, as
we have seen in the speeches of Lodge's Glaucus and of Shakespeare's
Venus, it is often subjected to an ironic exposure every bit as devastating
as that which it receives at the hand of the satirist. The epyllionic wooer,
as Lecocq points out, is usually the very opposite of the idealizing neo-
Platonic lover so common in the Petrarchan tradition. He—or she, as is
more often the case— has no need to discover with Sidney's Astrophel that
"Desire still cries 'Give me some food!'" The wooers of Elizabethan
epyllia are all too aware of the physical realities of sexual love. If for a
moment they indulge the illusion that their desires are not rooted in brute
physical immediacy, their own actions or the comments of the narrator
quickly remind the reader that he is in a poetic universe governed by
"sick-thoughted Venus" and by "gods in sundry shapes, / Committing
heady riots, incest, rapes." This strain of ironic, even cynical erotic
realism, coupled as it so often is with an exaggerated version of Ovid's
comic anthropomorphism in presenting the ancient myths, would indeed
appear to give the epyllion a certain invulnerability to satiric attack.

   In addition to their ironic sexual realism and their playfully
irreverent handling of classical deities, Elizabethan epyllia contain
specific satirical motifs of their own which would have insulated them
against certain kinds of satirical criticism. Two of these motifs may be
seen as complementary reflections of the University and Inns-Of-Court
background which many authors of epyllia shared with their immediate
audience. On the one hand there is the recurrent mockery of pedantry and
the witty, ironic appropriation of scholastic logic. Glaucus advises the
narrator of Lodge's epyllion, who sits dejectedly on the banks of the Isis,
to search "the schoolemens cunning noates" and, when he has instructed
himself in the capriciousness of fate, to "mourne no more, but moane my
hapless state" (ll. 37–42). Leander shows himself equally ready to
appropriate the wisdom of the "schoolemen" to his own rather
unacademic pursuits when he lectures Hero on the precept that "One is
no number" (I. 255), or when he deduces for her that virginity is nothing:

> This idol which you term virginity,
> Is neither essence, subject to the eye,
> No, nor to any one exterior sense,
> Nor hath it any place of residence,
> Nor is't of earth or mould celestial,
> Or capable of any form at all.[4]
>   (I. 269-274)

One does not have to be familiar with scholastic Aristotelianism and with
its application in the legal profession to appreciate the comedy of

Glaucus's or Leander's arguments, but it is clear that such arguments would have had a special appeal for Elizabethans who either were or had been subjected to the institutionalized propagation of such "reasoning."

The complementary counter-motif to this satirical exploitation of scholastic pseudo-learning is the praise of genuine learning, implied, for example, in Marlowe's playful account of the punishment of Mercury by the Fates:

> Yet as a punishment they added this,
> That he and Poverty should always kiss.
> And to this day is every scholar poor,
> Gross gold from them runs headlong to the boor.
> Likewise the angry Sisters thus deluded,
> To venge themselves on Hermes, have concluded
> That Midas' brood shall sit in Honour's chair,
> To which the Muses' sons are only heir:
>
> (I. 469–476)

Thomas Edwards echoes Marlowe's ironic lament for the neglect of learned, sophisticated poetry in *Cephalus and Procris*. In opposing the fashionable banalities and clichés of "Midas' brood" and appealing to a non-pedantic, open-minded erudition, the authors of epyllia were giving expression to some of the same concerns which one finds articulated with greater harshness and severity in Elizabethan satire.[5]

Having seen, then, that the epyllion was in some respects invulnerable to any very obvious form of satire, we may go on to reconsider the relationship between the Ovidian poems of Lodge, Shakespeare, Marlowe, and their followers and the various sorts of satirical writing which might be thought to have impinged upon them. There are two main currents in late Elizabethan literature to consider. The first, more common in drama, epigram, and prose than in formal verse satire, marks the beginning of what will become a major genre in later seventeenth-century literature: burlesque and travesty of classical myth. The second current is centered in one of the dominant preoccupations of formal verse satire in the late 1590s: violent denunciation of lust and of erotic poetry allegedly intended to titillate the sexual appetite. Although these two currents merge in some of the examples we shall be looking at, it is useful as a preliminary argumentative procedure to distinguish them.

The first thing to notice about the mythological parody of the 1590s is that in several instances this parody was produced by the authors of epyllia themselves. Shakespeare's plays of this period contain two quite familiar mythological parodies. "The most lamentable comedy, and most cruel death of Pyramus and Thisby" performed by Peter Quince and his company of "rude mechanicals" in *A Midsummer Night's Dream* is probably the best known parody of an Ovidian subject in English literature. The composition of the play is usually dated to 1594 or 1595,[6] only a year or two after *Venus and Adonis* and at a time when imitation of the epyllia of Shakespeare and Marlowe was at its height. In fact only a year later, in 1596, a narrative poem entitled *Pyramus and Thisbe*, containing numerous echoes of *Venus and Adonis* and *Hero and Leander*, was written by an otherwise unknown poet named Dunstan Gale.[7] It is unlikely that Shakespeare was familiar with Gale's poem when he wrote *A Midsummer Night's Dream*, unless he had seen it in manuscript or unless the play was written slightly later than the date usually conjectured for it (which is, of course, entirely possible). But whether intentionally or coincidentally, the satire of the "rude mechanical's" play effectively exposes the feebleness of Gale's handling of the subject. Here, for instance, is Gale's account of the lovers' attempt to kiss through the chink in the wall which separates them:

> Through this they kist, but with their breath they kist,
> For why the hindering wall was them betwixt.[8]

This ludicrous couplet is wonderfully deflated in the exchange between Bottom's Pyramus and Francis Flute's Thisbe:

> *Pyramus.* O, kiss me through the hole of this vile wall.
> *Thisbe.*   I kiss the wall's hole, not your lips at all.
> (V.i.200–201)

Though he may not have known Gale's poem, there is little doubt that Shakespeare was thinking of his fellow epyllion-writers in this part of the scene, for the lines just quoted are immediately preceded by bungled allusions to "Helen" and "Limander" (Hero and Leander) and to "Shefalus" and "Procus" (Cephalus and Procris). Here and in the earlier sections of the play devoted to the "tedious brief scene of young Pyramus, / And his love Thisbe" (V.i.56–57), Shakespeare is glancing satirically at the vogue of Ovidian narrative poetry he had done so much to establish by showing what happens to Ovidian subjects when they fall into the hands of "rude mechanicals."[9]

The other famous Shakespearian parody of an epyllionic subject is Rosalind's mockery of the Hero and Leander story in *As You Like It* (probably written in 1599 or 1600). Orlando has just sworn to the disguised Rosalind, who has decided to play herself for a moment, that he will die if she will not have him:

Rosalind.   No, faith, die by attorney. The poor world is almost six thousand
years old, and in all this time there was not any man who died in
his own person, videlicet, in a love-cause. Troilus had his brains
dash'd out by a Grecian club; yet he did what he could to die
before, and he is one of the patterns of love. Leander, he would
have lived many a fair year though Hero had turn'd nun, if it had
not been for a hot mid-summer night; for, good youth, he went
but forth to wash him in the Hellespont, and being taken with
the cramp was drown'd: and the foolish chroniclers of that age
found it was 'Hero of Sestos.' But these are all lies: men have died
from time to time, and worms have eaten them, but not for love.

(IV.i.86–99)

In this speech Shakespeare is taking advantage of perhaps the most
popular subject of mythological parody in the 1590s. Shakespeare himself
had already alluded satirically to the love of Hero and Leander in *The
Two Gentlemen of Verona* (I.i.20–24), in *Romeo and Juliet* (II.iv.47–48),
and in *Much Ado About Nothing* (V.ii.28). And towards the very end of
the century two more extended parodies appeared: one in an anonymous
verse satire called *Tyros Roring Megge* (1598);[10] a second, much more
successful one in *Nashe's Lenten Stuff* (1599), which concludes with the
gods turning Leander into a ling, Hero into a Cadwallader herring, and
Hero's old nurse into a mustard seed because she "was a cowring on her
backe side whiles these things were a tragedizing."[11] Rosalind's sarcastic
retelling of the story must be seen, then, as only one example of what had
become by the turn of the century a set piece of mythological satire.

The relation of these parodies to Marlowe's epyllion, at least in the
case of *Nashe's Lenten Stuff* and *As You Like It*, is deceptively
complicated. There can be no doubt that Nash and Shakespeare were
glancing at the popular success of *Hero and Leander*. They were looking
more directly, however, at the vulgar, sentimentalized conception of a
story which, as Abraham Fraunce said in 1592, a year before the
registration of Marlowe's poem, was "in every mans mouth."[12] Nash and
Shakespeare both focus on that portion of the story—the lovers' death—
which Marlowe, whether intentionally or not, did not treat. And they
both go out of their way in these same works to pay tribute to Marlowe's
poem. Nash begins his parody by praising Marlowe with the language of
Marlowe's own praise of Musaeus: "Let me see, hath anie body in
Yarmouth heard of Leander and Hero, of whome divine *Musaeus* sung,
and a diviner Muse than him, *Kit Marlowe?*"[13] Shakespeare's well-known
tribute comes in the scene just before Rosalind's mockery:

> *Phebe.* Dead Shepherd, now I find thy saw of might,
> "Who ever lov'd that lov'd not at first sight?"
>
> (III.v.80–81)

The important thing about both these tributes is that they are either directed to (Nash's) or projected through (Shakespeare's) unsophisticated readers who lack the ability to understand the irony of Marlowe's handling of the Hero and Leander story. Phebe obviously thinks she is quoting from an idealized romance; Nash is toying with much the same attitude towards the story when, in a passage recalling Fraunce's pronouncement, he tells the citizens of Yarmouth: "Twoo faithfull lovers they were, as every apprentice in Poules churchyard will tell you for your love, and sel you for your money."[14] In the popular imagination Hero and Leander had become what they never are in Marlowe's epyllion: ideally faithful lovers doomed to an early death. Nash and Shakespeare both indicate that it is primarily this simple-minded, popularized view of the myth, and not Marlowe's, which they are parodying.

If we look ahead briefly to a work which stands outside the chronological range of this chapter, Ben Jonson's *Bartholomew Fair*, we will find many of the points observed in the parodies of Nash and Shakespeare confirmed in John Littlewit's puppet show. Jonson's play, first performed in 1614,[15] was written at a time when verse parodies of Ovidian subjects had become at least as common as epyllia written in serious emulation of Shakespeare and Marlowe. It is all the more interesting, therefore, to see Jonson being even more careful than Nash and Shakespeare had been to distinguish Marlowe's poem (and Chapman's continuation, we must assume) from a version of the story comically appropriate to an unsophisticated audience. Bartholomew Coke asks Lantern Leatherhead if he will play Littlewit's entertainment "according to the printed book"—that is, according to the 1598 edition of *Hero and Leander*:

> LAN. By no means, Sir.
> COK. No? How then?
> LAN. A better way, Sir, that is too learned, and
> poeticall for our audience; what doe they know
> what *Hellespont* is? Guilty of true loves blood?
> or what *Abidos* is? or the other *Sestos* hight?
> COK. Th'art i' the right, I do not know my selfe.
> LAN. No, I have entreated Master *Littlewit*, to take
> a little pains to reduce it to a more familiar
> straine for our people.
>
> (V.iii.108–117)

Leatherhead may be no more capable than Shakespeare's Phebe or a Yarmouth fisherman of appreciating the irony and the mythological wit of Marlowe's epyllion. But he understands enough about the poem to know that it is beyond the grasp of St. Bartholomew fair-goers and that Littlewit's puppet scenario does indeed reduce the myth "to a more familiar strain"—at least in one sense of the word "familiar." By associating his parody with the theatrical efforts of another group of "rude mechanicals," Jonson, like Nash and Shakespeare, demonstrates his respect for the more sophisticated elaboration of the subject by a writer who would have been the first to enjoy the comedy of a Hero who woos her "amorous Leander" by casting at him "a Sheepes eye, and a halfe" (V.iv.125).[16]

It is reasonable to conclude that while Elizabethan parody of classical myth had the effect of making writers of Ovidian narrative poetry even more ironically self-conscious than they would have been otherwise, such parody reflected derisively only on bad imitations of Shakespeare and Marlowe and on the crude, sentimental popular conception of the better-known classical love stories. One is led to similar conclusions about the effect of satirical attacks on lust and erotic poetry, although the questions raised by these attacks involve ambiguities and contradictions of a more complicated and deep-lying kind.

In his book on *Comicall Satyre and Shakespeare's "Troilus and Cressida,"* O. J. Campbell remarks that Elizabethan satirists of the 1590s were so preoccupied "with the sins and perversions of sex . . . that a critic must assume either that the satirists, in particular Marston, were pathologically attracted to the unsavory subject or that lustful practices constituted in their time the most dangerous enemy to social decency. . . ."[17] More recent studies have called into question both of Campbell's alternative assumptions, but they have not controverted the fact that lust and sexual perversion do play a strikingly dominant role in Elizabethan satire. Even Joseph Hall, eventually to become Bishop of Norwich and of Exeter and along with Donne the most dignified satirist of the 1590s, attacks sexual debauchery with surprising verbal ferocity:

> Shall then that foule infamous *Cyneds* hide
> Laugh at the purple wales of others side?
> Not, if hee were as neere, as by report,
> The stewes had wont to be to the Tenis-court,
> Hee that while thousands envie at his bed,
> Neighs after Bridals, and fresh-mayden heade:
> While slavish *Juno* dares not look awry
> To frowne at such imperious rivalrye,

> Not tho shee sees her wedding Jewels drest
> To make new Bracelets for a strumpets wrest,
> Or like some strange disguised *Messaline,*
> Hires a nights lodging of his concubine;[18]
> > (*Virgidemiae* IV.i.92–103)

Hall's attacks are sedate and measured, however, compared to those of his arch-enemy Marston in *The Scourge of Villanie* (1598), of Marston's friend Everard Guilpin in *Skialetheia: or a Shadow of Truth* (1598), and of the young Thomas Middleton in *Micro-Cynicon* (1599). Marston is at his most savage when mocking homosexuality:

> Alack, alack, what peece of lustfull flesh
> Hath *Luscus* left, his *Priape* to redresse:
> Grieve not good soule, he hath his *Ganimede,*[19]
> His perfum'd shee-goate, smooth kembd & high fed.
> > (*The Scourge of Villanie,* Satyre III, ll. 37–40)

This same subject is developed at greater length in the fifth satire of Middleton's *Micro-Cynicon,* which in some passages reads like a satiric counterpart to Edwards' *Narcissus:*

> As it is *Sathans* usuall pollicie,
> He left an issue of like quallitie:
> The still memoriall if I aime aright,
> Is a pale chequered *Hermaphrodite:*
> . . . .
> Yet *Troynovant* that all admired towne,
> Where thousands still do travel up and downe,
> Of Bewties counterfets affords not one,
> So like a lovely smiling parragon,
> As is *Pyander* in a Nymphes attire,
> Whose rowling eye sets gazers harts on fire;
> Whose cherry lip, black brow & smile procure
> Lust burning buzzards to the tempting lure.[20]

Guilpin confines himself to attacking heterosexual lust, but his wit is every bit as scurrilous as that of Marston and Middleton:

> Since marriage, *Faber's* prouder than before,
> Yfayth his wife must take him a hole lower.[21]
> > (*Skialetheia,* Epigram 6)

Sexual vice had, of course, been a major theme in Roman satire: Hall, Marston, Guilpin, Middleton, and their fellow practitioners of satire and epigram could look back to Juvenal, Persius, and Martial to find classical precedents for their exposure of lust and for the frequently obscene verbal means by which they did so.[22]

The main problem which satire of this kind raises, of course, is the contradictoriness of its ultimate meaning and effect. In *The Cankered Muse*, Alvin Kernan articulates the problem in its broadest aspect:

> In order to attack vice effectively, the satirist must portray it in detail and profusion, and he must explore the nastiest activities of the human animal and describe them in ... revolting terms ... At times the satirist will go beyond mere prurience and appear pathological in his unending revelations of human nastiness and his paraded disgust with the ordure of the world. Trapped by his need for making sin appear hideous he seems always to be seeking out and thoroughly enjoying the kind of filth which he claims to be attacking. And at the same time that he opens himself to the charge of being a literary Peeping Tom, he also makes it possible to charge him with sensationalism, for the more effectively he builds up catalogues of human vice, the more it will appear that he is merely purveying salacious material to satisfy the meaner appetites of his audience.[23]

Late sixteenth- and seventeenth-century writers were highly conscious of the contradictions Kernan describes. John Davies of Hereford tries to obviate the charge of hypocritical sensationalism, for example, at the beginning of *The Scourge of Folly* (1611):

> The *Printer* praies me most uncessantly,
> To make some *lines* to lash at *Lechery*.
> . . . .
> Then, Reader, thinke when thou seest such a Straine,
> Its for the Lechers pain, and Printers gaine.[24]

Elizabethan and Jacobean writers were also keenly aware of the satirist's vulnerability to the charge of melancholy envy which Marlowe levels against Hero's rejected suitors with their ineffectual satires. Burton says of the envious man that "every word he speaks [is] a satire";[25] Weever, in one of his epigrams, equates "the Satyres venim'd bite" with "malecontented Envies poysned spight."[26] Only someone incapable of enjoying sex, the argument would have run, could spend so much energy degrading it. The fact that Elizabethan satirists went to considerable lengths to defend themselves against accusations that they were all envious malcontents, and even launched their own attacks against the "Vaine envious detractor," only testifies further to their sensitivity and vulnerability on this point.[27]

Without attempting to explain away the ambiguities and contradictions of late Elizabethan satire, or to dismiss the biographical interest of a figure like Marston, recent commentators have seen the problems as essentially literary rather than psychological or ethical, and have approached them with reference to Renaissance notions of satiric strategy, decorum, and persona. In the passage from *The Cankered Muse* quoted above, for instance, Kernan uses "satirist" to refer not to the author of a given poem but to the speaker, the consciously created satiric persona. The Elizabethans, along with most of their contemporaries on the Continent, identified the word "satire" etymologically and historically with "satyr" and believed that as a literary genre satire was descended from the satyr plays of Greek Old Comedy.[28] Kernan argues further that Elizabethan satirists wrote under the conviction that satire had originally been the utterance of satyrs. It was this conviction, he claims, which determined their satiric persona and their pervasive roughness, obscurity, obscenity, and preoccupation with sex: "The Elizabethan definition of satire as it appears in formal pronouncements amounts to little more than, 'a poem in which the author playing the part of the satyr attacks vice in the crude, elliptic, harsh language which befits his assumed character and his low subject matter.'"[29]

Lecocq advances some incisive criticism of Kernan's conception of the "satyr" persona and argues that the supposed connection between "satire" and "satyr" was only one of several important factors influencing the Elizabethan satirists' search for a fully coherent and controllable mode of expression.[30] Bridget Gellert Lyons has recently analyzed another of these important factors by showing how Marston and his contemporaries made use of Renaissance ideas of the melancholic personality in creating a satiric persona consciously endowed with an excessive verbal aggressiveness and an obsessive preoccupation with lust and other forms of human degradation—a persona, that is, whose "mind is a reflection of the world he portrays."[31] But the connection of the satyr figure with Elizabethan satire remains an indisputable fact. William Rankin introduces his *Seaven Satyres* (1598) by declaring "My shaggy Satyres doe forsake the woods, / . . . To view the manner of this humane strife" ("Induction," ll. 3-6); the speaker in Rankin's first satire announces "I am a Satyre savage in my sport" ("Satyr Primum," l. 40).[32] As we shall see, this entire question of the Elizabethan conception of satire, and particularly the "satire"-"satyr" connection, has an important bearing on Weever's *Faunus and Melliflora*, where the relationship between the sexually-preoccupied satire of the late 1590s and the epyllion is focused in a most interesting way. The general point I wish to make is that the ambiguity of satirical attacks on sexual indulgence can be approached as a question of poetic strategy and meaning without depending, as Campbell and others have done, on conjecture about the author's character or about the prevalence of sexual immorality in Elizabethan society.

Attacks on erotic poetry constitute a prominent sub-category of the general preoccupation with sexual vice in the satire of the late 1590s and accentuate many of the ambiguities and contradictions we have already observed. Attacks of this kind were of course not new. Stephen Gosson, whose pamphlet battle with Lodge was examined in Chapter I,[33] had denounced the "amarous Poets" in *The School of Abuse* by comparing them to pigs:

> It is . . . the maner of swine, to forsake the fayre fieldes, and wallow in the myre: and the whole practice of Poets, eyther with fables to shew theyr abuses, or with plaine tearmes to unfold theyr mischiefs, discover theyr shame, discredit themselves, and disperse theyr poyson through all the worlde.[34]

One of the things which distinguishes later Elizabethan satirists from writers like Gosson is the dazzlingly resourceful verbal wit with which they profess their disgust with erotic poetry. Hall devotes long sections of *Virgidemiae* to what he calls "such Litturs of new Poetry" (I.ii.28):

> Now is *Parnassus* turnéd to the stewes:
> And on Bay-stockes the wanton Myrtle growes.
> *Cytheron's* hill's become a Brothel-bed,
> And *Pyrene* sweet, turnd to a poysoned head
> Of cole-blacke puddle; . . .
>   (I.ii.17–21)

> Each bush, each banke, and each base apple-squire,
> Can serve to sate their beastly lewd desire.
> Ye bastard Poets see your Pedegree,
> From common Trulls, and loathsome Brothelry.
>   (I.ii.35–38)

Marston's denunciation of erotic poetry, particularly his attempts to dissociate himself from the salacious parts of his own *Pigmalions Image*, will be discussed fully in the next chapter. Guilpin, in the second epigram

of *Skialetheia,* invokes what should by now be the familiar notion of the
effeminizing effects of indulging in lust:

> Whose hap shall be to reade these pedler rimes,
> Let them expect no elaborat foolery,
> Such as Hermaphroditize these poor times
> With wicked scald jests, extreame gullerie:[35]
> ("To the Reader," ll. 1-4)

The striking thing about a passage like this is the way in which the satirist
imputes a familiarity with erotic poetry to his reader in order to display his
own witty command of sexual allusion in upsetting expectation.
Poetically, the poetry of Hall, Marston, and Guilpin is often cleverly
parasitic on the writing it condemns.

Whatever the intentions of the Elizabethan satirists, their scourging of
sexual vice and of the poets who allegedly catered to it produced a
contradictory public response in the form of an edict of censure issued on
June 1, 1599. Although the wording of the edict is confusing at several
points, its central concerns are clear: it forbids the further publication of
Hall's satires, Marston's *Pigmalions Image* and *Scourge of Villanie,*
Guilpin's *Skialetheia,* Middleton's *Micro-Cynicon,* the volume containing
Sir John Davies's *Epigrams* and Marlowe's translation of the *Amores,* and
several other volumes of satirical writing or writing presumed to be
obscene; it orders that no more satires or epigrams be published; it insists
that all "histories" and plays must be approved and registered before being
published; and it orders all existing copies of the books specifically named
to be brought to the Archbishop of Canterbury and the Bishop of London
to be burned.[36] A subsequent entry in the Stationers' Register tells us that
on June 4, copies of all the named works were burned except for Hall's
satires, Thomas Cutwode's *Caltha Poetarum,* and *Willoughby His Avisa*
(the latter had not been mentioned in the original edict).[37] There are, as
Lecocq points out, certain inconsistencies in the edict itself and in the
report of the burning, and John Peter probably oversimplifies the matter
when he says "it was not so much Satire itself that the Bishops were
opposing, but pornography and obscenity. . . ."[38] But it nevertheless does
appear that a major factor in the banning and burning of these books was
that the satirists' attacks on lust and erotic poetry had made their own
writing licentious in the eyes of the ecclesiastical authorities.

One may well ask with Lecocq[39] why neither *Venus and Adonis* nor
Hero and Leander nor any other Ovidian narrative poem of the early 1590s
was called in by the edict of 1599. It may simply have been that the bishops
were concerned with turning the most immediate tide of writing which

they found offensive. The poems mentioned in the edict were all published between 1597 and 1599, whereas *Venus and Adonis* had been publicly available since 1593. And Marlowe's *Hero and Leander,* when it finally appeared in print in 1598, was joined to Chapman's learned and elevated continuation. Imitation of Shakespeare and Marlowe had, moreover, diminished somewhat by 1599. Marston's *Pigmalion* was the only recent testimony to their influence which might have given offense, and the volume containing that poem appears at the top of the list of books actually destroyed.

There may also be a more significant literary reason for the bishop's apparent lack of concern with the epyllion. The poems of Lodge, Shakespeare, Marlowe, and their followers were for the most part cunningly indirect in their use of erotic detail compared to the raw verbal lewdness of Marston and Guilpin. Archbishop Whitgift might have missed the pornographic suggestiveness of Venus's invitation to Adonis, in her famous deer-park simile, to graze upon her "sweet bottom grass" (l. 236),[40] but he could hardly have overlooked Marston's much more explicit references to pederasty and masturbation:

> Fayth, what cares he for faire *Cynedian* boyes?
> Velvet cap'd Goates, duch Mares? tut common toies.
> Detaine them all, on this condition
> He may but use the Cynick friction.
> (*The Scourge of Villanie,* Satyre III, ll. 49-52)

It is, finally, Marston and Guilpin, not Shakespeare and Marlowe, who praise *"Aretines* great wit" (*Skialetheia,* Satyre Preludium). For all its potentially subversive exploration of the turbulence of erotic experience and its ironic attitude towards the allegorical and moralized approach to Ovidian myth, the Elizabethan epyllion posed less of a threat to accepted standards of public literary decency than did much of the satire which attacked it.

All the issues surveyed in this chapter will be examined in greater detail in the discussions of Marston's *Pigmalions Image* and Weever's *Faunus and Melliflora* in Chapters VI and VII. It should already be apparent, however, that whatever the effect of late Elizabethan satire on the epyllion, it was not that of exposing romantic mythological fictions to the harsh and deflating scrutiny of satiric realism and moral severity. It should also be apparent that the epyllia and the satire we have examined relate to each other in a complex pattern of conflict and convergence. Both types of poetry spring from the same immediate literary environment, from sophisticated writers with University backgrounds (Shakespeare is always the exception here) and with close ties either to one of the Inns of Court or to a literary coterie like that of Southampton. Lodge, although older than most of the writers with whom we are concerned, is a representative figure in this regard. The volume entitled *Scillaes Metamorphosis,* addressed to "the Gentlemen of the Innes of Court and Chauncerie," contained a poem called *The Discontented Satyre* as well as *Glaucus and Scilla. A Fig for Momus,* Lodge's most important satirical work, is advertised on the title-page as being "by T. L. of Lincolnes Inne Gent." Marston was at the Middle Temple from 1595 to 1606; Guilpin became a member of Gray's Inn in 1591.[41] *The Scourge of Villanie* and *Skialetheia,* no less than *Glaucus and Scilla* and *Venus and Adonis,* were designed to succeed initially with a relatively restricted and sophisticated audience. This was the audience of Donne's early poetry, much of it written while he was resident in Lincoln's Inn.[42] It was the audience of the "Prince d'Amour" revels held at the Middle Temple in 1597–98, which dramatize many of the elements common to epyllion and satire of the 1590s: the jokes intended to reflect on the rakish sexual lives supposedly led by the members of the audience; the mockery of the pseudo-Petrarchan posturing of the sonneteers; above all the pervasively ironic and often cynical attitude towards love.[43]

The conflict and convergence of epyllion and satire may also be related to their respective indebtedness to classical influences. Hall, Marston, and Guilpin were breaking away from the English "complaint" tradition and exploring the themes and poetic energies of the Roman satirists as they had not been explored in English before. In this respect they provide an important parallel to the Elizabethan Ovidian poets who were freeing themselves from the strictures of the moralizing and allegorical tradition and exploring Ovid's poetry with a new freedom and openness. Whatever their psychological or moral interest in sexual vice, late Elizabethan satirists were obviously attracted by the sheer poetic virtuosity, the savage verbal cleverness, with which the Roman satirists exposed erotic folly. Their interest in this strain in Juvenal, Persius, and Martial, like the epyllion-writers' interest in Ovid's sophisticated erotic ambivalence, may be seen as an expression of the cynical realism which developed in late Elizabethan and Jacobean literature in reaction to the prevailing Christian, humanist, and Petrarchan traditions of idealizing human sexual love.

Yet if the relationship of late Elizabethan satire to Roman poetry establishes an important parallel with the epyllion, this very relationship also brings the two poetic modes into apparent conflict. Juvenal's entire imaginative orientation towards erotic experience is significantly different from Ovid's. He is not positively concerned, as Ovid is, with the charm and pathos of sexual love or with the haunting archetypal erotic patterns embedded in the ancient myths. Even when Ovid's approach is overtly satirical and social, as in the *Amores* and the *Ars Amatoria*, his irony and cynicism do not obliterate his sensitivity to erotic sentiment and pathos. There is, then, an important literary tension between Elizabethan satire and epyllion which can in part be articulated in terms of the difference between Juvenal and Ovid. Approaching the situation in this manner does not explain away the confusions and contradictions of the satirical attacks on lust and erotic poetry or the conflict between satire and epyllion, just as the theories of satiric strategy and persona do not explain these problems away. But both approaches help to place the problems in a useful literary perspective—useful not just in reading the poems, but also in evaluating the biographical and historical factors involved. An emphasis on the literary dimensions of the situation enables one to imagine, for instance, that a sophisticated Elizabethan could enjoy Marston as well as Marlowe, that he could appreciate the poetic appeal of a Juvenalian as well as of an Ovidian perspective on sexual experience.

I have tried in this chapter to establish a context for understanding more fully than we have in the past the immediate post-Shakespearian and -Marlovian development of the epyllion and for reading Marston's *Pigmalions Image*, Weever's *Faunus and Melliflora,* and Beaumont's *Salmacis and Hermaphroditus* as the three most important expressions of the contending pressures on the Ovidian poet around the turn of the century. While the pressure which figures most prominently in the epyllia of Marston and Weever comes from the sexually-preoccupied satire we have just been looking at, in the case of Beaumont's poem we will need to return to the more diffuse influence of mythological parody.

Chapter VI

The Metamorphosis of
Pigmalions Image

❦

It is not surprising that the relationship between epyllion and satire described in the last chapter should have given rise to at least one singularly ambiguous performance. There has been nothing else in the interpretation of Elizabethan poetry quite like the critical debate over John Marston's *The Metamorphosis of Pigmalions Image*. Until the 1960s most critics held the poem to be a serious but rather poor attempt at an epyllion, and Marston to have been dishonest and hypocritical when he claimed, after the fact, that he had actually written a satirical exposure of amorous and erotic poetry.[1] The main dissenting voice was that of Douglas Bush. He was "inclined to believe" Marston's claims and saw the poem as an "ironic piece of studied excess" by an author who nevertheless "derived a vicarious gratification from detailed accounts of the vices he attacked. . . . "[2] In 1960 Bush's position was extended, without his lingering reservations, in an essay by Gustav Cross, who argued that *Pigmalions Image* was a thoroughgoing parody, a "mock-epyllion."[3] The next stage in the debate was in some ways predictable: Philip Finkelpearl proposed "to show that both sides in this controversy are partially right" and that the poem "is an attempt in the Ovidian mode . . . but that it also has satiric elements."[4] This attempt to resolve the controversy did not convince the authors of the two most recent studies of *Pigmalions Image*. Louis Lecocq[5] and John Scott Colley[6] both set out to clarify Marston's "intentions" and to defend the poem as a parody with strong moral implications. Yet the major discrepancies between their accounts suggest that a good deal of confusion remains. One can imagine Marston himself smirking sarcastically at his modern interpreters and pointing to the dedication of his 1598 volume "To the Worlds Mightie Monarch, Good Opinion," whom he addresses with proleptic irony as "perpetuall / Ruler of Judgement," as "Great Arbitrator, Umpire of the Earth."

To think that the discussion offered here could put an end to the critical confusion occasioned by *Pigmalions Image* would be both presumptuous and, in a sense, contrary to what I wish to say about the poem. I shall argue that *Pigmalions Image* is irreducibly ambiguous and that Marston was partly, but not entirely, in control of the ambiguity. The discussion is organized around the assumption that Marston's "external" comments on the poem's intended meaning and effect must be evaluated in terms of an "internal" understanding of what the poem actually does. I shall therefore begin by examining the "internal" sources of critical confusion—Marston's handling of his mythological subject, his style, and his narrative technique—and then measure this assessment of Marston's actual poetic performance against what he says "externally" in "The Author in Prayse of his precedent Poem," which appears immediately after *Pigmalions Image* in the 1598 volume, and in Satire VI of *The Scourge of Villanie*. This approach should enable us to test the validity of Arnold Davenport's judgment on the poem: "Had it appeared by itself, few readers, perhaps, would ever have suspected that it could be anything but a rather weak example of its *genre*. . . ."[7] I shall of course be concerned throughout this chapter to see the problems raised by *Pigmalions Image* in relation generally to what has been said about the Elizabethan epyllion so far and particularly to the conflicts and convergences of epyllion and satire described in the preceding chapter.

One of the major sources of confusion arises from the way in which Marston exploits his Ovidian source. While it is right to speak of Marston's "special treatment of the Pigmalion story," as Finkelpearl does,[8] one should add that the story is already special in Ovid, since it involves not a "downward" transformation from a higher to a lower form of life but an unusual kind of "upward" transformation from an inanimate but humanly created object to a living person. Ovid's own relation to his Hellenistic source is in this instance particularly significant. An earlier version of the Pigmalion story appeared in the *Kypriaka* of Philostephanus, a follower or perhaps friend of Callimachus.[9] Here, according to Brooks Otis, the Pigmalion story was merely one of a group of sensationalistic erotic tales which dealt with sexual intercourse between men and statues or with the use of artificial objects as sexual stimulants.[10] In Philostephanus's version, Pigmalion simply satisfied himself by making love to a statue of Aphrodite. It is only with Ovid that the statue becomes Pigmalion's own personal amatory ideal and is transformed through the power of Venus into a real woman.

Ovid has, as Otis says, eliminated or at least greatly reduced the element of sensationalistic perversion in his source, but he has not

eliminated the erotic dimension altogether. He has, however, made this
dimension far more complex. The story of Pigmalion, like that of Adonis,
is part of the song of Orpheus in Book X of the *Metamorphoses*. As we
observed in Chapter III, Orpheus's song comes after the loss of Eurydice,
when he has "shunned all love of womankind" and "set the example for
the people of Thrace of giving his love to tender boys" (X. 79-85).[11] Most
of the tales in Orpheus's song have to do either with homosexuality or
with female sexual corruption. The Pigmalion episode is no exception,
although it relates to these two motifs in a special and more indirect way.
Pigmalion had been disgusted by the Propoetides, the maidens of
Amathus who were turned into prostitutes by Venus for denying her
divinity (X. 220-242).[12] Pigmalion's response to the sexual degradation of
the Propoetides was to shun all contact with women, to withdraw into the
world of art, and eventually to carve an ivory figure "more perfect than
that of any woman ever born" ("qua femina nasci / nulla potest," X. 248-
249). He fell in love with his statue and prayed to Venus that she give the
statue life. This Venus did: Pigmalion and his beloved were married and
soon produced a daughter called Paphos, whose name was eventually
given to one of Venus's island abodes. What Ovid has done, then, is to
take a story of artificial erotic fulfillment and convert it into a story of
alienated and repressed sexuality transformed by art into genuine erotic
fulfillment.[13] In Philostephanus art was, perversely, the *source* of erotic
fulfillment; in Ovid art provides the *means* by which Pigmalion moves
from sexual hatred to love. It is the interrelationship of artistic and erotic
imagination which stands at the center of Ovid's story, along with the
ambivalent power of Venus. It was Venus's punishment of the Propoetides, we recall, which caused Pigmalion to hate women in the first place;
it is subsequently the intervention of a beneficent Venus which brings
about the miraculous transformation of art into life.

Medieval and Renaissance adaptations of Ovid's Pigmalion episode
are more relevant to understanding Marston's approach than one might
at first think, although very few of these adaptations demonstrate much
sensitivity to the complexity of Ovid's narrative. In this case, even more
clearly than in the case of the Salmacis and Hermaphroditus episode
which we shall examine later, there is a dual tradition of positive and
negative adaptation. On the one hand writers in the medieval courtly
tradition tend to present Pigmalion as a positive type of the ardently
persistent lover. Gower's Confessor in the *Confessio Amantis* praises
Pigmalion's passionate wooing:

> And if he wolde have holde him still
> And nothing spoke, he scholde have failed:

> But for he hath his word travailed
> And dorste speke, his love he spedde,
> And hadde al that he wolde abedde.[14]
>
> (IV. 426–430)

Writers with a more severe moral perspective, on the other hand, such as Arnulf of Orleans, condemn Pigmalion as an example of irrational erotic folly and idolatry.[15] Jean de Meung follows and transforms this tradition in his brilliantly satirical adaptation of the story in the *Roman de la Rose* (ll. 20815–21175).[16] This dualistic approach continues into the Renaissance. For sixteenth-century lyric poets Pigmalion is time and again the ideal lover who serves as a foil for the eternally frustrated wooer of the Petrarchan tradition, since he finally succeeds in getting his literally idolized but hard-hearted mistress to yield. Here is Samuel Daniel's version of the conceit in sonnet XIII of *Delia* (1592):

> Behold what happe *Pigmaleon* had to frame,
> And carve his proper griefe upon a stone:
> My heavie fortune is much like the same,
> I worke on Flint, and that's the cause I mone.
> . . . .
> And stille I toile, to chaunge the marble brest
> Of her, whose sweetest grace I doe adore:
> Yet cannot finde her breathe unto my rest,
> Hard is her hart and woe is me therefore.
> O happie he that joy'd his stone and arte,
> Unhappy I to love a stony harte.[17]

A very different view of the the myth is suggested in Golding's "Epistle to Leicester," although he does not bother to comment specifically on the Pigmalion story itself:[18]

> The tenth booke cheefly dooth containe one kynd of argument
> Reproving most prodigious lusts of such as have been bent
> To incest most unnaturall.
>
> (ll. 213–215)

By making love to his own artistic creation, Golding implies, Pigmalion is engaging in a form of incestuous sexual madness. Marston's approach has a good deal in common with this tradition of negative interpretation, as we shall see, although he is much closer to Jean de Meung's satirical version of it than to the somber pronouncements of Arnulf of Orleans or Golding. And he also draws ironically on the tradition of Pigmalion as an ideal lover expressed in Daniel's sonnet.

Marston begins with a prose "Argument" which demonstrates his familiarity with the *Metamorphoses* episode and raises expectations that he may be returning to those Ovidian motifs which most later adaptors had disregarded. The idea of sexual alienation and repression is suggested in the opening words: *"Pigmalion* whose chast mind all the beauties in Cyprus could not ensnare. . . . " This idea appears again in the first stanza of the poem proper:

> *Pigmalion,* whose hie love-hating minde
> Disdain'd to yeeld servile affection,
> Or amorous sute to any woman-kinde,
> Knowing their wants, and mens perfection.
> (St. 1, ll. 1-4)

There are also suggestions at the beginning that Marston is concerned with Ovid's integration of artistic and erotic imagination. Pigmalion became "deeplie enamored on his owne workmanship," he says in the "Argument," and in stanza 3—

> Hee was amazed at the wondrous rarenesse
> Of his owne workmanships perfection.
> He thought that Nature nere produc'd such fairnes
> In which all beauties have their mantion.
> And thus admiring, was enamored
> On that fayre Image himself portraied.

These passages lead one to expect that Marston will take up the themes which figure so importantly in earlier epyllia and which link the Pigmalion episode with other epyllionic subjects. Like Adonis and Narcissus, Pigmalion is excessively resistant to the attractions of women. His "hie love-hating minde" recalls Adonis ("love he laugh'd to scorn," l. 4); his passion for his sculpture affords a clear parallel to Narcissus's love for his own reflected image.[19] By the fourth or fifth stanza, however, it becomes apparent that the primary direction of Marston's poem is tending elsewhere—that he is interested in exploring these Ovidian themes only insofar as they relate to an essentially satirical conception which has much more to do with Jean de Meung's adaptation and with Daniel's *Delia* XIII than with the episode in the *Metamorphoses*.

For Marston, as Finkelpearl was the first to point out, Pigmalion is a comic embodiment of the pseudo-Petrarchan wooer. The basic situation alluded to in Daniel's sonnet is dramatized and exaggerated to satiric proportions. Where the Petrarchan lover's mistress is figuratively as hard and unyielding as stone, Pigmalion's statue is literally that way.[20] Marston is thus able to ridicule many of the clichéd devices of bad Petrarchan poetry by having Pigmalion see in his statue what the sonnet lover sees in his mistress:

> He thinks he see'th the brightnes of the beames
> Which shoote from out the fairnes of her eye:
> At which he stands as in an extasie.

> Her Amber-coloured, her shining haire,
> Makes him protest, the Sunne hath spread her head
> With golden beames, to make her farre more faire.
> (St. 5, ll. 4-6; St. 6, ll. 1-3)

Finkelpearl elucidates many ways in which the verbal strategies of Petrarchan poetry are parodied in Pigmalion's wooing. Of course satire and parody of such strategies were by no means new in 1598: Sidney had scorned those who "poor Petrarch's long deceased wooes / With new born sighs, and denizen'd wits do sing" (*Astrophel and Stella*, sonnet XV, ll. 7-8), and Shakespeare's sonnets in praise of dark beauty partake of what by the end of the sixteenth century was a well-established anti-Petrarchan tradition. Yet the verbal ploys of Marston's satire are frequently original and clever. Finkelpearl does not mention, for example, the way in which the multiple meanings of words like "imagery" and "conceit" are exploited to support the implied parallel between Pigmalion's love "Of his owne workmanships perfection" and the Petrarchan poet-wooer's love—not of any real woman—but of the fictional mistress who exists only through his language. The modern rhetorical meanings of "image" and "imagery" were just evolving during the sixteenth century, but they were available to Marston, along with the literal meanings referring to carved statues.[21] In several passages Marston seems to be playing upon the double sense of these words to expose Pigmalion as a comic actualization of the Petrarchan poet-lover:

> O what alluring beauties he descries
> In each part of his faire *imagery*!
> (St. 4, ll. 3-4; my italics)

> He wondred that she blusht not when his eye
> Saluted those same parts of secrecie:
> *Conceiting* not it was *imagerie*
> That kindly yeelded that large libertie.
> (St. 11, ll. 1-4; my italics)

It is more certain that in this last passage and elsewhere in the poem
Marston is punning to similar effect on "conceit" ("A fancy, ingenious, or
witty expression" as well as "That which is conceived in the mind" and
"A fanciful notion . . . a whim"):[22]

> Then view's her lips, no lips did seeme so faire
> In his *conceit*, . . .
> (St. 7, ll. 1-2; my italics)

The verbal means by which Marston metaphorically converts Pigmalion
from an artist in stone to an artist in words make his satire more
sophisticated than it has sometimes been acknowledged to be. Francis
Bacon will articulate the underlying idea of Marston's strategy in *The
Advancement of Learning* (1605): "Here therefore is the first distemper of
learning, when men study words and not matter; . . . It seems to me that
Pygmalion's frenzy is a good emblem or portraiture of this vanity: for
words are but the images of matter; and except they have life of reason and
invention, to fall in love with them is all one as to fall in love with a
picture."[23]

   That Marston uses Pigmalion's deluded wooing to satirize the clichés
of the sonnet and of other amorous lyrics of the sixteenth century is
beyond question. But how does this satire relate to Pigmalion's eventual
success in realizing his love when his statue is brought to life? And what
other possibilities, in addition to anti-Petrarchan satire, does Marston see
in the myth? Finkelpearl's answer to the first of these questions is that the
satire is confined to the first half of the poem, before Pigmalion realizes
the folly of loving a statue and prays to Venus that his creation be made
human: "Up to this point Pigmalion is certainly an object of satire, but a
change now occurs . . . Pigmalion refuses to be rebuffed; he insists on
fulfillment. As a result . . . Pigmalion is no longer an object of satire; he is
a mirror, an amatory model."[24] Finkelpearl is certainly right in noting a
shift in the poem's presentation of Pigmalion, but he is wrong, I think, to
see that shift as a movement from Pigmalion as an "object of satire" to
Pigmalion as a serious "amatory model." I would argue instead that the
shift is from one satirical perspective to another, from an exposure of the
artist-wooer's foolish love of his own work to a culminating demonstration that lust, and not aesthetic aspiration, has been Pigmalion's
dominant motivation all along. Surely the handling of Pigmalion's
prayer to Venus is as comically satirical as anything earlier in the poem:

> Thou know'st the force of love, then pitty me,
> Compassionate my true loves ardencie.

> Thus having said, he riseth from the floore,
> As if his soule divined him good fortune,
> . . . .
> And therefore straight he strips him naked quite,
> That in the bedde he might have more delight.
>   (St. 24, ll. 5-6; St. 25, ll. 1-2, 5-6)

The detail of Pigmalion stripping himself naked in response to his "soule's" divination of good fortune is not in Ovid; it is as much a part of Marston's comic and satirical transformation of the story as are the Petrarchan clichés. And the puns from the first part of the poem extend into the later stanzas to emphasize the connection as well as the contrast between Pigmalion's wooing of his statue and his wooing of his newly humanized mistress:

> Yet all's *conceit*. But shadow of that blisse
> Which now my Muse strives sweetly to display
> In this my wondrous metamorphosis.[25]
>   (St. 28, ll. 1-3; my italics)

> He's well assur'd no faire *imagery*
> Could yeeld such pleasing, loves felicity.
>   (St. 31, ll. 5-6; my italics)

It is Pigmalion's statue, not his attitude, that has been transformed. As Donne so often suggests in the *Songs and Sonnets*, the poetic wooer is quite happy to engage his mistress physically rather than verbally if he is only granted the opportunity.

To argue that a comic and satirical exposure of the postures and language of the Petrarchan poet-lover is a major literary consequence of Marston's handling of the Pigmalion story is not to argue that this is the only consequence. The erotic description in the poem, which is far more explicit and extensive than it is in Ovid's or in any other poet's handling of the story, has to be accounted for. After all, Thomas Cranley, writing early in the next century, would list *Pigmalions Image*, along with *Venus and Adonis* and *Salmacis and Hermaphroditus*, as one of the "amorous Pamphlets" which the prostitute Amanda keeps on the shelf near her bed.[26] Marston's erotic description is perhaps more conspicuous near the end of the poem, where it functions as part of the ironic celebration of Pigmalion's sexual fulfillment, but it also figures prominently in earlier stanzas, in the account of Pigmalion's wooing of his statue. Here Marston's description moves very skillfully from voyeurism to physical

immediacy. The early emphasis is on Pigmalion's foolish attempt to see
by stealth what he himself has made in the first place:

> Thus fond *Pigmalion* striveth to discry
> Each beauteous part, not letting over-slip
> One parcell of his curious workmanship.
>
> Untill his eye discended so farre downe
> That it discried Loves pavillion:
> Where *Cupid* doth enjoy his onely crowne,
> And *Venus* hath her chiefest mantion:
> There would he winke, & winking looke againe,
> Both eies & thoughts would gladly there remaine.
>   (St. 8, ll. 4-6, St. 9)

Pigmalion soon becomes dissatisfied with just looking, however, and
decides to take fuller advantage of his erotic toy:

> She with her silence, seemes to graunt his sute.
> Then he all jocund like a wanton lover,
> With amorous embracements doth salute
> Her slender wast, presuming to discover
> The vale of Love, where Cupid doth delight
> To sport, and dally all the sable night.
>   (St. 16)

This movement from voyeurism to immediacy prepares the reader for the
final account of Pigmalion's enjoyment of his newly humanized mistress,
where everything is tactile and physical for Pigmalion and where the
voyeurism is shifted entirely to the narrator and, through him, to the
reader. While Pigmalion then finds his mistress "Yeelding soft touch for
touch, sweet kisse, for kisse" (St. 31, l. 4), the reader is placed by the
narrator in Pigmalion's original position and invited to "conceit but
what himselfe would doe / When that he had obtayned such a favour" (St.
34, ll. 1-2).

Whatever the ultimate significance of the eroticism in *Pigmalions
Image*, it clearly extends the poem's range of meaning, including its range
of satirical meaning, beyond the requirements of Marston's anti-
Petrarchan theme. The poem's three most conspicuous references to non-
literary social experience, for example, are all presented in similes which
stand in deliberately shocking contrast to stanzas of explicit erotic
description.[27] The account of Pigmalion's foolishly furtive leering at his

statue's pudenda in stanza 9 is followed by the allusion in stanza 10 to the "subtile Citty-dame" who peers through her fingers in church "When that her eye, her mind would faine bewray." Pigmalion's lustful fondling of his statue in stanza 13 is compared in stanza 14 to the behavior of "peevish Papists" who

> kneele
> To some dum Idoll with their offering,
> As if a senceles carved stone could feele
> The ardor of his bootles chattering,[28]
> (St. 14, ll. 1-4)

Finally, in a simile which is not in itself satirical but which presents an even more sensationally irreverent contrast to the eroticism than the two similes just cited, Pigmalion's joy when he embraces his statue's "naked wast" and finds that "Each part like Waxe before the sunne did melt" (St. 29) is compared to

> a Mothers passing gladnes,
> (After that death her onely sonne hath seazed
> And overwhelm'd her soule with endlesse sadnes)
> When that she sees him gin for to be raised
> From out his deadly swoune to life againe:[29]
> (St. 30)

All these comparisons—the first two, at any rate—might be seen as consistent with and even as extensions of the anti-Petrarchan satire, but such an explanation would hardly account for their total effect. Nor can they simply be passed off as instances in which Marston has suddenly decided to broaden the scope of his satire. The three similes are preceded in each case by particularly explicit passages of erotic description, and their function as dramatically daring contrasts cannot be ignored.[30]

Although recent readings of *Pigmalions Image* have diverged widely in their interpretation of the erotic description, they all see this aspect of the poem as central to determining its relation to previous Ovidian poetry. For Finkelpearl the celebration of Pigmalion's sexual fulfillment confirms Marston's serious participation in the "Ovidian mode": "Venus, the goddess of healthy, sensual, propagative love, becomes the heroine, or, perhaps the conqueror of the poem. . . . *Pigmalion* is an orthodox Ovidian amatory poem, its attitudes virtually epitomizing the *genre*."[31] Two immediate objections may be raised against this position.

The first is that Elizabethan epyllia almost never take as their theme the fulfillment of "healthy, sensual, propagative love." In all the poems we have looked at, sexual fulfillment is either tragically frustrated or severely qualified by an emphasis on the comic, violent, and grotesque aspects of erotic experience. The second objection is that whatever the nature of Pigmalion's love, the way in which that love is presented by the narrator, in the later as well as in the earlier stanzas of the poem, raises questions which Finkelpearl's account tends to gloss over. It is precisely in this aspect of the poem—for instance, in the narrator's manner of presenting Pigmalion's lovemaking—that Lecocq and Colley see the greatest evidence for reading the poem as a satire and parody of Ovidian poetry. It is therefore essential to take a close look at the attitude of Marston's narrator towards Pigmalion, towards the reader, and towards himself. The way in which the narrator relates to these three basic determinants of the rhetorical situation has been the greatest single source of confusion about *Pigmalions Image*.

In his relationship to Pigmalion the narrator is clearly Marston's main instrument of satire. In stanza after stanza in the first part of the poem he insists upon the folly of Pigmalion's delusion either through ironic praise ("O what alluring beauties he descries / In each part of his faire imagery!" St. 4), through sarcastic exposure of the fact that Pigmalion's love is all mental "conceit" ("He thought he saw the blood run through the vaine . . . "; "He thinks he see'th the brightnes of the beames . . . ," St. 5), or through direct and concentrated satirical summaries:

> And thus enamour'd, dotes on his owne Art
> Which he did work, to work his pleasing smart.
>
>   (St. 12)

In the second half of the poem, as we have already observed, the narrator's attitude towards Pigmalion continues to be ironic, although the terms of the irony have to change since Pigmalion is now making love to a real woman and not to a statue. And it is here, at the beginning of the final description of Pigmalion's lovemaking, that the narrator's irony begins to be directed towards the reader:

> And now me thinks some wanton itching eare
> With lustfull thoughts, and ill attention,
> List's to my Muse, expecting for to heare
> The amorous discription of that action
>   Which *Venus* seekes, . . .
>
>   (St. 33, ll. 1-5)

Since Marston goes on to provide four stanzas of "amorous discription," the key question is this: how does the narrator's apparent taunting of the reader relate to his exuberant account of Pigmalion's lovemaking?

The most recent answer offered to this question is that Marston is titillating the reader's erotic interest for the sole purpose of ridiculing and embarrassing him, thereby providing the concluding strategy for "a burlesque of an overworked literary form. . . ."[32] This is not, I would suggest, an adequate account of Marston's performance and of its relation to previous Ovidian poetry. What one in fact finds in stanzas 33-38 is an extended display of an old Ovidian device used less conspicuously by Thomas Edwards and, in a subtly indirect way, by Marlowe:

> Fast to his girted side she neatly clings,
> Her hair let loose about his shoulders flings;
> Nay 'twere immodest to tell the affection
> That she did show, least it draw to action.
> (*Cephalus and Procris*, ll. 355-358)

> Leander now, like Theban Hercules,
> Enter'd the orchard of th'Hesperides;
> Whose fruit none rightly can describe, but he
> That pulls or shakes it from the golden tree.
> (*Hero and Leander*, II. 297-300)

Having one's erotic imagination encouraged ("Let him conceit but what himselfe would doe / When that he had obtayned such a favour," St. 34, ll. 1-2) and then frustrated ("O pardon me / Yee gaping eares that swallow up my lines / Expect no more," St. 38, ll. 1-3) is certainly nothing new for a reader familiar with classical and Renaissance erotic poetry. As Lecocq points out, the question with which Marston begins stanza 38— "Who knowes not what ensues?"—is itself a convention of erotic poetry derived ultimately from the *Amores* (I.v.25: "cetera quis nescit").[33] The point to be made, then, is that the narrator's ironic taunts to the reader do not in themselves undermine the poem's eroticism, nor do they prove that the poem is a satire against erotic poetry. Only an extremely unsophisticated reader—one who really does "seek sexual satisfaction second-hand from a poem"—could be duped by Marston's strategy. In fact the fictional duping of such a reader may be part of the joke Marston is sharing with readers familiar with the strategies of the erotic poet. The prominence Marston gives to the titillation-frustration strategy is one of the things that distinguishes *Pigmalions Image* from previous Elizabethan epyllia, and I shall have more to say about this later. But it is not in itself evidence that the poem is a parody of an epyllion or that Marston's eroticism has no function except as bait to dupe a witless reader.

So far we have been concerned with Marston's narrator as an *instrument* of satire. But Lecocq's reading of the poem as a satiric parody of the "disciples of Ovid," as he calls them,[34] is based primarily on a notion of the narrator as an *object* of satire. Some of the evidence he offers is stylistic, and this we shall examine in a moment. But he also places great emphasis on the narrator's self-presentation—especially on his numerous addresses to "his mistress" and on his comments about women. These addresses and comments contradict the narrator's ironic exposure of Pigmalion's folly, according to Lecocq; they show that irony to be cheap and hypocritical, and they puncture the narrator's pose as the sophisticated and experienced Ovidian commentator on love. When in stanza 32 the narrator imagines himself in the same situation with his mistress as Pigmalion realizes with his statue, Lecocq argues, he allows himself to be deluded by the very folly which he criticizes so sarcastically in his hero.[35]

A close look at the way in which Marston develops the narrator's addresses to and comments on "his mistress" during the course of the poem suggests that Lecocq has exaggerated the extent to which the narrator is an object of Marston's irony and has underestimated the degree of ironic self-consciousness invested in him. The reader is meant to retain a certain amused distance on the narrator's "swaggering humor" (see "The Authour in prayse of his precedent Poem," l. 8), much as he is meant to see the vulnerabilities and biases of the ironic and often cynical narrator of *Hero and Leander*. But it is a distortion to see the narrator of *Pigmalions Image* as a fatuous pseudo-gallant who undermines his own ironic pretensions. It is even more misleading to identify him with the "Labeo" attacked in "The Authour in prayse" (ll. 29–30), as Lecocq does, since the speaker of "The Authour in prayse" continually refers to *Pigmalions Image* as "my" poem. And it is apparent in the sixteen-line address "To his Mistress" which precedes the poem that the narrator's attitude towards this special member of his audience is far from straightforward. Not only does he present his poem as a persuasion to sexual submission, but instead of disguising his sexual interests, he flaunts them in the very first line:

> My wanton Muse lasciviously doth sing
> Of sportive love, of lovely dallying.
>
>   (ll. 1–2)

Unlike Pigmalion, Marston's narrator openly acknowledges his erotic motives from the beginning and thus obviates the hypocrisy of his subsequent idealized and spiritualized references to "his mistress":

> O beauteous Angell, daine thou to infuse
> A sprightly wit, into my dulled Muse.
> I invoke none other saint but thee,
> To grace the first bloomes of my Poesie.
>
> (ll. 3–6)

One cannot take seriously such etherealizing professions from a speaker who has just confessed that his "wanton Muse lasciviously doth sing"— the bogus idealism is part of a cleverly self-conscious performance. The narrator is confident, moreover, that "his mistress" will inspire him with the "sprightly wit" he needs to seduce her. The question is not "if," but "when":

> Then when thy kindnes grants me such sweet blisse,
> I'le gladly write thy metamorphosis.
>
> (ll. 15–16)

The sexual frankness with which the narrator addresses his mistress is hardly surprising in the work of a poet undoubtedly familiar with and impressed by Donne's early lyrics.[36] Of course in *Pigmalions Image*, as in the *Songs and Sonnets*, no actual mistress is being addressed at all. "She" is merely another aspect of a fictive rhetorical situation.

Only by acknowledging the sexual frankness which characterizes the game the narrator is playing with his mistress can one make sense of the "asides" directed to her in the poem proper. The first of these "asides" is, appropriately enough at such an early stage in the poem, a straightforward compliment: the narrator simply says that his mistress's face is more beautiful than the face of Pigmalion's statue (St. 2). The second "aside," however, offered as a comment on Pigmalion's voyeuristic enjoyment of his statue, is much less innocent:

> O that my Mistres were an Image too,
> That I might blameles her perfections view.
>
> (St. 11, ll. 5–6)

The point of this couplet depends upon the contrast between the narrator's awareness of his mistress and Pigmalion's deluded leering at his statue. In the fictional world of the poem it is the understanding that the narrator's mistress is not an "Image"—not merely a product of "his own workmanships perfection" (St. 3, l. 2)—which gives him his satirical leverage.

As Pigmalion moves closer and closer to sexual success, the narrator's comments become increasingly explicit in their sexual innuendo. They also become increasingly impersonal, indicating that the mistress is being used primarily as a ploy in the narrator's self-presentation rather than as a genuine focus for a poem of sexual persuasion. She is in fact addressed directly in the second person only at the beginning of the poem, in stanza 2. Thereafter she is always referred to in the third person. This process of impersonalization can be seen at the turning point in the poem, when Pigmalion decides to persist in his wooing despite the fact that he now realizes his previous delusion about his statue. As Pigmalion prepares to pray to Venus for sexual fulfillment, the narrator feels free to forget his mistress altogether for the moment and to comment nonchalantly to the "Ladies":

> And therefore Ladies, thinke that they nere love you,
> Who doe not unto more than kissing move you.
> (St. 20, ll. 5-6)

Yet near the end of the poem, when Pigmalion's statue has been turned into a living woman, the narrator brazenly refers to his mistress again as "my Love":

> O wonder not to heare me thus relate,
> And say to flesh transformed was a stone.
> Had I my Love in such a wished state
> As was afforded to *Pigmalion*,
>> Though flinty hard, of her you soone should see
>> As strange a transformation wrought by mee.
> (St. 32)

The narrator's swaggering confidence here at the end is in keeping with his attitude towards his mistress all along: he has used her to establish and maintain his persona and to participate ironically in romantic postures which Pigmalion takes seriously. Looking back, one sees that the narrator had anticipated the entire development of his rhetorical relationship to his mistress in the prefatory address. The couplet of stanza 32 echoes quite closely the concluding lines of "To his Mistress":

> Then when thy kindnes grants me such sweet blisse,
> I'le gladly write thy metamorphosis.
>
>   ("To his Mistress," ll. 15–16)

> Though flinty hard, of her you soone should see
> As strange a transformation wrought by mee.
>
>   (St. 32, ll. 5–6)

Marston's narrator is far more self-aware than Lecocq's analysis allows. His seductive asides to his mistress are nothing more than self-dramatizing flourishes, and he knows it.

A final source of critical confusion about *Pigmalions Image* has been the writing itself. Many readers have complained that Marston's stylistic control in this poem is inadequate;[37] Lecocq goes much further and argues that the writing is deliberately bad. Lecocq's analysis of specific passages is seriously weakened, however, by his tendency to disregard rhetorical structure and context. "What writer not totally deprived of poetic talent," he asks, "would have used the words *fair* or *fairness* five times, the words *beauty* or *beauteous* seven times, in the first five stanzas of his poem?"[38] The answer: a twenty-one-year-old poet like Marston trying to demonstrate his skill in handling the highly patterned rhetorical artifice of Shakespeare's *Venus and Adonis* sixain and at the same time to establish, admittedly for satirical purposes, certain conventional pseudo-Petrarchan postures. Five of the seven variants on "beauty," for instance, are used up in two passages which Puttenham might well have praised as examples of the rhetorical figure known as *traductio*, or "the tranlacer":[39]

> That never yet proudest mortalitie
> Could show so rare and *beautious* a creature,
> (Unlesse my Mistress all-excelling face,
> Which gives to *beautie*, *beauties* only grace.)
>
>   (St. 2, ll. 3–6)

> Her nakednes, each *beauteous* shape containes.
> All *beautie* in her nakednes remaines.
>
>   (St. 4, ll. 5–6)

As for "faire" and "fairness," the former is used in each case in conjunction with "image" or "imagery," suggesting that Marston is developing a kind of reiterated formula to establish his main satiric counters. And one of the two appearances of "fairness" (St. 3, l. 3) is there to rhyme with "rarenesse." My argument is not that these rhetorical repetitions are in themselves poetically effective or that they have nothing to do with Marston's satiric purposes, but simply that one is not justified in calling such writing deliberately bad. To do so is to obscure the means by which Marston generates his satire. To cite just one more example, when Lecocq points out that the phrase "Compassionate my true loves ardencie" is repeated twice (St. 15, l. 6 and St. 24, l. 6) and varied a third time to "satiat his loves ardencie" (St. 20, l. 4),[40] he fails to notice that the two exact repetitions are spoken by Pigmalion and represent part of his foolish romantic posturing, while the variation to "satiat" and the dropping of "true" in stanza 20 shows the narrator mocking Pigmalion's rhetoric and articulating the basic carnality of his longing. One does not have to defend Marston's writing as being consistently good—in fact it is often quite awkward—to question the notion of deliberate badness, except occasionally when Pigmalion's own verbal wooing is concerned.

Another feature of Marston's writing which is of major significance in deciding about the extent of his literary satire and in determining the relation of *Pigmalions Image* to other Elizabethan epyllia is the echoing of Shakespeare and Marlowe. Lecocq makes curiously little of these echoes, but Bush and others after him have spoken of "parody" and "burlesque" of passages from *Venus and Adonis* and *Hero and Leander*. Perhaps the first thing to note about these echoes is that there are far fewer of them than in the epyllia of Heywood and Edwards, or of Weever and Beaumont.[41] Had Marston been primarily interested in trying to parody the epyllia of Shakespeare and Marlowe, one would have expected much more verbal imitation. Still, there are a few conspicuous examples. Pigmalion is admiring his statue early in the poem:

> Then view's her lips, no lips did seeme so faire
> In his conceit, through which he thinks doth flie
> So sweet a breath, that doth perfume the ayre.
> (St. 7, ll. 1-3)

This is a clear echo of Marlowe's Hero portrait, and its function in the ironic exposure of Pigmalion's folly is obvious.[42] But does it burlesque Marlowe's language?

> Many would praise the sweet smell as she pass'd,
> When 'twas the odour which her breath forth cast.
> And there for honey bees have sought in vain,
> And beat from thence, have lighted there again.
> (I. 21-24)

The ironically extravagant wit of Marlowe's narrator in praising Hero's deceptive charms makes Marston's passage appear almost restrained and a bit labored by comparison.[43] And the irony Marlowe's narrator directs against Hero's admirers is much the same as that directed by Marston's narrator against Pigmalion. There is no question in this case of burlesque or parody.

A stronger suspicion of parodic intent might arise in the stanza describing Pigmalion's going to bed with his statue just after his prayer to Venus. As in the previous passage, there is obvious irony at Pigmalion's expense:

> Then thus, Sweet sheetes he sayes, which nowe doe cover,
> The Idol of my soule, the fairest one
> That ever lov'd, or had an amorous lover.
> Earths onely modell of perfection,
> Sweet happy sheetes, daine for to take me in,
> That I my hopes and longing thoughts may win.
>
> (St. 26)

Marston is thinking here of Leander's request to Hero as he sits on her bed, exhausted from his swim across the Hellespont:

> Whereon Leander sitting thus began,
> Through numbing cold, all feeble, faint, and wan:
> 'If not for love, yet, love, for pity sake,
> Me in thy bed and maiden bosom take;
>
> (II. 245–248)

Marston exaggerates the comedy of this moment in *Hero and Leander*, but does he burlesque Marlowe's writing? Again I would argue that Marlowe's own wit makes his passage invulnerable to any parodic reverberations created by Marston's exaggerated imitation. Leander's ability to summon up his amorous sophistry even in a state of physical exhaustion is much more effectively comic than Pigmalion's ludicrous apostrophe to his "Sweet sheetes."[44]

There is only one likely echo in *Pigmalions Image* of the language of *Venus and Adonis*:

> No wanton love-trick would he over-slip,
> But full observ'd all amorous beheasts.
> Whereby he thought he might procure the love
> Of his dull Image, which no plaints coulde move.
>
> (St. 13, ll. 3–6)

The verbal motif of a "dull Image" appears in Venus's denunciation of Adonis's ideal but unresponsive beauty, a passage in which Shakespeare was himself certainly thinking of the Pigmalion story:

> "Fie, lifeless picture, cold and senseless stone,
> Well-painted idol, image dull and dead,
> Statue contenting but the eye alone,
> (ll. 211–213)

Here, as in the borrowings from Marlowe, the irony of Marston's earlier epyllionic model is far more complex than that of his own passage. Venus is in love not with an actual work of art but, as she herself is all too aware, with a mortal as beautiful and as erotically unresponsive as a work of art. Her unrepressed frustration and anger in this passage place her in critical opposition to Pigmalion's deluded wooing and hyperbolic praise. Marston's lines cannot be read as a burlesque, either deliberate or fortuitous, of Venus's accusations.

The final piece of evidence always emphasized by those who want to read *Pigmalions Image* as a parody of Ovidian poetry is Pigmalion's absurdly anachronistic apostrophe to Ovid himself:

> But when the faire proportion of her thigh
> Began appeare. *O Ovid* would he cry,
> Did ere *Corinna* show such Ivorie,
> When she appear'd in *Venus* livorie?
> (St. 12, ll. 1–4)

Since none of the epyllia we have looked at refers directly to Ovid or makes use of the fictional situation of the *Amores* alluded to here, it would be difficult to maintain that Marston's passage reflects parodically on them in any specific way. In fact the closest parallel to Marston's stanza in previous Elizabethan poetry is a passage from Sidney's famous blazon in the *Arcadia*:

> Yet never shall my song omitte
> Those thighes, for *Ovid's* song more fitte.
> (ll. 87–88)

If Marston is attempting to burlesque Sidney's poem, he has chosen rather crude poetic means for doing so. Nothing self-serious or indulgent is exposed by Marston's joke, either in Sidney or in the passage from *Amores*

I.v to which both poets are alluding. I quote from Marlowe's translation of the *Amores*, since some of the phrasing reappears in *Hero and Leander*:

> How smooth a belly under her wast saw I?
> How large a legge, and what a lustie thigh?
> To leave the rest, all lik'd me passing well,
> I cling'd her naked body, downe she fell,
> Judge you the rest: being tirde she bad me kisse,
> *Jove* send me more such after-noones as this.[45]
>
> (ll. 21-26)

Marston has simply used an allusion to two much more deftly clever passages as an occasion for a rather broad joke. The strategy of "Judge you the rest," incidentally, is another example of the Ovidian invitation to erotic imagination which Marston exploits so conspicuously at the end of *Pigmalions Image*. And this is not the only bit of ironic wit which Marston copies from Ovid. The "aside" discussed earlier—"And therefore Ladies, thinke that they nere love you, / Who do not unto more than kissing move you" (St. 20, ll. 5-6)—is a reworking of *Ars Amatoria* I. 669-670:

> Oscula qui sumpsit, si non et cetera sumet,
> Haec quoque, quae data sunt, perdere dignus erit.

[He who has taken kisses, if he take not the rest beside, will deserve to lose even what was granted.]

Ovid is the source, rather than the butt, of much of Marston's irony in *Pigmalions Image*.

Taken on its own terms, then, *Pigmalions Image* emerges as an Ovidian narrative poem in which the ironic exposure of erotic idealism and the playful alternation between arousing and frustrating the reader's erotic imagination figure much more prominently than they had in previous epyllia. Equally important, these elements are not balanced or supplemented by any attempt to generate a sense of serious erotic pathos or to enlarge and complicate the meaning of the main narrative through inventive mythological digression. *Pigmalions Image* is about one-third the length of other epyllia, and this is mainly because Marston's interests in exploring his Ovidian subject are much more circumscribed than those of his predecessors. Finally, there is no internal evidence to justify our calling *Pigmalions Image* a parody of *Venus and Adonis*, of *Hero and*

Leander, or of any other epyllion. It shares with these poems, and intensifies, their satirical exposure of the clichéd rhetoric of the love lyric, and it exaggerates their comedy and eroticism. It is primarily Marston's exaggeration of the satirical, comic, and explicitly erotic possibilities of his subject which has given rise to so much critical confusion. But *Pigmalions Image* cannot be said to represent a parody of the Ovidian narrative poetry of the 1590s. The poetic result of Marston's exaggerations will not support such a reading.

With this view of *Pigmalions Image* before us, let us go on to look at those notorious comments on the poem which appear elsewhere in Marston's writing. We must remind ourselves straightaway that we have no more right to assume that Marston the man is the speaker of these comments in his satires than we do to assume that he is the narrator of *Pigmalions Image*. This even applies to "The Authour in prayse of his precedent Poem." The author of the entire volume entitled *The Metamorphosis of Pigmalions Image and Certaine Satyres* is designated after the dedication "To Good Opinion" as "W. K.," the initials of Marston's mysterious satirical pseudonym, "W. Kinsayder." The first thing that strikes one about "The Authour in prayse" is the excessive sarcasm with which "Kinsayder" or "W. K." ridicules "his precedent Poem":

> Now *Rufus*, by old *Glebrons* fearefull mace
> Hath not my Muse deserv'd a worthy place?
> Come come *Luxurio*, crowne my head with Bayes,
> Which like a Paphian, wantonly displayes
> The Salaminian titillations,
> Which tickle up our lewd Priapians.
> Is not my pen compleate? are not my lines
> Right in the swaggering humor of these times?[46]
>
> (ll. 1–8)

It is already apparent that "Kinsayder's" account of "his precedent Poem" is not going to be a very complete or objective one. Except perhaps in the phrase "swaggering humor,"[47] there is no mention of the comedy, wit, and irony in *Pigmalions Image*; the poem is described as sheer erotic titillation, and nothing more. "Kinsayder" acknowledges his authorship of *Pigmalions Image*, but he consistently refuses to attribute any satirical wit or irony to his performance in that poem. He mocks the idealizing praise in the address "To his Mistress," for example, without allowing for the fact that his romantic flattery was placed in a rather suspect light by his opening confession that "My wanton Muse lasciviously doth sing":

> Doe not I flatter, call her wondrous faire?
> Vertuous, divine most debonaire?[48]

(ll. 13–14)

"Kinsayder" goes on to a derisive description of "my stanzaes":

> Glittering in dawbed lac'd accoustrements,
> And pleasing sutes of loves habiliments.
> Yet puffie as Dutch hose they are within,
> Faint, and white liver'd, as our gallants bin;
> (ll. 21–24)

Not a word is said about the way in which the final couplet in the sixains of *Pigmalions Image* is often used for witty asides and ironic summaries. Eventually "Kinsayder" confesses the motive behind this exercise in self-criticism:

> Now by the whyps of *Epigramatists,*
> Ile not be lasht for my dissembling shifts.
> And therefore I use Popelings discipline,
> Lay ope my faults to *Mastigophoros* eyne:
> Censure my selfe, fore others me deride
> And scoffe at me, as if I had deni'd
> Or thought my Poem good, . . .
> (ll. 35–41)

Arnold Davenport argued that Marston was responding in this poem to an actual epigrammatic attack, by Joseph Hall, on a conjectured earlier edition of *The Metamorphosis of Pigmalions Image and Certain Satyres.*[49] That curious rhyme-word "deni'd" (l. 40) makes the above passage annoyingly ambiguous, but apart from this obscurity, the lines clearly suggest that the purpose of "The Authour in prayse" is to anticipate rather than to respond to such an attack ("Censure my selfe, fore others me deride"). The anticipation has taken the form of feigned, and rather confused, self-criticism. It is not really clear, for instance, whether "Kinsayder" thinks of "his precedent Poem" as one which genuinely fulfills the requirements of a type of poetry he despises, as one which does not fulfill those requirements and therefore has certain "faults" which he wants to "lay ope" (l. 38), or as a deliberate parody in which the "faults" are actually "dissembling shifts" (l. 36). Even more

importantly, "Kinsayder" makes no mention of "his" former ironic
relationship to Pigmalion, to "his Mistress," and to the reader in "his
precedent Poem." He quotes from the ironic self-praise with which Ovid
opens Book II of the *Ars Amatoria* (*"Io bis dicite,"* ll. 9–10) without
acknowledging that he had already made use of this and other bits of
Ovidian cynicism in *Pigmalions Image* itself.[50]

A somewhat sharper but no more accurate denunciation of *Pig-*
malions Image appears only a few months later in Satire VI of *The*
Scourge of Villanie. Now "Kinsayder" does appear to be responding to
attacks on his earlier poem:[51]

> O stay me, least I raile
> Beyond *Nil ultra,* to see this Butterflie,
> This windie bubble taske my balladry
> With sencelesse censure.
>
> (ll. 2–5)

By this point in *The Scourge* "Kinsayder" is in the full swing of his
savage attacks on lust, and as he begins to denounce *Pigmalions Image,*
his voice becomes strident and brutal:

> Yet deem'st that in sad seriousnes I write
> Such nastie stuffe as is *Pigmalion?*
> Such maggot-tainted lewd corruption?
>
> (ll. 6–8)

There seems to be a clearer notion operating here of *Pigmalions Image* as
a parody—as a deliberately bad amorous poem and not simply a typical
example of a corrupt genre. But "Kinsayder" still emphasizes the
amorous and erotic elements of *Pigmalions Image* and refuses to
acknowledge its internal irony and satire. Perhaps to do so would expose
the excessiveness of his disclaimer and of the amount of energy he invests
in the language of sexual loathing:

> Think'st thou, that I, which was create to whip
> Incarnate fiends, will once vouchsafe to trip
> A Pavins traverse? or will lispe (*sweet love*)
> Or pule (*Aye me*) some female soule to move?
> Think'st thou, that I in melting poesie
> Will pamper itching sensualitie?
> (*That in the bodyes scumme all fatally*
> *Intombes the soules most sacred faculty.*)
>
> (ll. 15–22)

"Kinsayder" uses a phrase like "itching sensualitie" without ever acknowledging that in doing so he sounds very much as he did in *Pigmalions Image* when he taunted his reader's "wanton itching eare" (St. 33, 1. 1).

In the next forty lines or so of Satire VI Marston's speaker claims that he wrote *Pigmalions Image* to expose "the odious spot / And blemish that deformes the lineaments / Of modern Poesies habiliments" (ll. 24–26) and goes on to conjure up examples of these poetic deformities. It is here that he may be alluding to Nash's *A Choise of Valentines* ("Here's one must invoke some lose-legg'd dame, / Some brothell drab," ll. 33–34) and perhaps also to Edwards' *Cephalus and Procris* ("Another yet dares tremblingly come out, / But first he must invoke good *Colyn Clout*, ll. 37–38).[52] It is also here that he "explains" the joking anachronism of having Pigmalion call upon Ovid:

> Another makes old *Homer, Spencer* cite
> Like my *Pigmalion*, where, with rare delight
> He cryes, *O Ovid*.
>
> (ll. 59–61)

But it is really the stupidly admiring reader, much more than the amorous poet or the reader who censures *Pigmalions Image* for being obscene, who arouses "Kinsayder's" gall and contempt:

> . . . these Nilus Rats,
> Halfe dung, that have their life from putrid slime,
> These that doe praise my loose lascivious rime:
> For these same shades I seriously protest
> I slubber'd up that Chaos indigest,
> To fish for fooles, . . .
> *Capro* reads, sweares, scrubs, and sweares again,
> Now by my soule an admirable straine,
> Strokes up his haire, cryes passing passing good,
> Oh, there's a line incends his lustfull blood.[53]
>
> (ll. 66–77)

Now more than ever one sees the continuity between the "W. Kinsayder" of *The Scourge* and the "W. K." of *Pigmalions Image*, with his sarcastic apology: "O pardon me / Yee gaping eares that swallow up my lines" (St. 38, ll. 1–2). But this continuity is something the speaker of *The Scourge* will never allow. For him *Pigmalions Image* is a "loose lascivious rime" in which his satiric "*Genius*" (ll. 12, 109) could not find expression.

How are we to account for this discrepancy between "Kinsayder's" actual performance in *Pigmalions Image* and what he says about that performance in "The Author in prayse" and in Satire VI of *The Scourge*? There are three ways of accounting for it. None of them requires that we charge Marston himself with moral and psychological confusion, as some of his critics have done. The possibility of a certain amount of poetic confusion is, however, another matter.

First of all, it is not uncommon for the author of an erotic poem to deny the worthiness of his endeavor or the seriousness of his intention. Such denials distance the author from his poem, but they do not undermine—nor are they meant to undermine—the appeal of his eroticism. Nash's *The Choise of Valentines* provides an interesting parallel to Marston's case in this respect. Nash, of course, is a writer willing to assume almost any stance to meet the requirements of immediate literary effect or of patronage. In the *Anatomy of Absurditie*, one of his earliest works (published 1589/90), he could rail like Gosson himself against mythological love poetry:

> Are they not ashamed in their prefixed posies, to adorne a pretence of profit mixt with pleasure, when as in their bookes there is scarce to be found one precept pertaining to vertue, but whole quires fraught with amorous discourse, kindling *Venus* flame in *Vulcans* forge, carrying *Cupid* in tryumph, alluring even vowed *Vestals* to treade awry, inchaunting chaste mindes and corrupting the continenst.[54]

This is the same Thomas Nash who will begin *The Choise of Valentines* (written sometime before 1597)[55] with a sonnet addressed "To the right Honorable Lord S." in which he "apologizes" in advance for the most obscene Elizabethan poem known to us:

> Although my Muse devor'st from deeper care
> Presents thee with a wanton Elegie,
> Ne blame my verse of loose unchastitie
> For painting forth the things that hidden are,
> Since all men acte what I in speache declare,
> Onelie induced by varietie.
> . . . .
> Accept of it Dear Lord in gentle gree,
> And better lynes ere long shall honor thee.[56]

In the poem itself Nash's speaker tells the story of his visit on St. Valentine's Day to a brothel, where his "lady" has been forced to seek refuge from "Good Justice Dudgein-haft, and crab-tree face" (l. 21). There he pays a fancy price to enjoy his "mistris Francis," and after some initial embarrassment when his "limm's" (all of them) ". . . spend their strength in thought of hir delight" (ll. 125–126), he finally recovers and makes love to her. But unfortunately he fails to satisfy "Mistris Francis," and she bids him farewell, saying that she will no longer trust men to give her pleasure: "My little dildo shall suplye their kinde" (l. 239). The narrative ends with Mistress Francis's celebration of the dildo and with the speaker claiming that he wrote the poem "onelie for my self" (l. 297), to give vent to his sexual discouragement. Then Nash concludes with a second sonnet in which he acknowledges his debt to Ovid ("He is the fountaine whence my streames doe flowe," l. 5) and once again apologizes for his "wanton Elegy":

> My mynde once purg'd of such lascivious witt,
> With purifide word's, and hallowed verse
> Thy praises in large volumes shall rehearce,
> That better maie thy graver view befitt.
> Meanwhile yett rests, yow smile at what I write,
> Or for attempting, banish me your sight.
> (ll. 9–14)

One doubts that "Lord S." (both Southampton and Ferdinando, Lord Strange have been suggested)[57] or any other sophisticated Elizabethan reader would have been confused by Nash's "apologies." They would have seen them as part of the poem's humor (the pun on "large volumes" in the passage above is indicative of Nash's tone) and as a conventional device by which the author dramatizes his distanced control over the entertaining eroticism. But would a sophisticated Elizabethan reader have been confused if Nash had presented his poem not simply with witty "apologies," but with a sarcastic claim such as Marston's that his poem was nothing more than a "dissembling shift" designed to snare the lewd-minded reader who looks to poetry only for erotic stimulation? Is it possible that a reader like "Lord S." would have taken "Kinsayder's" disclaimers no more seriously than he took Nash's "apologies"? Of course one cannot answer such questions with certainty. One can say, however, that Marston must have been aware of the convention of the disingenuous apology and disclaimer, and that if "Kinsayder's" commentary on *Pigmalions Image* is to be seen as an exploitation of this convention, it is an exploitation which places the convention under considerable strain.

A second way of approaching the problem of "Kinsayder's" comments on *Pigmalions Image* is suggested in Bridget Gellert Lyons's observation that "Marston is never too confident of his irony in the satires. . . ."[58] He appears to be even less confident, one might add, of his irony in *Pigmalions Image*. This may be one reason why Marston does not allow the poem's own internal wit and satire to indicate to the reader that he is not being offered a straightforward capitulation to amorous and erotic indulgence, but instead delivers a proleptic denunciation of the poem's "faults." An intensification of the ironic and satirical aspects of the epyllion was not enough to insure protection against readers who would either attack him for obscenity or witlessly praise him for his "Salaminian titillations." Marston had to make doubly sure, as it were, and in doing so he had to obscure some of the complexities of his narrative technique in *Pigmalions Image* itself.

This last point leads to a third perspective on Marston's puzzling and seemingly contradictory performance, a perspective already suggested in what was said earlier about Marston's satiric persona. Marston's experiments in Juvenalian satire virtually demanded that "Kinsayder" attack *Pigmalions Image* and that in doing so he make it out to be a much simpler and more indulgent piece of eroticism than it really is. It is the function of the whipping, scourging satiric speaker to lash out at anything associated with erotic indulgence and to refuse to grant his enemies the slightest claim to a defensible position, for to do so would weaken the force and poetic energy of his attack. In the case of Marston's "Kinsayder" this holds true even when the enemy is none other than "Kinsayder" himself, in his role as the poet-narrator of *Pigmalions Image*. The decorum of late Elizabethan satire invited Marston to turn back against himself in this way. In launching his poetic career with an exercise in Ovidian poetry (*The Metamorphosis of Pigmalions Image* is given far greater prominence on the title-page and in the arrangement of the 1598 volume than the *Certain Satyres*), Marston was in a sense providing "Kinsayder" with his first satirical target. But he was also giving his first volume of satires the added attraction of a sophisticated Ovidian narrative poem. Marston, one may assume, was concerned with literary success, even if "Kinsayder," by his own protestations, was not.[59]

What, then, is one to conclude about Marston's curious poetic debut? *Pigmalions Image*, I have tried to show, is neither a parody of an epyllion nor an indulgent sop to lecherous readers. It is a highly self-conscious and unevenly written exercise in Ovidian narrative poetry in which Marston intensifies both the satirical and the explicitly erotic aspects of the epyllion and avoids any serious interest in erotic pathos and any attempt at narrative and thematic complexity through digression or allusion (not one other classical myth is mentioned). The result is undeniably ambivalent, but the ambivalence is a reduced and impoverished version of the rich, haunting Ovidianism of *Venus and Adonis* and *Hero and Leander*. *Pigmalions Image* is the kind of epyllion one would expect from a writer in 1598 whose main poetic interests were satirical. Even without "Kinsayder's" commentary, the poem epitomizes the ambiguous pattern of convergence and conflict between epyllion and satire in the late 1590s. "Kinsayder's" denunciations of *Pigmalions Image* may be understood as an exaggeration of the conventional distancing device in which the erotic poet "apologizes" for his poem, as an indication of Marston's poetic nervousness and lack of confidence in his own ironic control, and as a consequence of his experiments with an expressively distorted and unbalanced satiric persona. If the entire performance is also characteristically Marstonian, this is not because "Kinsayder's" perplexingly ambiguous attitude towards sexual experience tells us anything directly about Marston's own "divided soul"[60] or his "secret disgust for readers, for amorous man, and for sex itself."[61] It is rather because "Kinsayder's" particular combination of sophisticated ironic titillation and savage, obsessive revulsion anticipates the attitudes of some of Marston's most striking characters in the plays of the next decade.[62]

Chapter VII

Faunus and Melliflora

❧

John Weever's *Faunus and Melliflora* reflects even more extensively and explicitly than Marston's *Pigmalions Image* the pressures exerted by late Elizabethan satire on Ovidian narrative poetry at the turn of the century. Yet Weever's response to those pressures differs strikingly from Marston's. The differences between them may be related in a rudimentary way to contrasting biographical circumstances. Marston, a resident student at the Middle Temple when he wrote *Pigmalions Image* and *The Scourge of Villanie*, was intimately involved in the London literary life centered around the Inns of Court.[1] His early writing is pervaded by a hypersensitive attention to the expectations and "opinion" of this extremely sophisticated and often cynical audience. Weever, on the other hand, seems deliberately to have avoided the London milieu with which Marston was so closely connected. In 1598 he apparently left Queens' College, Cambridge, where he had been admitted in 1594, without ever having visited London.[2] And instead of going from Cambridge to London to make his name as a writer, as Marlowe, Thomas Heywood, and a number of other late Elizabethan poets had done, he retired for several years to his family home in Lancashire. It was at this considerable distance (both literal and figurative) from the London literary scene that Weever began his career as a writer and as a scholar of English literature and antiquities. He is best known today for his first published work, *Epigrammes in the Oldest Cut and Newest Fashion,* which appeared in 1599 and contains important early comments on Shakespeare, Spenser, Jonson, Marston, Daniel, Drayton, Warner, Middleton, and other writers.[3] Already in the *Epigrammes* Weever exhibits a comprehensive, distanced, idiosyncratic perspective on the contemporary state of English poetry which was to emerge again the following year in his next publication, *Faunus and Melliflora, or the Origin of Our English Satyres* (1600).[4] Taken in its entirety, this volume provides nothing less than a summarizing assessment by an informed contemporary of the problematic relationship between satire and erotic poetry at the end of the sixteenth century.

Weever's 1600 volume, like Marston's *The Metamorphosis of*

Pigmalions Image and Certaine Satyres, combines erotic mythological poetry and satire in a kind of composite or hybrid volume anticipated by Lodge in *Forbonius and Prisceria* (1584) and in *Scillaes Metamorphosis* (1589).[5] But as Weever's title itself suggests, the constituent poems of his volume are interrelated as they are not in the works of Lodge and Marston. After an epistle to Edward Stanley and five short poems in praise of the author which are themselves of some critical interest, the volume opens with a mythological narrative poem in Marlovian couplets entitled *Faunus and Melliflora.* This poem concludes with an account of how the unborn son of Faunus and the nymph Melliflora was transformed by a vindictive Diana, whose rule of chastity is subverted in the course of the poem, into a monstrous little satyr who ran off into the woods and "Joyned issue with the Satyres and the Faunes" (l. 1042). When Brutus came to England five generations later and founded "Troynovaunt," he brought with him several satyrs descended from Faunus's transformed son. Diana was still vengeful, and she obtained a promise from Jove that these new English satyrs should be the "utter enemies" of "lovers pastimes" and of all other "sportfull veneries" (ll. 1069-1070). Through the false Renaissance etymological identification of "satyr" and "satire," Weever is able to end *Faunus and Melliflora* with an account of the attacks on the realm of Venus by the "jerking sharp fang'd poesie" of these English "satyres" (l. 1073) and with a final promise that he will now go on to introduce the reader to the descendants of those "satyres" which "Brutus left behind in *Italie*" (l. 1088). The volume then continues with Weever's own English translations of the first satire of Horace and the first satire of Persius. He begins the first satire of Juvenal, but after ten lines he breaks off and resumes the fiction of *Faunus and Melliflora.* Venus, as it happens, was not about to submit passively to Diana's vengeful assault. She came to England and contrived that "all the Satyres then in England living / Should sacrifisde be . . . in the burning fire" (ll. 1673-1674)[6] and that from the ashes of the sacrificed "satyres" a new "satyre" would arise which would oppose the "snarling" attacks of its predecessors. Weever concludes his volume with a poem called *A Prophesie of this present yeare, 1600,* in which the speaker takes up the cause of Venus by turning the "satyres'" own "snarling," "jerking" methods against them and by claiming that "There is no lewdnesse in these *Halcyon* times" (l. 9).

The only previous attempt to account in any detail for Weever's curious volume appears in Arnold Davenport's introduction to his edition of *Faunus and Melliflora* (1948). Davenport begins by rejecting the idea that Weever was simply following Marston's example in the *Pigmalions Image* volume and trying "to exploit simultaneously the attractions of eroticism and satire":

A more plausible explanation is that Weever had, in June, 1599, two unfinished works in his desk; one an erotic poem very nearly completed, and the other a collection of fragments towards a book of satires translated and original. On 1 June, 1599, the Bishop of London and the Archbishop of Canterbury, alarmed by the increase of erotic literature, and even more by the dangerously overt attacks in contemporary satire on persons and on social abuses, ordered the Stationers' Company to print no more satires and directed certain satirical and erotic publications to be called in and burned. Valentine Simmes, Weever's printer [for the *Epigrammes* and for the *Faunus* volume], was one of the 'untrustworthy' printers who were individually warned by the Stationers about the new orders. Weever may well have been disquieted when he realised that both his projected books were threatened by these orders . . . It is quite credible that Weever should have attempted to evade the ban by cobbling together his two works in such a way that the erotic poem might pass as a mythological account of the origin of satire and the satires themselves be presented as a deprecation of satire.[7]

It may be apparent from the brief description I have already given of the *Faunus and Melliflora* volume that this is in fact not an adequate or fully "credible" account of Weever's volume or of the motives behind it. Davenport was certainly right to argue that Weever's writing was conditioned by the edict and the book-burning of June 1599 and that some of the connections among the constituent poems are, as he says, "forced and awkward." It is also possible that Weever had begun work on a collection of satires before he conceived of the composite volume. But to see the volume merely as the result of Weever's having "cobbled together" previously existing and entirely unrelated poems is to overlook the work's most interesting and important sources of unity. It is particularly misleading to conclude that when Weever wrote the "greater part" of his erotic narrative poem he had no idea of using it as an epyllionic prelude to a survey of the current state of English satire.[8] The most obvious features of *Faunus and Melliflora* call such a conclusion into question.

Faunus and Melliflora stands out among Elizabethan epyllia in that its main narrative subject is not derived from Ovid or from any other classical source. The principal figures themselves are largely Weever's own invention, as the author of one of the complimentary poems at the beginning of the volume indirectly acknowledges:

> *Faunus* a silvan god, and *Melliflora*
> A sacred Nymph, that usde among the woods,
> Rose every morning with the bright *Aurora,*
> To gather garlands made of muskrose buds:
> . . . .

> Oblivion buried them in their chiefe pride:
> So all men die whom no sweete Muse doth cherish:
> This *Aesculapius* by his cunning pen,
> Revives the dead from their obscured grave,[9]
>
> (ll. 1-4, 7-10)

In calling Faunus "a silvan god," Weever's friend is obviously thinking of the mythological Faunus, a woodland deity with oracular powers who was often identified with Pan. There was also a legendary Faunus, an ancient king of Latium who married the nymph Marica and produced a son, Latinus, the father of Romulus and Remus.[10] Although Weever's Faunus is primarily an invented figure who owes more to Shakespeare's Adonis and Marlowe's Leander than to either of these classical traditions, both the mythological and the legendary associations are invoked in the poem and indicate clearly that Weever had the idea of "satyre" in mind when he created his protagonist. The fact that the mythological Faunus was traditionally thought of as a satyr, like Pan, made it plausible for Weever to depict his Italian and English "satyres" as the descendants of Faunus. And by invoking the legendary Faunus at the end of his narrative, Weever is able to move from the remote mythological past to the immediate present in England where Faunus's transformed descendants are "Scourging the lewdnesse of damnd villany" (l. 1076). However contrived these mythological connections may seem, they are undeniably rooted in the name and identity of Weever's epyllionic protagonist.

There are other prominent features of *Faunus and Melliflora* which show that it was written with an awareness of the satire which follows it. Weever begins the poem by telling of Faunus's father, Picus, whose descent from "aged *Saturne*" (l. 5) and whose dislike of women ("The wood-Nymphes woo'd him, yet not won of any," l. 20) will be developed in a key episode later in the poem, where Picus speaks against love and women with the voice of the saturnine, cynical satirist. More significant still is the rivalry between Diana and Venus, a motif woven through the entire poem and extended into the rest of the volume to provide a mythological basis for the enmity between satire and erotic poetry. It is of course possible that Weever made all these changes after the edict and book-burning, as Davenport suggests. If so, *Faunus and Melliflora* was completely rewritten with the design of the entire volume in mind. It was not simply tacked on in a "nearly completed" state to the beginning of "a book of satires" to which it originally bore no relation.

The over-arching and controlling idea of Weever's volume is that erotic, romantic love inevitably gives rise to jealous, resentful, and frequently hypocritical attacks by those excluded for various reasons from the pleasures of "sportfull venery." The function of *Faunus and Melliflora* itself in this overall design is suggested in another of the volume's prefatory poems:

> Methinks I heare some foule-mouth'd Momus say,
> What have we here? a shepheards roudelay?
> More love-tricks yet? will this geare never end,
> But slight lascivious toyes must still bee pend?[11]
>
> (ll. 1–4)

The author of this poem, obviously aware of the Elizabethan satirists' violent attacks on amorous poetry, goes on to defy "Momus" and to defend Weever's effort "to write of Love, and Loves delights" (l. 7) and "To blazon forth the love of shepheard swaines" (l. 15). In some respects the emphasis of this prefatory poem is not misplaced. In *Faunus and Melliflora*, more clearly than in any other epyllion we have looked at, youthful love is seen to thrive and to satisfy the promptings of an erotically charged pastoral world. Neither the lovers' own comic naiveté, nor the various jealous and mean-minded obstructions which confront them, nor even the fact that their first offspring is turned into a monstrous enemy of "lovers pastimes" (l. 1070) can undermine the fulfillment of their love.

Weever's narrative is more eventful and episodic than that of other epyllia and is organized around the ancient idea of a pastoral love affair overcoming a series of obstacles to its success.[12] After a twenty-five line introduction, the love story is set in motion with extended portraits of Faunus and Melliflora and with an account of their first meeting. At about line 200, however, the love story gives way to a sequence of episodes which keep the two lovers at a distance and which provide Faunus with a kind of education in love. These episodes include (1) Faunus's visit to the valley of the nymphs and his participation in their games (ll. 199–439); (2) the attack of the boar, and Faunus's encounter with Adonis and Venus (ll. 440–514); (3) Faunus's return home and confrontation with his father Picus (ll. 515–590); (4) Cupid's appeal to the Destinies on behalf of Faunus (ll. 591–672). At line 672 the love story is resumed: the lovers' portraits are redone in miniature (ll. 678–720), and after some gratuitously elaborate wooing and a few Hero-like second thoughts on Melliflora's part, they are married "by one of *Vestaes* Nuns" (ll. 999–1000). It is at this point in the poem that Weever begins the transitional conclusion which leads into the rest of the volume.

In *Faunus and Melliflora* the imitativeness which has been a major feature of the Elizabethan epyllion from the beginning attains a new range of eclecticism and a new level of self-conscious, and often playful, virtuosity. Weever borrows extensively from *Venus and Adonis* and *Hero and Leander*. But even more extensive are his borrowings from Sidney's *Arcadia*, a work which has figured prominently in the background of the epyllion all along and which in *Faunus and Melliflora* becomes a direct source of verbal and narrative detail. Especially in the first half of the poem, in the introduction of the main characters and in the pastoral episode of Faunus's visit to the valley of the nymphs, Sidney is the dominant influence on Weever's writing.

The Faunus portrait (ll. 26–80) provides a good indication of the degree of success Weever is able to achieve in synthesizing details from Sidney, Shakespeare, and Marlowe to create figures and episodes with their own distinctive interest and function. The portrait opens with a passage recalling both Leander's "dangling tresses" (I. 55) and Adonis's wind-blown "locks" (ll. 1087–1090) and suggesting that perhaps masculine physical beauty is going to be praised in the extravagant homoerotic terms of Marlowe's Leander portrait:

> *Faunus* a boy whose amber-stragling haires,
> So straungely trammeld all about his eares,
> The crisp dishevel'd playing with the winde,
> Among the thickest, never way could finde,
> But sweetest flowers would leape from *Floraes* lap,
> And so themselves within his tresses wrap.
> That glad he was those lockes (those lockes alone,
> Those lockes that lockt in bondage many one:)
> With carelesse art, or artlesse care infolde,
> And draw them in a coronet of golde.
>
> (ll. 29–38)

The pastoral hyperbole and the rather awkward attempts at highly patterned rhetorical ornament already indicate that Sidney's prose is as conspicuous a source for Weever here as Shakespeare's sixains or Marlowe's couplets.[13] Accordingly, after an apology imitated from Marlowe ("His eies were such, my Muse hardly can / Emblazon forth the beauty of a man," ll. 45–46),[14] Weever's narrator suppresses the Marlovian emphasis on masculine sensuality and focuses instead on Faunus's ornate costume in a passage derived largely from a well-known description of the enamored hero Pyrocles in his feminine "Zelmane" disguise in Book I, Chapter 12 of the *New Arcadia*.[15] In the *Arcadia* the comic and ironic effects of Pyrocles's feminine disguise are controlled to a certain degree by the thematic significance of a love-sick young man who has temporarily abandoned the active heroic life for the seductive charms of love and pastoral retirement.[16] But in *Faunus and Melliflora* Sidney's thematic emphasis is altered. Faunus's attire is not a feminine disguise; it is his own clothing. And although he wears tokens of many "faire Ladies" (ll. 61-68), he has not yet fallen in love. Faunus's elaborate costume belongs not to a tested hero "effeminized" by love, but to a naive and bashful "boy" (ll. 26, 29) whose masculinity has yet to be proven through experience. When Sidney tells us that "Zelmane's" mantle was fastened with "a very riche jewell" on which was depicted "a *Hercules* made in little fourme, but a distaffe set within his hand," he is giving us an emblem of the immediate threat which love poses to Pyrocles's masculine virtue.[17] But when Weever gives Faunus a jewelled clasp which also shows "Great *Hercules* with distaffe in his hand" (l. 58), he is projecting a possibility that his hero has yet to encounter. The image of subjugated heroism only calls further attention to Faunus's youth and inexperience. Unlike Shakespeare's Adonis, Faunus's masculinity is not undermined by an excessive aversion to women or to love. It is merely swathed in the foppish elegance of youthful dandyism:

> His ivory feete, appearing unto sight,
> In murrey[18] velvet buskins rich were dight,
> The middle slits with tyrian Bisse were laced,
> Whose prettie knots his man-like legge embraced.
> (ll. 75-78)

The way in which Weever adapts Sidney's "Zelmane" portrait to his own narrative and integrates it with Shakespearian and Marlovian motifs is indicative of his technique throughout the poem.

The portrait of Melliflora (ll. 129-166), which follows a forty-five line description of Faunus's wandering among the "Latian mountaines" (l. 82) filled with echoes from the *Arcadia*, parallels the Faunus portrait and calls further attention to the self-dramatizing virtuosity of Weever's imitative technique. Details from Marlowe's opening portraits are not only borrowed and reworked—in some instances they undergo a process of sexual transposition:

> Amorous Leander, beautiful and young,
> (Whose tragedy divine Musaeus sung)
> (Marlowe, I. 51-52)

> Faire *Melliflora*, amorous and yong,
> Whose name, nor story, never Poet sung:
> (Weever, ll. 131-132)

Weever's "Faire Melliflora" may recall Marlowe's "Hero the faire" (I. 5), but the rest of the couplet is a witty emulation of Marlowe's introduction of Leander. A similar transposition in the other direction occurs in the Faunus portrait:

> Hir kirtle blue, whereon was many a stain,
> Made with the blood of wretched lovers slain.
> (Marlowe, I. 15-16)

> With purple coloured silke it had beene wrought:
> But (ah alas) it was the crimson staine,
> Of goddesses, which *Faunus* lookes had slaine:[19]
> (Weever, ll. 70-72)

These transpositions are interesting not only for what they suggest about Weever's relationship to his sources, but also for the way in which they anticipate Beaumont's more complex exploitation of this "mannerist" device in *Salmacis and Hermaphroditus*.[20] The few critics who have commented on *Faunus and Melliflora* have diverged widely in their assessment of such imitativeness. At one extreme Hallett Smith calls the poem "the most slavish of all the imitations of Marlowe's masterpiece";[21] at the other extreme, Helmut Castrop sees the imitations as "highly accomplished parody."[22] It seems to me that Weever's imitative passages are neither "slavish" nor really "parodic." He regards his model with a witty detachment and transforms what he borrows with a display of self-conscious cleverness. But there is no sense that he is attempting to ridicule or mock *Hero and Leander*.

Weever's pervasive borrowing will inevitably restrict one's assessment of his originality. But it is important to recognize the extent to which the borrowings are purposively assimilated into a distinctive mythological narrative. For example, Weever describes the traditional dress of Diana worn by Melliflora in a way which anticipates the subversions of Diana's law of chastity in the next episode:

> Strange were her weedes to *Faunus,* yet not strange,
> For in such weedes the wood-Nymphes use to range,
> A petticote tuckte even with the knees,
> Garnisht about with leaves of sundry trees:
> And sometimes like a net drawne up, and wrought,
> (Which net the eagle-*Jove* might well have caught)
> And all her garments made so light and thin,
> (Who could restraine, but thinke what was within?)
> (ll. 153-160)

Most of these details are taken from Sidney's description of Philoclea's "nimphe-like apparell":

> . . . her haire (alas too poore a word, why should I not rather call them her beames) drawn up into a net, able to take *Jupiter* when he was in the forme of an Eagle; her body (O sweet body) covered with a light taffeta garment, so cut, as the wrought smocke came through it in many places, inough to have made your restraind imagination have thought what was under it. . . .[23]

By transferring the conceit of "a net, able to take *Jupiter*" from Philoclea's hair to Melliflora's skirt tucked up Diana-fashion above her knees, Weever calls attention to the latent erotic power of Diana's supposedly chaste followers. He may even be toying with the idea of Venus disguised as Diana which we noted earlier in connection with Marlowe's Hero.[24] Certainly Venus's influence already seems to have invaded Diana's domain.

Faunus's response to Melliflora recalls Leander's first sight of "Venus' nun" and anticipates the main thematic function of the episode in which he visits the valley of the nymphs: *"Faunus* kneel'd downe and unto *Venus* prayde"* (l. 181).[25] He follows a "rose strowne way / Into the valley" and finds the frolicking nymphs "Accosted all with *Venus* and the Graces" (ll. 199–201), another clear indication that while they wear Diana's garb and apparently follow her rule of spartan chastity (the narrator calls them a "bevie of faire virgins," l. 343), their behavior and abode is fraught with erotic encouragement. Melliflora is designated to ask Faunus to spend the night, and in her invitation she gives away her sexual curiosity—not with one slip of the tongue, like Marlowe's Hero, but with two (ll. 229–236). Faunus is led to the nymphs' lodging and "summer hall," which is modelled on the pastoral abode of King Basilius in the *Arcadia*.[26] To heighten the erotic ambient of the nymphs' hall, Weever makes the stream which flows under it (Basilius had contrived an artificial water work for his hall) a replica of Sidney's River Ladon, which in a later episode of the *Arcadia* so gratefully receives the naked bodies and the splashings of Pamela and Philoclea.[27]

Melliflora leads Faunus on to a gallery, where the only work of art described depicts the nymphs' patron goddess in a most compromising moment:

> There was *Diana:* when *Acteon* saw her,
> Bathing her selfe (alas he did not know her):
> (A goldsmiths wife once nakt without her pearle,
> Hard to be knowne is from a countrie gerle.)
> (ll. 275–278)

The narrator's asides here point up the way in which Diana's dignity is threatened in this episode. Weever's passage is especially interesting for the way in which it reflects upon the Faunus episode in the "Mutabilitie Cantos" of Spenser's *Faerie Queene*. Spenser's episode is, of course, a comically debased adaptation of the Actaeon myth: his Faunus is a foolish lecher who is punished when he dares to intrude upon divine beauty.[28] Weever's Faunus, by contrast, is the naive and unwitting agent of Venus who stimulates a spontaneous erotic excitement that makes Diana look foolish. The motive for Diana's revenge is being planted here and will be taken up at the end of the poem. But there too her dignity will be undermined, and her counter-attack against Faunus and his goddess Venus will be exposed as hypocritical and ineffective.

As Faunus's visit among the nymphs continues, he falls more deeply in love and gradually loses some of his callow naiveté when he participates in the nymphs' boisterous country games. The idea for these games comes from an unfinished poem by Sidney added to the "First Eclogues" in the expanded 1593 edition of the *Arcadia*.[29] Sidney had used the country game of Barley-break as an elaborate comic framework in which Strephon and Klaius pursue their beloved Urania (ll. 208–416). Weever reverses the direction of the sexual pursuit, as it were, and shows the nymphs enacting their desire for Faunus through this "prettie pastime" (l. 355). English country games were notoriously lustful, as William Ringler notes, and Weever, by heightening the sexual puns and elaborating his descriptions of Faunus tumbling about with the nymphs, gives the games an even stronger erotic significance than they have in Sidney.[30] Faunus's education in love is taking place, ironically, under the tutelage of Diana's own nymphs. Rolling on the grass in country games seems to be just what this ivory-skinned boy with his excessively elegant costume needs: when the games are over "Shamefastnesse" continues to prevent Faunus from openly expressing his "bold" desire, but he has grown sufficiently aggressive to ask Melliflora for a private rendezvous (ll. 416–424).

Melliflora complies with Faunus's request by asking him to help her find her necklace and caul, which she has conveniently managed to lose in the woods (ll. 425–436). The second of the poem's main episodes now begins as Faunus and Melliflora are attacked by a "fierce wild boare" just as they are about "To plucke the sweetes (how sharpely sweetes will grow:) / From sharpest stinging hawthorne as they go" (ll. 437–441)— Weever's language again makes the sexual symbolism of this moment in the narrative difficult to miss. The idea of interrupting a carefree idyl with an attack by a savage beast comes from the end of Book I of the *Arcadia*, where the wooing of Philoclea and the disguised Pyrocles is disrupted by

the attack of a lion.[31] By changing Sidney's lion to a boar, a traditional
symbolic embodiment of male lust, and by emphasizing that Faunus and
Melliflora are on the verge of realizing "how sharpely sweetes will grow"
(1. 438), Weever suggests momentarily the intrusion of threatening sexual
violence into youthful and idealized romantic passion. The appearance of
the boar also indicates something else, however—the temporary emer-
gence of Shakespeare's *Venus and Adonis* as the dominant influence on
Weever's narrative.

Faunus's encounter with Adonis and Venus themselves after he has
killed the boar but lost Melliflora in the process (ll. 461-468) is perhaps
the most problematic section of the narrative. In it Weever appears to
move closer to travesty than any other follower of Shakespeare and
Marlowe. In assessing the effect of Weever's narrative here, however, it is
helpful to observe that while Shakespeare's influence in the episode
eventually eclipses that of Sidney, it is the lion attack in the *Arcadia*
which in a sense establishes the opening tone of Weever's episode. And
Sidney's own account is a mixture of heroic seriousness and erotic
comedy. Having dispatched the lion after receiving only a scratch on the
shoulder, "Zelmane" turns to present Philoclea with the lion's head and
finds her still running away in terror: " . . . her light apparell being
carried up with the winde, that much of those beauties she would at
another time have willingly hidden, was present to the sight of the twise
wounded *Zelmane*."[32] Weever imitates this passage, with some added
erotic detail about Melliflora's panting and about the "wanton wind"
being "like to some pleasant civit smelling breath," and places it before
the killing of the boar (ll. 447-460). But the mixture of seriousness and
comedy extends into Faunus's encounters first with the dead Adonis and
then with a saddened but still lustful Venus.

The lines on Adonis are conceived in the manner of a Marlovian
etiological conceit, in which a witty new causality is attributed to a
commonly known or evident phenomenon:

> . . . within a grove he found
> Love-sicke *Adonis* lying on the ground.
> For hating Love, and saying *Venus* nay,
> Yet meeting *Melliflora* in his way:
> Love made (Love weepe to see thy tyrannie,)
> *Adonis* frustrate his vow'd chastitie:
> Whilst narrowly upon her lookes he spide,
> Strooke with loves arrow, he fell downe and dide.
>
> (ll. 471-478)

One could of course say that the Venus and Adonis story is trivialized in this passage, much as one could say that it is trivialized in Marlowe's ironic account of its depiction on the sleeve of Hero's gown (I. 11-14), or that Marlowe's conjectural allusion to Hippolytus ("Had wild Hippolytus Leander seen / Enamour'd of his beauty had he been," I. 77-78) trivializes that story. But to do so would be to misapprehend the mythological wit of the Elizabethan epyllion. A clever recasting of a traditional myth need not imply a denial or mockery of its serious, even tragic, possibilities. The interesting thing about Weever's passage is how aware he is of the themes and ironies of Shaespeare's epyllion. In applying the term "love-sicke" to Adonis (it was Shakespeare's Venus, we recall, who was "sick-thoughted") and then reminding us that Shakespeare had placed great emphasis on Adonis "hating love, and saying Venus nay," Weever is actually extending—admittedly in a comic direction—Shakespeare's own irony in having Adonis declare, "I know not love . . . / Unless it be a boar, and then I chase it" (ll. 409-410). Weever's Adonis is killed not by the boar's tusk, but by Cupid's arrow: the spirit of the variation is not very far from Sidney's observation that in being clawed by the lion and smitten by Philoclea's naked charms, Pyrocles is "twise wounded."

Faunus's encounter with Venus (ll. 481-512), to whom he had prayed for success in love not so long before, shows even more clearly how Weever works a comic variation on Shakespeare's much darker irony without ridiculing or mocking the original and without obliterating our sense of its complex expressiveness. Weever begins by having Venus mistake Faunus for Adonis, a maneuver which in itself represents a witty acknowledgment of his indebtedness to Shakespeare. Still unaware of Adonis's death, Venus assumes that he has had a change of heart, and she assails Faunus with résumés of those persuasions to love which Shakespeare had given her:

> Or give, or take, or both, relent, be kind,
> Locke not Love in the paradize of thy mind:
> Is *Venus* lovely? then *Adonis* love her.
> Is she the Queene of love? then what should move her
> To sue and not command? Is shee Loves mother?
> Shall she be loath'd, which brings love to all other?[33]
>
> (ll. 497-502)

Weever surrounds Venus's speech with humorous indications that once again the Queen of Love is going to undermine her persuasions with her own sexual aggressiveness, if not, as in *Venus and Adonis,* with her physical grossness as well. Before beginning her persuasions she "stript all to the smocke" (1. 488); at the conclusion, enflamed by her own rhetoric, she

> doft all to the Ivorie skinne,
> Thinking her naked glorie would him winne.[34]
> (ll. 503–504)

When Faunus smiles at her exuberance, Venus recognizes that he is not Adonis, but she tries to make love to him anyway. The narrator's comment—"Thus women will one for another take" (l. 508)—may again seem to trivialize the story, but of course one of the points Shakespeare makes about Venus at the end of his poem is that it is part of her nature as the embodiment of sexual love to take love where she can find it, to pluck the flower which reminds her of Adonis rather than to let it "grow unto [it]self" (l. 1180). When the "shamefac't *Faunus*" resists Venus, she ceases to woo him and flies away in her dove-drawn chariot, reassuming her dignity as a goddess much as she does at the end of *Venus and Adonis.* Weever has used this comic but non-parodic imitation of Shakespeare to carry Faunus's erotic education still further, and to show that although he has overcome some of his earlier naive shyness, he is still "shamefac't " when confronted with love in all "her naked glorie."

The next two episodes in *Faunus and Melliflora* are as dependent on Marlowe as the pastoral and the Venus and Adonis episodes are on Sidney and Shakespeare. Up to this point the only impediment to Faunus's love, apart from the boar, has been his own shyness. But now, having been solicited and embraced by Venus herself, he encounters the opposition of parental disapproval, and of fate. The first of these episodes, Faunus's return home and interview with his father Picus (ll. 512–590), is based upon Leander's return to Abydos and confrontation with his father after the first visit to Hero's tower (II. 103 ff.). Picus's initial reaction to the evident effects of seven days and nights of lovesickness is to chide Faunus "mildely" (l. 520), much as Leander's father "mildly rebuk'd his son / Thinking to quench the sparkles new begun" (II. 137–138). But Picus quickly warms to his work, and it becomes apparent that Weever's conception of him bears a special relation to the warfare between Venus and her enemies which unites *Faunus and Melliflora* with the rest of the volume. We were told at the beginning of the poem that Picus was the offspring of Saturn (ll. 5–8), a figure whose traditional associations include strong ties to satire and to a hatred of love and women.[35] It should not come as a total surprise, therefore, that Picus is made to speak to Faunus in the voice of the saturnine satirist:

> Fond Boy, quoth hee, and foolish cradle witted,
> To let base love with thy yong years be fitted:
> This upstart love, bewitcher of the wit,
> The scorne of vertue, vices parasite:
> The slave to weaknesse, friendships false bewrayer,
> Reasons rebell, Fortitudes betraier:
> The Church-mens scoffe, court, camp, and countrie's guiler,
> Arts infection, chaste thoughts and youth's defiler.
> And what are women? painted weathercocks,
> Natures oversight, wayward glittering blocks:
> True, true-bred cowards, proude if they be coide,
> A servile sex, of wit and reason voide:
>
> (ll. 521–532)

The narrator's comment on Picus's speech indicates the connection Weever wants to establish between this episode and the derisive exposure later in the poem and in the volume of those satirists obsessively bent on "Lashing and biting *Venus* luxurie" (l. 1074):

> Thus in our find-fault age, many a man
> Will fondly raile with foule-mouth'd *Mantuan*.[36]
> Some sharpe witted, only in speaking evill,
> Would prove a woman worse than any divell
> With prating *Picus*: . . .
>
> (ll. 535–539)

When Faunus suggests that he is in love not with an ordinary woman but with a nymph, Picus's response aligns him even more solidly with those whose antipathy to love is a sign of their own hypocrisy and mean-mindedness. Weever is also able to work in here the comment on the mistreatment of poets which had become almost a signature of the Elizabethan epyllion since *Hero and Leander:*

> Nymphes are like Poets, full of wit, but poore,
> Unto thy kingdom, adde a kingdome more
> By marriage: let *Pycus* counsel thee,
> Looke not (my boy) at wit, and Poetrie.
>
> (ll. 567–570)

"Prating *Pycus*" will receive his just deserts later in the poem. But his cynical, saturnine, and hypocritical denunciation of the love by which

Faunus is inspired is already a substantial confirmation that Weever's epyllion is constructed with the design of the entire volume firmly in mind.

Faunus's reaction to the "blasphemie / Pronounc'd by *Pycus* gainst his deitie" (ll. 589–590) is predictably governed by the principle laid down by Marlowe's narrator: "But love resisted once, grows passionate, / And nothing more than counsel, lovers hate" (II. 139–140). At this point Cupid himself intervenes on behalf of Faunus and makes an appeal to the "seld-prevented Destinies" (l. 592) in an episode which derives from Cupid's similar appeal in *Hero and Leander* (I. 377 ff.). The idea of destiny or fate is never given the significance in *Faunus and Melliflora* that it has in *Hero and Leander,* and to a certain extent the mythology of Weever's episode seems rather gratuitous. But it is important to observe that the debate between Cupid and the Destinies continues the argument of the preceding episode and provides further links with the overarching theme of love's battle against its opponents and detractors. Cupid's speech also brings out a key difference between Weever's version of the ambivalent Ovidian attitude towards love and that of his predecessors in the epyllion. Cupid proposes an ideal of playful, generous, unthreatening erotic freedom which contrasts sharply with the compelling, violent, often threatening erotic power which pervades other epyllia:

> Love's will was this, that maides should have their will,
> Not overmuch, but to restraine from ill.
> Ill kept-in-thoughts, with vertuous companie,
> Restraining not from well-rulde libertie.
>
> (ll. 609–612)

> (So then twixt *Faunus* and faire *Melliflore,*
> Love told the Love,) and fearing fathers ire,
> Love is defeated of his chiefe desire.
> This kind unkindnesse children yet must take,
> Until their parents price of them do make,
> As in a market: . . .
>
> (ll. 636–641)

Cupid's attack on Picus's kind of narrow cynicism and his plea that young love be granted a humane and generous freedom seem at first to move the Destinies, and they "did somewhat pittie youth" (l. 650). Their unanimous decree, however, is a perverse and contradictory overreaction:

These statutes should for ever be decreed:
That man for his unmanlike treacherie
Should be tormented with vile jealousie,
That maids from honest libertie restrained,
Should alway thinke from what they thus refrained:
(ll. 653-656)

These thoughtes awaked, women growe manwood,
Nor can these thoughts from actions be withstood.
(ll. 661-662)

That shrewdnesse should possesse the womans heart,
In stubbornnesse the husband act his part:
Thus drawing opposite in one yoke, alive
Long might they live, but they should never thrive:
(ll. 667-670)

Weever's Destinies thus condemn the world to a domestic version of the turbulent erotic chaos which rules the universe of late Elizabethan Ovidian poetry. Weever has retained the ambivalence so fundamental to the Ovidian attitude towards love, but the negative aspects of that ambivalence impinge on the main love story in a different way than they do in other epyllia. Although Faunus had "turnd to hate / His fathers words, and grew passionate" (ll. 675-676) before Cupid could return with the Destinies' decree, hate, jealousy, and destructive pride are not forces which will continue to enter the consciousness and behavior of Faunus and Melliflora as they do that of Glaucus and Scilla, Venus and Adonis, or Hero and Leander. Weever's lovers continue to operate very much within Cupid's ideal of happy, "well-rulde" erotic liberty. It is the enemies of Venus and her lovers—Diana, Deiopeia, Picus, and above all the "satyres"—who become the primary agents for the negative aspects of love.

Most of the rest of the poem, up to the concluding mythical genealogy of satire, is devoted to the reunion of Faunus and Melliflora and to the happy fulfillment of their love. Faunus leaves his father's court, this time dressed in a garment "more rich than glaring" whose embroidered decoration of "birdes, and beasts" and flowers (ll. 688-698) suggests a closer association with the pastoral world of the nymphs than did his previous lavish attire. There is a great deal of playfully distanced imitation of both *Venus and Adonis* and *Hero and Leander* in the scene which follows. Melliflora comes upon Faunus, who has fallen asleep on the grass, and first mistakes him for Adonis (ll. 725-726). When she recognizes that it is Faunus and that he has not been murdered by the boar, she tries to revive him in a passage typical of Weever's rather precious eroticism:

> With that she joynd her corrall lips to his,
> Sucking his breath, and stealing many a kisse:
> Wishing the life of a Camelion,
> That she might onely live his breath upon:
>   (ll. 733-736)

Melliflora wakes Faunus by beginning to woo him (ll. 755-786). Since her speech contains many echoes from the attempts by Shakespeare's Venus to persuade Adonis to love,[37] one can see another of Weever's witty acknowledgments of his source in the fact that the aroused Faunus first mistakes Melliflora for Venus and runs away, remembering Venus's overly aggressive solicitations (ll. 803-812). Melliflora divulges her true identity by calling out his name, and the lovers finally embrace passionately. But Faunus insists on wooing Melliflora, even though she "was already wonne" (l. 850) in a much more complete sense than Marlowe's Hero (I. 330). Melliflora plays along with Faunus and, like Hero but somewhat more rationally in view of her association with Diana, claims that she has vowed "To die a virgin" (ll. 905-906). This gives Faunus an opportunity to attack the unnaturalness of a life devoted to virginity in an argument which contains, in addition to borrowings from Leander's "bold sharp sophistry" (I. 199-294, 299-310, 315-340), several very interesting echoes from the speeches against chaste, studious seclusion in Shakespeare's Love's Labor's Lost.[38] The important thing to notice about this entire scene of elaborate wooing is the way in which the element of serious psychological tension and vulnerability, so crucial to the confrontation between Hero and Leander, has been reduced and transformed into what both lovers recognize as an elaborate amatory game. When Faunus and Melliflora see that they are about to be discovered by the nymphs, they quickly put an end to their contrived love-debate and, when night comes, fly away together (ll. 945-956). Once again we see Weever minimizing the problems and maximizing the comic happiness of his young lovers.

The marriage which Melliflora insists on before she will allow Faunus to seal "with the cheefest armes / Of his desire, the waxe that Venus warmes" (ll. 992-1006) is set between two passages of special importance in refocusing the rivalry between Venus and Diana and in preparing for the genealogy of satire with which the poem concludes.

First, Diana's vengeful opposition to the love of Faunus and Melliflora is
secured by Deiopeia, the most aggressive of the nymphs in her pursuit of
Faunus earlier in the poem (ll. 314–340) but now bitterly jealous when she
realizes that he has run away with Melliflora. Diana is angry when she
hears from Deiopeia of *"Mellifloraes* perjury" (l. 978):

> She sware her priests and huntsmen would not tarrie,
> If thus her chastest Nymphes beganne to marrie.
> (ll. 983–984)

Much of what happens in the rest of Weever's volume derives from the
angry opposition to Venus which is here seen to arise from the jealousy of
those deprived of love. But Venus is already beginning her counter-attack.
As a gesture of approval after the marriage of Faunus and Melliflora,

> . . . *Venus,* to encrease their amitie,
> Considering words against her deitie
> Were spoken by *Pycus:* she incontinent,
> In heate of rage her indignation spent:
> Transforming him into a bird of th'aire,
> And where before, of al hee was most faire,
> She makes him blackest, keeping nothing white,
> But breast and bellie (for there dwelt delight)
> And by her power divine she so hath framed,
> That by his owne name hee is ever named.
> (ll. 1007–1016)

In the *Metamorphoses* (XIV. 320–396) Ovid tells how Picus was changed
into a woodpecker by Circe for rejecting her love. Weever changes the
transforming goddess to Venus and the motive to punishment for
hypocritical, narrow-minded opposition to love. Venus leaves Picus's
breast and belly white as an ironic manifestation of the falseness of his
chastisement of Faunus. For as a young man this saturnine detractor of
love had not only enflamed the desire of nymphs and goddesses with his
beauty but had himself surrendered to his desire for the nymph Canens
(see ll. 21–26), Faunus's mother. So if Deiopeia embodies the jealousy of
those opposed to love, Picus embodies the hypocrisy. With Venus's
transformation of him, the warfare between love and its detractors is fully
joined.

The conclusion to *Faunus and Melliflora* is clearly designed to serve
as a transition to the poems which follow, and in some respects it is

contrived and far-fetched. What cannot be disputed, however, is that Weever has been leading up to this conclusion throughout the entire poem. In lines which harken back to the picture in the nymph's gallery of "*Diana:* when *Acteon* saw her" (l. 275), "Chaste *Diana* on fell mischief bent" now enters the court ruled by Faunus, who has taken possession of his father's throne. Her "mischief" is directed against Melliflora's unborn son:

> And so (to ease her hate which inly burned)
> The faire childe to a monster she hath turned:
> His head was garded with two little hornes,
> A beard he had, whose haires were sharp as thornes,
> Crooked his nose: his necke, his armes, and breast
> Were like a man, but like a goate the rest.
> No sooner was the faire Nymphs wombe cut ope,
> To give the monster largest roome and scope,
> But out he flies, and to the woods doth runne,
> (For there *Diana* pointed he should come)
>
> (ll. 1031–1040)

Faunus's bemonstered son "Joynd issue" with other similar woodland creatures to produce a whole race of "Satyres," the living embodiments of a vindictive and distorted hatred of love's natural fulfillment. Many years later Brutus, the legendary great-grandson of Aeneas and hence one of Faunus's undeformed descendants,

> . . . at our English *Dover*
> Landed, and brought some Satyres with him over,
> And nimble Faeries.
>
> (ll. 1053–1055)

The "Faeries proved full stout hardy knights, " we are told, "As *Spencer* shewes" (ll. 1057–1064). But Diana continues to use the "Satyres" as agents of her "fell mischief":

> This boone *Diana* then did aske of *Jove*,
> (More to be venged on the Queene of Love,)
> That *Faunus* late transformed sonnes Satyres,
> (So cald because they satisfide her ires)
> Should evermore be utter enemies,
> To lovers pastimes, sportfull veneries.
> *Jove* granted her this lawful just demand,
> As we may see within our Faerie land:
> The satyres jerking sharp fang'd poesie,
> Lashing and biting *Venus* luxurie,
>
> (ll. 1065–1074)

The etymology of "satyre" offered here in line 1068[39] epitomizes Weever's playful variation on the Renaissance theory that "satire" originally derived from the ancient Greek "satyr play" and hence possessed an inherent connection with the mythological "satyr."

The attitude towards these "jerking sharp fang'd" English "satyres" expressed by the narrator in the final lines of *Faunus and Melliflora* is extremely important to understanding the relationship between Weever's erotic mythological narrative and the satirical writing which follows it:

> If this praise-worthy be, then first of all
> Place I the Satyre Academicall,
> His Satyres worthy are (if any one)
> To be ingrav'd in brasse, and marble stone:
> Detracting nothing from the excellencie,
> Of the *Rhamnusian* Scourge of Villanie,
> But I was borne to hate your censuring vaine,
> Your envious biting in your crabbed straine.
> (ll. 1079–1086)

Throughout the poem the narrator has been partial to Venus and the two young lovers and openly scornful of Diana and her allies, Picus and Deiopeia. He is fully in character, therefore, when he confesses his hatred of satire. But this confession is preceded by praising allusions to Hall ("the Satyre Academicall") and to Marston ("the *Rhamnusian* Scourge of Villanie").[40] This praise is heavily qualified[41] ("If this praise-worthy be, " " if any one"), but it nevertheless stands as an indication of the narrator's attempt to avoid the rash extremism of the "satyres" themselves. He admits his partiality—he is going to take the side of Venus against Diana, and particularly against the "envious biting" and "crabbed straine" of her "satyres." But satire does have a right to exist, he implies; Diana's request to Jove was a "lawful just demand" (l. 1071). The Elizabethan satirist, despite his commitment to truth, will never grant his enemy any claim to justification or validity. His attacks are always extreme, absolute, uncompromising.[42] By acknowledging the legitimacy of satire and by openly confessing his own partiality to satire's enemy, Weever's narrator adopts (at least at this stage) a much more balanced and forthright strategy, a strategy in keeping with Love's own ideal of a benevolent, "well-rulde libertie" (l. 612).

A certain principle of balance may in fact be seen to operate throughout the *Faunus and Melliflora* volume. Not only is the erotic mythological narrative set off against the inimical "satyre," but at the very end of the poem we are invited to see the "jerking sharp fang'd" English "satyre" set off against his Italian counterpart:

> Now let us shew the Satyres enmitie,
> Which *Brutus* left behind it *Italie*.
>   (ll. 1087–1088)

The translations which follow of the first satires of Horace, Persius, and Juvenal serve not only to show what the English and Italian (or Latin) "satyres" have in common, but where they differ. For among the Latin "satyres" themselves there is yet another partly balanced contrast which Weever will use in his assessment of contemporary English satire. Nothing could be further from the "envious biting," "crabbed straine," and obsessive hatred of "*Venus* luxurie" displayed by the English "satyres" than the first satire of Horace.⁴³ There is only one brief mention of "whores and bawds" (l. 1261) in the entire poem. For the most part Horace is concerned here with the follies of wealth and avarice. And near the end of the poem Horace offers the famous principle of moderation which is as antithetical to the spirit of the English "satyre" as it is to the greed and avarice he is attacking:

> A meane there is in all things, bonds be pight
> On this side or beyond which nought stands right.
>   (ll. 1266–1267)

In contrast to Horace, Persius is extremely close to the English "satyre, " both in subject matter and in tone. Amorous and erotic poetry and the corrupted, decadent taste to which it appeals are the major concerns of his first satire:

> O slight regard of sots, or brainlesse men!
> How great their blindfold vanities are, when
> Naught they applaud but tingling Poesie,
> Lulling the sence with itchfull ribaudry.
>   (ll. 1295–1298)

Weever accentuates the continuity on this point between Persius and the English "saytres" like Marston and Guilpin by expanding the attacks on erotic folly (he uses 295 lines of English couplets to render 134 lines of Persius's Latin) and, even more interestingly, by echoing Marston's own writing in his translation:⁴⁴

> Old-ore-worne truncke, and dost thou lay the baite,
> For tickling eares, for eares which itching waite,
>   (Weever's *Persius*, ll. 1345–1346)

> And now me thinks some wanton itching eare
> With lustfull thoughts, and ill attention,
> List's to my Muse, . . .
> > (*Pigmalions Image*, St. 33, ll. 1-3)

> The Salaminian Titillations
> Which tickle up our lewd Priapians.
> > ("The Author in prayse of his precedent Poem," ll. 5-6)

Davenport's assessment of the quality of Weever's translations may be accurate: "One cannot praise the translations of Horace and Persius. It is worth noting that though Weever was a fairly good Latinist, and dealt with Horace quite closely and faithfully, he groped and fumbled when he tackled Persius."[45] But the way in which the translations of these two satires function within the design of the entire book is interesting and important nonetheless. Weever has shown that while the English "satyres" have much in common with the harsh, sexually-preoccupied Persius, they have little in common with the more restrained, urbane, and wide-ranging Horace. These two translations demonstrate, in other words, that there is an alternative form of satire to the "jerking sharp fang'd" English variety and its obsession with "Lashing and biting *Venus* luxurie."

Weever's translation of Juvenal's first satire is broken off after only ten lines. Why? Davenport suggests that Weever's printer, Valentine Simmes, had interrupted work on the translation with the news that he had received a special warning from the Stationers' Company on behalf of the ecclesiastical authorities against his printing any more satires and epigrams. Simmes did in fact receive such a warning[46] and this very well could have influenced Weever's work. But Davenport's conjecture does not explain why a completed translation of Juvenal would have made Weever's book any more susceptible to censure than it already was with the translations of Horace and Persius. Perhaps Weever simply decided that Juvenal would have required more time and effort than he wanted to expend: the first satire is longer than Persius's (171 lines) and the Latin would have been just as difficult for an Elizabethan translator. Or perhaps he thought that since Juvenal's first satire is modelled on the first satire of Persius and is equally concerned with attacking amorous and erotic poetry, a complete translation of it would have upset the balance established by the Horace-Persius contrast. In any case the use Weever makes of his ten-line fragment of Juvenal is inventive. We are told that

Venus, seeing the attack of the English "satyres" against "sportfull venerie" about to be augmented by the Englishing of yet another of her Italian detractors ("glowming *Juvenall*"), "entreates my Muse, that for a while she would leave him in his English tongue unperfect. . . ." The narrator's further comment on his Muse once again shows Weever's concern to establish a pose of balance and independence: " . . . yet to *Venus* she makes a vow, that *Juvenall, Horace,* and *Persius* shall hereafter all be translated." Weever may merely be trying to stake out his claim here to a projected translation of the three main Latin satirists.[47] But the vow to Venus also serves another more immediate purpose. Although the narrator has declared his hatred of satire's "crabbed straine" and indicated time and again his partiality to Venus, he is committed here, as at the end of *Faunus and Melliflora,* to the idea of displaying the full range of the "Satyres enmitie" (1. 1088).

Weever now resumes his narrative of the warfare between Venus and her Diana-inspired detractors. Venus has been listening to the "satyres" "maligne, snarle, raile, and bite" (1. 1602) and has decided to use "All possible meanes for revengement" (1. 1605). Her first step is taken against the Italian "satyres":

> Thus much by much entreatie she obtainde:
> Or by her owne powre she thus much then gainde,
> I know not whether, that (for Satyres spight)
> Italians should in fond loves take delight.
> In stranger sinnes, sinnes which she was ashamed,
> Among th'Italians rightly should be named.
> . . . .
> And (to be breefe) that lustfull venerie,
> Should be the downfall of all *Italie:*
> This is the cause Italians to this day,
> Are ever readie, apt and prone that way.
>
> (ll. 1612–1625)

Weever is doing something more here than simply invoking the traditional Elizabethan view of Italy as a den of lechery and vice. He is preparing for the final poem in the volume where he will directly contradict the English "satyres'" claims that "the lewdnes of Britania" (Marston, "Proemium in librum primum," *The Scourge of Villanie,* 1. 2) needs to be exposed and punished. The way in which Venus next takes her revenge against these English "satyres" is Weever's most direct and daring allusion to the late Elizabethan controversy over satire and erotic poetry and to the edict and book-burning of June, 1599. Having traveled in all her "naked beautie" and with all her accoutrements "to our English clime" (ll. 1627–1660), Venus begins

> Using all mischiefe gainst her enemies,
> Thrusting her selfe in baudy elegies,
> Polluting with her damned luxury,
> All eares which vowd were unto chastity,
> And evermore thus on fel mischiefe bent
> Until she found (she never was content:)
> Some of her Saints (belike) who every day,
> Unto her shrine their orizons did say:
> Which for she askt, this boone to her was giving,
> That all the Satyres then in England living
> Should sacrifisde be in the burning fire,
> To pacifie so great a goddesse ire,
>
> (ll. 1664–1675)

The ecclesiastical authorities behind the 1599 censorship of satire—indeed the Archbishop of Canterbury and the Bishop of London themselves!—are here shown to be the secret agents of Venus's revenge. The audacity of Weever's strategy is heightened by the narrator's ironic assumption, for a brief moment, of the satirists' own denigrating attitude towards Venus's influence. The authorities are put in the position of praying and lending their support to a goddess who is "Polluting with her damned luxury / All eares which vowd were unto chastity."

Weever's wittily subversive version of the edict and book-burning of 1599 points up more clearly than any other factor how misleading Davenport's assertion is that Weever "attempted to evade the ban by cobbling together" an erotic poem and a group of satires. No one attempting to win the approval of the censors would have made the censors themselves the butt of such an irreverent satirical joke. Weever's audacity is so striking that Lecocq wonders whether or not "he benefited from some singularly powerful protection, or from an exceptional clemency. . . ."[48] It is more likely, however, that Weever and Simmes evaded the censors by totally circumventing the official instrument of their authority, the Stationers' Company, with a small, private, unregistered printing. The fact that the *Faunus and Melliflora* volume is not entered in the Stationers' Register would not normally be of much significance, since only about two-thirds of the books actually published in the sixteenth century were so registered.[49] But since the edict of 1 June 1599 issued by the Stationers' Company had laid particular stress on the requirement that "any book of the nature of these heretofore expressed . . .

shall not be printed untill the masters or wardens have acquainted the
said Lord Archbishop or the Lord Bishop with the same . . . ," the failure
of Simmes to register Weever's book may be understood as an attempt to
publish it without attracting the attention of the authorities. The fact that
only a single copy of the book survives (now in the Huntington Library)
also suggests that Weever and Simmes were relying upon a small,
inconspicuous printing, rather than upon friends in high places or the
composite nature of the book itself, to keep them from punishment. The
enterprise nevertheless does seem extremely risky. There can be little
doubt about what Archbishop Whitgift's or Bishop Bancroft's reaction
would have been had they found themselves depicted as Venus's "Saints . . .
who every day / Unto her shrine their orizons did say" (ll. 1670–1671).

Weever looks forward to the final poem of the *Faunus and Melliflora*
volume, "A Prophesie of this present yeare, 1600,"[50] in the couplet which
concludes his account of how the English "satyres" were sacrificed "in the
burning fire":

> And from their Cyndars should a Satyre rise,
> Which their Satyricke snarling should despise.
> (ll. 1676–1677)

Weever has been concerned all along with the possibility of an alternative
satiric mode, and although his approach in "A Prophesie" does not
correspond entirely to the Horatian alternative he had presented earlier, it
is based on an ironic opposition to the "Satyricke snarling" so obsessively
inimical to Venus:

> Cease cease to bawle, thou wasp-stung Satyrist,
> Let none so testy petulant insist:
> Hold, stay thy lashing hand, and jerking rimes,
> There is no lewdnesse in these *Halcyon* times.
> (ll. 6–9)

These four lines contain the two principal features of Weever's satiric
alternative. First, there is the open denunciation of satire itself as it is
currently practiced, a strategy which Weever will extend even further in
his next publication, *The Whipping of the Satyre* (1601). The narrator's
attitude has undergone something of an alteration since the end of
Faunus and Melliflora. There his confessed hatred of satire was balanced
by his qualified compliments to Hall and Marston; here his attack on the
"satyres" is much sharper, much less restrained. But the shift in tactics

should not obscure the underlying perception which links *Faunus and Melliflora* with "A Prophesie"—that the "satyre's" violent denunciations betray an envious and hypocritical fascination with the human experiences he holds up to ridicule:

> Not for a world of Indian treasury,
> Would I the world in tearmes so villifie,
> Or prove it in my wrangling poesie,
> A Brokers shop of vile iniquitie:
> Nor should my lavish and malignant tongue,
> Teare out the bowells of sinnes hidden long,
> Hooke out abhoring-nature strange delights,
> Drownd in the dead sea with the Sodomites.
> For whilst such covered sinnes you do unvaile,
> Crabbde reprehension sets them but to sale.
>
> (ll. 76–85)

Weever's writing is as effective here as it is anywhere in the entire volume, partly because of the clever way in which he takes up the "satyres" own savage language ("Teare out the bowells," "Hooke out nature-abhoring strange delights") and turns it against them. This technique is perhaps inherent in the tradition which Lecocq calls "satire du satirique," and it is not without its own pitfalls.[51] But Weever is able to exert a distanced control over the "Satyricke snarling" he has all along professed to hate by obviating the suspect motives behind such writing.

The second principal feature of Weever's approach in "A Prophesie," the apparent praise of contemporary English society, is even more deceptive.[52] It does seem clear, however, that lines such as "There is no lewdnesse in these *Halcyon* times" are meant to be read ironically, since Weever's narrator acknowledges and catalogues just as many vices as Hall, Marston, and Guilpin. But the narrator refuses to scourge the vices he names because, he says in a memorable couplet,

> Sinne's like a puddle or a mattery sincke,
> The more we stirre them, stil the more they stincke.
>
> (ll. 106-107)

Weever has, of course, gone Marston one better and contrived a way of writing sensationalistic satire while denying that he is doing so. He reverses the strategy of *Pigmalions Image*. Marston's "Kinsayder" claimed he was being satirical when he wrote erotic poetry; Weever's narrator disclaims any satiric intention as he delivers a biting satirical portrait:

O could the circuit of my pulsive braine,
Harbour but in it such a cinicke straine,
I would have scourgde self-blind *Bravortian,*
Keeping in Newgate his lewd curtezan,
So lushiously with sacke, and marrow pies,
Whilst in the Fleete his Unkle starving lies,
There fleete, or sincke, or drowne, his care is more,
To snort in th'armes of his shape-altring whore.
(ll. 108–116)

This is fine satirical writing, without the satirist's egotistical presumption to moral truth and rectitude. It is the kind of satirical writing one would expect from an advocate of Love's "well-rulde libertie," much as *Pigmalions Image* is the kind of erotic poetry one would expect from that saturnine malcontent "Kinsayder." Ultimately, of course, one may find the ironic optimism of Weever's narrator ("But Vice this yeare of Vertue makes an end," l. 154) as unconvincing and as disingenuous as "Kinsayder's" indulgent cynicism. But the point to remember is that neither Weever nor Marston is offering us personal manifestos. They are offering us clever, highly self-conscious poetic performances, performances which may very well reflect but certainly do not equal the author's own deepest convictions about poetry, society, and morality.

The *Faunus and Melliflora* and *Pigmalions Image* volumes represent contrasting attempts by two wily young Elizabethan writers to contend with the conflict and convergence of satire and erotic poetry at the turn of the century. Weever's distinctive approach was determined partly, one imagines, by a temperament very different from Marston's, partly by the fact that he was writing at a greater distance from the London literary scene and from the cynical, jaded Inns-of-Court wits whose "opinion" the young Marston was so sensitive to, and partly by the sheer force of historical circumstances, which provided him with an opportunity to distinguish himself from those "snarling Satyres" who had been "lashing and biting *Venus* luxurie." Weever is far from being a great poet—he is less good than Marston at his best. But Weever's hybrid volume of 1600 displays a thematic unity and a grasp of the main issues involved in the controversy over satire and erotic poetry which Marston's *Pigmalions Image* volume lacks. The most impressive thing about *Faunus and Melliflora* itself is the way in which each of its main episodes is made to contribute to the central argument of the volume as a whole: that satirical denunciations of sexual love betray an envious and hypocritical alienation from the human pathos and comedy such love can generate. The writing in Weever's epyllion is at times labored and inept; his imitation of Sidney, Shakespeare, and Marlowe, though never "slavish," can become mere clever pastiche. And in concentrating on the attractive passion and comedy of young love, Weever has simplified that Ovidian erotic ambivalence which in other Elizabethan epyllia also includes the violence, grotesqueness, and inevitable disappointments of sexual experience. Yet *Faunus and Melliflora* remains an inventive contribution to the Elizabethan epyllion, a highly original poem despite its pervasive dependence on the work of three much greater writers.

Chapter VIII

Salmacis and Hermaphroditus

❧❦❧

Poetically as well as chronologically, *Salmacis and Hermaphroditus* marks the transition from the Elizabethan epyllion to its Jacobean sequel. The epyllion had survived the controversy over satire and erotic poetry of the late 1590s and would continue into the seventeenth century, but not without having internalized many of the pressures exerted on it by the "Satyres jerking sharp fang'd poesie." The tendencies toward parody and explicit satire, present in the epyllion from the beginning and intensified by Marston and Weever, would become dominant in the majority of Jacobean mythological narrative poems. *Salmacis and Hermaphroditus* perpetuates the heightening of these tendencies and does indeed look forward, as Bush suggests,[1] to seventeenth-century Ovidian poetry. But it also retains deep affinities—deeper than those of either *Pigmalions Image* or *Faunus and Melliflora*—with the tone and the thematic concerns of *Venus and Adonis* and *Hero and Leander*. It offers, in fact, a more complexly wrought and accomplished version of Elizabethan Ovidian ambivalence than any other epyllion except those of Shakespeare and Marlowe.

The 1602 edition of *Salmacis and Hermaphroditus* is anonymous.[2] In 1640 the poem was reprinted as the work of Francis Beaumont in a small volume of his collected poetry,[3] and it has subsequently appeared under Beaumont's name in Dyce's edition of *The Works of Beaumont and Fletcher* (1846), in Donno's *Elizabethan Minor Epics,* and in Alexander's *Elizabethan Narrative Verse*. Some scholars have remained skeptical of the attribution,[4] but as Philip Finkelpearl argues in the most recent and complete assessment of the question, explicit links between *Salmacis and Hermaphroditus* and the mock-Ovidian *Metamorphosis of Tobacco*, also published anonymously in 1602 but ascribed by a contemporary to John Beaumont, virtually confirm the former as the work of the eighteen-year-old Francis.[5] The two Beaumont brothers, both in residence at the Inner Temple, seem to have engaged in friendly rivalry by writing Ovidian and mock-Ovidian poems at the same time, publishing them anonymously, and exchanging complimentary verses for them.[6] The entire situation is suggestive generally of the status of the epyllion after the turn of the

190

century, and particularly of the way in which *Salmacis and Hermaphroditus* incorporates, without completely giving itself up to, the heightened tendency towards mythological parody.

Two preliminary observations may be made about Beaumont's choice of subjects. First, it is only a slight exaggeration to say that the story of Salmacis and Hermaphroditus had been present in the Elizabethan epyllion all along as a kind of latent poetic paradigm. Certainly no other Ovidian episode crystallizes so mysteriously that key epyllionic pattern of delicate, chaste male beauty under assault from aggressive female libido. Shakespeare's interest in the story is implicit throughout *Venus and Adonis*, as numerous critics have observed,[7] and Marlowe alludes to it at a key moment in *Hero and Leander* (II. 45-48).[8] Beaumont may thus be said to have elaborated an Ovidian source of special importance for the entire development of the epyllion. Secondly, along with this latent paradigmatic status, the conclusion of the tale of Salmacis and Hermaphroditus has an undeniable element of erotic sensationalism about it and might well have seemed to the young Beaumont to offer a daring and piquant way of appealing to readers whose taste for more straightforward erotic subjects had by 1602 become a little jaded. Having said this, one must immediately add that Beaumont declines to take advantage in any obvious way of the more lurid possibilities of his subject. *Salmacis and Hermaphroditus* is much further from cynical pornography than Marston's *Pigmalions Image*. But it would be misleading not to acknowledge the distinctive character of Beaumont's epyllionic subject from the outset. Beaumont could have counted on a special interest in his poem without having to cater to that interest blatantly or crudely.

Along with its erotic sensationalism, Beaumont's subject—particularly the concept of the hermaphrodite itself—carried an ancient and complex history of attempts to sublimate that erotic sensationalism through moralized interpretation and allegory. During the Renaissance, as Edgar Wind and others have shown, Neoplatonic, Biblical, and even alchemical traditions converged to produce a philosophical myth of the original, and hence ideal, androgyny of man.[9] Poetic appropriation of this symbolic tradition was quite widespread in the sixteenth century, but the extent to which a given poet was concerned with bringing the intricacies of hermaphroditic symbolism into play varied a great deal. For the French Pléiade poets the "androgyne" became an almost habitual metaphor for the ideally hoped for union of the male lover with his female counterpart—his "moitié."[10] In Elizabethan poetry, a writer like

Weever, in telling us that Faunus and Melliflora "with their kisses made
two bodies one" (l. 827), could take up the hermaphroditic metaphor with
little evident concern for philosophical symbolism. Spenser, on the other
hand, draws in a rich and complicated way on such symbolism, as we
shall see in the conclusion to this study when we compare the expressive
concerns of Spenser's poetry with those characteristic of the epyllion.

Ovid's story of Salmacis and Hermaphroditus (*Metamorphoses* IV.
285-385), though obviously connected in a general way to the various
symbolic meanings of the hermaphrodite, has a largely independent
interpretive history. The story does not figure prominently in Neoplatonic discussions of the hermaphrodite, and indeed there is every indication
that it proved difficult, if not impossible, to accommodate within the
positive theories of androgyny. In the *Genealogia Deorum* Boccaccio
gathers together several rather bizarre geographical and physiological
explanations of the myth, but he is clearly not convinced by any of them.[11]
In the sixteenth century, in contrast to the consistently positive meanings
invested in the hermaphrodite itself [see Figs. 8 & 9], the prevailing
interpretations of Ovid's story of Salmacis and Hermaphroditus were
negative. Barthélemy Aneau illustrates his emblem "Fons Salmacidos,
Libido Effoeminans" ("the fountain of Salmacis is the emasculating
libido") with a woodcut showing a terrified Hermaphroditus trying to
escape from the clutches of an enflamed Salmacis [Fig. 10].[12] Golding's
version of this negative moralization has already been cited:

> Hermaphrodite and Salmacis declare that idlenesse
> Is cheefest nurce and cherisher of all volupteousnesse,
> And that voluptuous lyfe breedes sin: which linking all toogither
> Make men to bee effeminate, unweeldy, weake and lither.
> ("Epistle to Leicester," ll. 113-116)

Thomas Peend, who published his translation of the Salmacis and
Hermaphroditus episode in 1565 to arouse interest in a projected English
version of the entire *Metamorphoses*, is even more severe than his rival
translator:

> By *Salmacis*, intende eche vyce
>   that moveth one to ill.
> And by the spring the pleasant sporte,
>   that doth content the wyll.[13]

One's first reaction to moralized commentaries such as those of Aneau,
Golding, and Peend is to dismiss them as hopeless distortions of Ovid's

8. Barthélemy Aneau, "Matrimonii Typus" (woodcut). *Picta Poesis ut Pictura Poesis Erit*, Lyon, 1552, p. 14.

9. Barthélemy Aneau, "Humana Origo et Finis" (woodcut). *Picta Poesis ut Pictura Poesis Erit*, Lyon, 1552. p. 50. Photo British Museum.

episode, as indeed they are in some respects. But it would be a mistake to reject them as entirely irrelevant. For one thing, these moralizations often exhibit a telling preoccupation with the sexual reality they condemn. Aneau, for instance, is quite explicit in identifying the fountain of Salmacis with the vagina.[14] Ovid's own narrative, moreover, is offered as an explanation of the harmful effect of the fountain in Caria, which is "infamis" because it "enervates with its enfeebling waters and renders soft and weak all men who bathe in it . . . " ("male fortibus undis / Salmacis enervet tactosque remolliat artus," IV. 285–286). What really distinguishes Ovid from most of his medieval and Renaissance commentators is the attitude he generates towards the events leading up to the final transformation and to the spell cast on the fountain by Mercury and Venus. Where late Christian writers see a lamentable example of masculine virtue overcome by feminine lust, Ovid sees a much more ambiguous and ironic situation in which Hermaphroditus's extraordinary beauty and his extreme aversion to sexual love are as much responsible for the final unfortunate conclusion of the episode as is the uncontrollable passion of Salmacis.[15]

Beaumont's prefatory "Lines to the reader" offer an important indication of the approach he will take to Ovid's story and of where he stands in relation to the various interpretive traditions impinging on his subject:

> I sing the fortunes of a lucklesse payre,
> Whose spotlesse soules now in one body be:
> For beauty still is *Prodromus* to care,
> Crost by the sad starres of nativitie;
> And of the strange inchauntment of a well
> G'in by the gods my sportive Muse doth write,
> Which sweet-lipt *Ovid* long ago did tell,
> Wherein who bathes, strait turnes *Hermaphrodite*.
> I hope my Poeme is so lively writ,
> That thou wilt turne halfe-mayd with reading it.

Beaumont is looking back past hermaphroditic allegory and moralizing denunciations of lust to "sweet-lipt *Ovid*," and he is being guided by a "sportive Muse"[16] which will grant him the freedom not only to retell the original story but to elaborate on it as he sees fit. The jaunty panache of the last five lines should not blind one, however, to the more somber overtones of the first five. The pair Beaumont writes of were "lucklesse," their innocent beauty linked inevitably to "care" and "Crost by the sad

starres of nativitie." Beaumont has his eye on the darker dimensions of
Ovid's narrative lurking beneath the languidly beautiful and sophisticated surface. Although his epyllionic elaborations are indeed "sportive," he
never loses touch with the disturbing dimension of Ovid's poetic world, a
world governed by irrational and irresponsible erotic energies, a world in
which the only consistently operative rule is ironic coincidence and
contradiction. The ambivalence of this address to the reader extends into
the opening lines of the poem proper:

> My wanton lines doe treat of amorous love,
> Such as would bow the hearts of gods above.
>
> (ll. 1–2)

The pointed ambiguity of the second line of this opening couplet should
make one pause and reconsider the swaggering flourish of the first line.
The hearts of the gods may be bowed in erotic sympathy, or they may be
bowed in pitying sadness. In either case, the reader has to reorient his
expectations about what Beaumont's "wanton lines" are going to offer.
Without duplicating the narrative conciseness and tone of Ovid's episode,
Beaumont nevertheless manages to establish from the outset an ambivalent perspective on the myth which is deeply Ovidian.

The "sportive" yet subtly foreboding way in which Beaumont will
explore the multiple ironies of his subject becomes evident in the opening
portrait of Hermaphroditus (ll. 13–94). The portrait begins with three
couplets (ll. 13–18) which correspond very closely to Ovid's initial
description (IV. 288–291) and which establish two basic motifs: first,
Hermaphroditus is the offspring of Mercury and Venus, a fact reflected
both in his name and in his appearance;[17] secondly, he has been brought
up by the nymphs of Ida in an entirely feminine environment. Both
motifs set in motion the central irony of Beaumont's handling of
Hermaphroditus—he is androgynous and effeminate long before his
identity merges with that of Salmacis. Beaumont goes on to develop this
central irony through a series of deftly varied strategies. Lines 19–42,
which are entirely Beaumont's own invention and have no equivalent in
Ovid, praise the bisexual attraction of Hermaphroditus's "wondrous"
beauty by recounting the effect it has had on two mythological figures
who come to play significant subsidiary roles in the poem. We are first
told how Diana almost slew Hermaphroditus because, like Weever's
Faunus, he was distracting her nymphs from the chase. But she too was
captivated by his beauty, and when she finally let loose an arrow, she "did
of purpose misse him":

10. Barthélemy Aneau, "Fons Salmacidos, Libido Effoeminans" (woodcut). *Picta Poesis ut Pictura Poesis Erit*, Lyon, 1552, p. 32.

Photo British Museum.

> Shee turn'd againe, and did of purpose kisse him.
> Then the boy ran: for (some say) had he stayd,
> *Diana* had no longer bene a mayd.
>
> (ll. 32-34)

Only Hermaphroditus's chaste shyness prevents Diana herself from losing her virginity. And the effect of his beauty on a masculine deity is no less powerful: his beautiful face has lured Apollo away from "fayre *Leucothoes* side" (l. 37—the implied feminine comparison is significant), and since Hermaphroditus's death, we are told, the sun-god's daily flight around the earth has really been determined by his endless search for "this lovely boy" (ll. 39-42). The ironic implications of both these early allusions will be taken up later in the poem.

The opening portrait continues with a 36-line catalogue of Hermaphroditus's physical charms and confirms the notion already hinted at that his remarkable beauty deserves the kind of celebration normally reserved for feminine beauty. Each of the enumerated features provides an occasion for an extended conceit in Marlowe's wittily extravagant manner. As in Marlowe, the conceits are not just rhetorical hyperbole— the comparisons with other mythological figures all contribute to Beaumont's pervasive irony. Hermaphroditus's severe chastity, for instance, is shown to be distinctly contradictory when we learn that Venus has given him Cupid's "sparkling eyes" (ll. 59-74), even though he was already "farre fairer than the god of love" (l. 78). Like Shakespeare's Adonis, everything about Hermaphroditus conspires to excite the erotic attention which so repels him. The similarities between Adonis and Hermaphroditus are also relevant to the concluding section of the opening portrait (ll. 79-94), as Beaumont picks up Ovid's narrative again (at IV. 292 ff.) and begins to move into the story proper:

> When first this wel-shapt boy, beauties chief king,
> Had seene the labour of the fifteenth spring, . . .
> He gan to travaile from his place of birth,
> Leaving the stately hils where he was nurst,
> And where the Nymphs had brought him up at first:
> He lov'd to travaile to the coasts unknowne,
> To see the regions farre beyond his owne,
>
> (ll. 79-86)

Beaumont follows Ovid in giving Hermaphroditus a specific age, sixteen, which places him in the ambiguous transitional stage between boyhood and early manhood. Like Adonis, he is old enough to be sexually

motivated but too young to have had any sexual experience. His latent
sexual energy is being directed towards an approved "masculine" outlet—
adventurous exploration and travel—which, as in the case of Adonis's
boar hunting, will have disastrous sexual consequences. For it is
Hermaphroditus's desire "to know the wealthy Carians utmost bounds"
(l. 94) which leads him to the spring inhabited by Salmacis.

The introduction of Salmacis, although it is interrupted after only
twenty-one lines by the first of the poem's major digressions, extends and
complicates the ironic strategies of the Hermaphroditus portrait. Already
in the relatively brief preliminary section (ll. 95-116) one can see
Beaumont elaborating a complex reciprocal relationship between his
protagonists which will culminate in their eventual union. The catalogue
of Salmacis's charms echoes, rhetorically and through specific descriptive
detail, the earlier praise of Hermaphroditus's beauty:

[Hermaphroditus]	So wondrous fayre he was, . . . (l. 19)
[Salmacis]	So faire she was. . . . (l. 105)

[Hermaphroditus]	His legge was straighter than the thigh of *Jove*: (l. 77)
[Salmacis]	So straight a body, and so sweet a face,
	So soft a belly, such a lustie thigh,

(ll. 106-107)

[Hermaphroditus]	His haire was bushie, but it was not long,
	The Nymphs had done his tresses mighty wrong:
	For as it grew, they puld awaie his haire,
	And made abilliments of gold to weare,

(ll. 55-58)

[Salmacis]	Her haire as farre surpast the burnished gold,
	As silver doth excell the basest mold:

(ll. 115-116)

The conventional status of some of these details in the language of
Elizabethan love poetry only reinforces the sense of bisexual similarity
and parallelism between the two figures. Beaumont reserves Salmacis's
most significant physical similarity to Hermaphroditus until after the
digression which interrupts her portrait. Only then are we told how she
"washes o're her snowy limmes" in her "cristall fountaine" (ll. 375-376),
a passage which corresponds exactly to Hermaphroditus's search for
"cleare watry springs to bathe him in: / (For he did love to wash his ivory
skinne)" (ll. 87-88).

There is an additional level of reciprocal irony in the portraits of
Salmacis and Hermaphroditus which suggests that Beaumont may have
studied Weever's technique in *Faunus and Melliflora*. The sexual
transposition of details borrowed from Marlowe's portraits of Hero and
Leander occurs again in *Salmacis and Hermaphroditus*, and here the
device takes on a greater thematic significance than it had in *Faunus and
Melliflora*. The Marlovian details in the Salmacis portrait are taken not
from the description of Hero, as one might expect, but from the
description of Leander. Salmacis's "straight" body (l. 106) recalls
Leander's, which "was as straight as *Circes* wand" (I. 61), as well as
Hermaphroditus's "legge . . . straighter than the thigh of *Jove*" (l. 77); her
"soft . . . belly" (l. 107) recalls Leander's "white . . . bellie" (I. 66); her
"smooth . . . breast" (l. 109) recalls "How smooth [Leander's] breast was"
(I. 66). If we look back now to the Hermaphroditus portrait, we find
similar transpositions in the other direction. The phrase "so wondrous
fayre he was" (l. 19) is closer than the parallel phrase applied to Salmacis
("So faire she was . . . ," l. 105) to what I have suggested is the key line in
the Hero portrait: "So lovely fair was Hero, Venus' nun" (I. 45). And it
echoes even more precisely those famous lines in Leander's later praise of
Hero: "But you are fair (aye me) so wondrous fair / So young, so gentle,
and so debonair" (I. 287–288). Another important echo from the Hero
portrait occurs in the line about Hermaphroditus's hand: "For his white
hand each goddesse did him woo" (l. 75). This recalls Marlowe's praising
description of Hero's hands:

> She ware no gloves, for neither sun nor wind
> Would burn or parch her hands, but to her mind,
> Or warm or cool them, for they took delight
> To play upon those hands, they were so white.
> (I. 27–30)

The narrator also praises the whiteness of Salmacis's hand at a key
moment (l. 395), and he later tells how Phoebus "would ofttimes in his
circle stand / To sport himselfe upon her snowy hand" (ll. 465–466). But
the most strikingly sensual adaptation of Marlowe's conceit is reserved for
Hermaphroditus, just before he dives into Salmacis's pool:

> . . . he did begin
> To strip his soft clothes from his tender skin,
> When straight the scorching Sun wept tears of brine,
> Because he durst not touch him with his shine,
> For feare of spoyling that same Iv'ry skin,
> Whose whitenesse he so much delighted in.
> (ll. 837–842)

Beaumont is doing more than simply playing with the metaphorical details of *Hero and Leander,* although the element of verbal play in his reiterated imitations is certainly a part of the poem's appeal. Salmacis and Hermaphroditus are shown to be not only like each other physically, but also like their corresponding sexual opposites in Hero and Leander. By transposing and sharing borrowed Marlovian detail, Beaumont heightens the sense of a similar bisexual beauty which unites Salmacis and Hermaphroditus descriptively and metaphorically long before they are united physically and literally.

In the delayed completion of the Salmacis portrait (ll. 357 ff.), Beaumont develops another motif, already hinted at in the Hermaphroditus portrait, which suggests a familiarity with Weever's *Faunus and Melliflora.* This is the conflict between Diana and Venus. Salmacis, we learn, is the only nymph who refused to take part in "the savage and the bloudy sport / Of chaste *Diana*"[18] (ll. 362–363) and who "unto chaste *Diana* was unknowne" (l. 368). The other nymphs urged her to join in their chase, but Salmacis refused, preferring instead to swim in her "cristall fountain" or to admire her own beauty reflected in the water:

> Oft in the water did she looke her face,
> And oft she us'd to practise what quaint grace
> Might well become her, and what comely feature
> Might be best fitting so divine a creature.
>
> (ll. 383–386)

The way in which Salmacis's narcissistic pursuits parody the chaste pursuits of Diana establishes a complicated parallel with Hermaphroditus's relationship to his mother Venus. As the son of Venus, it was ironically appropriate that Hermaphroditus should have so attracted Diana that she was ready to surrender her virginity. But Hermaphroditus also contradicts the fundamental significance of Venus by rejecting the erotic attentions of others and by directing his energy towards vigorous exercise and adventure, much as Salmacis contradicts the values of Diana with her languid indulgence. There is one activity, however, which unites the parallel and contrasting pursuits of Hermaphroditus and Salmacis:

> (For he did love to wash his ivory skinne)
>
> (l. 88)

> And oft she washes o'er her snowy limmes:
>
> (l. 376)

Through the ambivalent symbolism of water and bathing, suggestive of purity and virtuous exercise on the one hand and of sexual indulgence and narcissism on the other, Hermaphroditus's sublimated and redirected inheritance from Venus merges with Salmacis's subversion of the activities of Diana.

Most of the middle portion of *Salmacis and Hermaphroditus*, and almost half of the entire poem, is taken up by the two extended digressions. These digressions are, as Castrop has noted, the most original feature of Beaumont's epyllion.[19] Though obviously indebted to Marlowe's two digressions in *Hero and Leander*, they are even freer in execution. At times one is reminded of the most extravagant narrative excursions of Ariosto, or of Chaucer—but Beaumont is even more self-consciously and elaborately whimsical than they are. If literary "mannerism" may be said to characterize the epyllion from the beginning, this "mannerist" element culminates in Beaumont's digressions. Yet the apparently whimsical narrative manner (what Lecocq calls "badinage érotico-mythologique"[20]) disguises a high degree of internal organization and extensive thematic connections with the main narrative. Both digressions are presented as elaborate etiological conceits. The tale of Jove's visit to the palace of Astraea and of his altercation with Venus and Vulcan (ll. 117-356) grows out of the Salmacis portrait and purports to explain why she is so extraordinarily beautiful:

> Therefore the god no more did woo or prove her,
> But left to seeke her love, though not to love her.
> Yet he forgot not that he woo'd the lasse,
> But made her twise as beauteous as she was,
> Because his wonted love he needs would shew.
>   (ll. 351-355)

The second digression, which tells of the rivalry among Bacchus, Mercury, and Phoebus (ll. 405-614), "explains" how Hermaphroditus happened to come to Salmacis's pool:

> But the fayre Nymph had never seene the place,
> Where the boy was, nor his inchanting face,
> But by an uncouth accident of love
> Betwixt great *Phoebus* and the son of *Jove*,
> Light-hearted *Bacchus*: . . .
>   (ll. 405-409)

The two digressions are approximately the same length (240 lines and 210 lines respectively) and are laid out so as to parallel each other at several points. Each digression is composed of a primary plot invented entirely by Beaumont and a secondary plot which has definite classical antecedents but which Beaumont reworks playfully and ironically. Thus in the first digression the invented tale of Jove's appeal to Astraea that he be allowed to turn Salmacis into a star is interwoven with the familiar antagonism of Venus and Vulcan.[21] In the second digression, the "uncouth accident of love" in which Bacchus rivals Phoebus as the wooer of Salmacis is interwoven with an elaboration of the traditional enmity between Phoebus and Mercury and with a parody of Vulcan's fabrication of the chariot of the sun.[22] Both digressions present a mythological universe ruled by gods whose lechery is at once comic and threatening and whose particular fondness for Salmacis predisposes them, ominously, to grant her every wish.

In *Hero and Leander* Marlowe had used Jove's sexual exploits to suggest that the entire universe was subject to violent and chaotic erotic power.[23] Beaumont develops much the same idea in his first digression, but with some additional satiric irony. The digression evolves out of the Salmacis portrait through an account of how Jove once offered to forego his usual brutal deceptions and to love Salmacis as an equal:

> Telling this lovely Nymph, that if he would,
> He could deceive her in a showre of gold,
> Or like a Swanne come to her naked bed,
> And so deceive her of her maiden-head:
> But yet, because he thought that pleasure best,
> Where each consenting joynes each loving brest,
> He would put off that all-commaunding crowne, . . .
> To taste the amorous pleasures of her bed:
>
> (ll. 121–132)

Jove's temporary abdication of supremacy merely shifts the exercise of erotic tyranny to Salmacis, and this "proud lascivious Nymph" begins to wield her power by demanding that Jove get Astraea's approval for his promises to place her as a star "in heavens vault" (l. 134). The narrator indicates parenthetically that Jove's surrender of power will have disturbing consequences:

> (Just times decline, and all good dayes are dead,
> When heavenly othes had need be warranted)
>
> (ll. 147–148)

The tone and generalizing judgment of this aside set the stage for the playfully subversive satire in the lines which follow.

Jove's visit to the palace of Astraea is the most conspicuously topical of any of the satirical episodes in the Elizabethan epyllion. Mythologically, Astraea is the virgin goddess who, as Ovid says in Book I of the *Metamorphoses*, lived on earth during the Golden Age but retired into the heavens during the Age of Brass.[24] Allegorically, as Frances Yates has shown in massive detail, Astraea became for the Elizabethans the chief symbolic embodiment of the Queen, "the imperial virgin who brings in the golden age of pure religion and national peace and prosperity."[25] Although Elizabeth had been celebrated as Astraea from the very beginning of her reign, this particular symbolic identity became especially prominent in the years following the Armada, when George Peele, Sir John Davies, and above all Spenser celebrated the Queen under this name.[26] It is Astraea who, in Book V of *The Faerie Queene*, instructs Artegall in the "discipline of justice" and makes him her earthly instrument:

> For *Artegall* in justice was upbrought
> Even from the cradle of his infancie,
> And all the depth of rightfull doome was taught
> By faire *Astraea*, with great industrie,
> Whilst here on earth she lived mortallie.
> (V.i.5.1-5)

The Astraea whom Jove seeks in Beaumont's epyllion seems at first to accord perfectly with her traditional identity:

> . . . she had long since left this earthly bowre,
> And flew to heaven above, lothing to see
> The sinfull actions of humanitie.
> (ll. 152-154)

But it soon becomes apparent that this Astraea's palace is a very strange abode of justice indeed—that Beaumont's episode is nothing less than a satirical parody of the conventional Elizabethan allegorical celebration of the Queen as the virgin goddess of justice.[27]

Beaumont's satirical technique in the Astraea episode has little in common with the "jerking sharp fang'd poesie" of the English "satyres" criticized by Weever. As Jove arrives at Astraea's "stately towre" (l. 159) and struggles to make his way to her throne, one is reminded instead of Chaucer's slyly benevolent manner in *The House of Fame*:[28]

> . . . from the palace side there did distill
> A little water, through a little quill,

The dewe of justice, which did seldome fall,
And when it dropt, the drops were very small.
Glad was great *Jove* when he beheld her towre,
Meaning a while to rest him in her bowre;
And therefore sought ѓo enter at her dore:
But there was such a busie rout before;
Some serving men, and some promooters bee,
That he could passe no foote without a fee:
But as he goes, he reaches out his hands,
And payes each one in order as he stands;
And still, as he was paying those before,
Some slipt againe betwixt him and the dore.
At length (with much adoo) he past them all,
And entred straight into a spacious hall,
Full of darke angles and of hidden wayes,
Crooked Maeanders, infinite delayes;
And which delayes and entries he must passe,
Ere he could come where just *Astraea* was.

(ll. 161–180)

Given the pervasive late sixteenth-century identification of Elizabeth with Astraea, there can be little doubt that Beaumont is here giving us a satirical account either of the court of Elizabeth itself, as Professor Bush has suggested,[29] or of one of the courts of law which theoretically represented an extension of the Queen's authority as the supreme dispenser of justice. When Jove finally reaches Astraea, he finds her listening to the complaints of Venus, Hermaphroditus's own mother, against "blacke *Vulcan*, that unseemely groome" (l. 198). The parody of legal procedure in the action which follows would have had a special appeal for Beaumont's fellow students at the Inns of Court.[30]

But topical satire is not Beaumont's only—perhaps not even his primary—poetic concern in the account of Jove's appearance before Astraea. An important thematic significance begins to emerge in the description of Astraea's throne:

Then she descended from her stately throne,
Which seat was builded all of Jasper stone,
And o're the seat was paynted all above,
The wanton unseene stealths of amorous *Jove;*
There might a man behold the naked pride
Of lovely *Venus* in the vale of Ide,[31]

(ll. 211–216)

Like the Fates in *Hero and Leander*, the Goddess of Justice in *Salmacis and Hermaphroditus* is shown to be inextricably linked with the disorder and irrationality inherent in erotic power, with Jove's "wanton unseene stealths" and with Venus's "naked pride." Astraea proceeds to enact the symbolism depicted over her throne by listening sympathetically to Jove's account of his latest amorous exploit and by agreeing to support his absurd bargain with Salmacis (ll. 251–252).

With Jove's "hopes and feares" momentarily "eas'd," Beaumont shifts the focus of his inset drama of fickle and irrational erotic power to Venus, whose presence above Astraea's throne suggests that she too will receive a sympathetic hearing in her case against Vulcan. But Venus has lost interest in her original complaint, for her "naked pride" has been wounded by Jove's praise of Salmacis and by his intention to place this "wanton Nymph" (l. 271) "in heaven above" (l. 266). Venus appeals directly to Jove in a speech which, in view of the speaker's identity and motives, may be read as a parody of the position one might have expected Astraea to have taken:

> . . . she griev'd to see
> The heaven so full of his iniquity,
> Complayning that eche strumpet now was grac'd,
> And with immortall goddesses was plac'd,
> Intreating him to place in heaven no more
> Eche wanton strumpet and lascivious whore.
>   (ll. 273–278)

Jove's response to Venus's appeal, or rather his failure to respond, occasions one of Beaumont's finest couplets:

> *Jove* mad with love, harkned not what she sayd,
> His thoughts were so intangled with the mayd,
>   (ll. 279–280)

Jove speeds "furiously" away to his own palace, where Astraea has promised to come "and set her hand / To what the love-sick god should her command" (ll. 289–290). Venus is left with no alternative but to devise a counterplot.

Venus prepares her revenge by reconciling herself with Vulcan in a passage which anticipates, through precise metaphorical parallels, Salmacis's final embracing of Hermaphroditus:

> For *Venus* so this night his sences pleas'd,
> That now he thought his former griefs were eas'd.
> She with her hands the black-smiths body bound,
> And with her Iv'ry armes she twyn'd him round,

> And still the faire Queene with a prety grace,
> Disperst her sweet breath o're his swarty face:
> Her snowy armes so well she did display,
> That *Vulcan* thought they melted as they lay.[32]
>
> (ll. 311–318)

For the moment Vulcan forgets his old jealousy and agrees to help Venus. They return to Astraea's palace the next day and with "othes that *Jupiter* himselfe doth feare" (l. 328), threaten to deprive Jove of his source of thunderbolts if he goes ahead with his plan to stellify Salmacis.[33] The comic power struggle among these deities governed by lust and sexual pride has now come full circle: Jove originally began his wooing of Salmacis by temporarily relinquishing his omnipotence; he has now been forced by a jealous Venus either to accept defeat in his amorous adventure and return to his old "wanton unseene stealths," or to give up his instruments of power and run the risk that "mortall men would plucke him from his throne" (ll. 337–338). The alternatives confronting Jove are expressive of an irrational, violently disordered universe appropriately presided over by an Astraea whose very throne is surmounted by pictorial representations of such irrationality and disorder. Jove's decision to cease wooing Salmacis but to make her "twise as beauteous as she was" (l. 354) completes the promised etiological function of the digression and projects the theme of frustrated erotic egotism into the rest of the poem. We are left with a sexually unsatisfied Jove and with a Salmacis twice as capable as before of inspiring the sort of ruthless amatory rivalry we have just witnessed.

I have examined Beaumont's first digression in considerable detail because it is so indicative of the spirit and technique of the poem as a whole. The playfully subversive satire of the traditional Elizabethan Astraea symbolism in the first part of the digression is fully in keeping with the way in which Beaumont's approach to the Salmacis and Hermaphroditus story itself exposes the distorting narrowness of the accepted Christian moralizations of Ovid's episode. The account of Astraea's court and of Jove's dispute with Venus is more broadly comic and more overtly parodic than anything we have seen in the epyllion before. Yet the entire digression from beginning to end is informed by an ominous and threatening sense of irresponsible erotic pride and exploitation. Finally, while the digression seems on the surface to flaunt narrative whimsy, it is in fact composed of a surprisingly elaborate tissue of mythological, metaphorical, and thematic ties to the main subject.

The second digression follows quickly on the first, after only a 48-line resumption of the introduction of Salmacis. Here Beaumont's subject is the rivalry of Bacchus and Phoebus for the love of Salmacis, and his manner is even more extravagantly capricious than in the first digression. But once again a surprisingly complicated integration of primary and secondary narrative material emerges when one looks beyond the immediate impression of poetic "sportiveness." The key to the artistic integrity of this digression is the indirect but multiple use Beaumont makes of the rich narrative context within which Ovid's episode of Salmacis and Hermaphroditus is set.

Ovid's framing narrative for the beginning of Book IV of the *Metamorphoses* is the story of the three daughters of King Minyas—the Minyades. The three sisters refuse to participate in the worship of Bacchus and, in defiance of his divinity, stay at home at their looms and amuse themselves by telling stories (IV. 1-42). Arsippe begins by telling the story of Pyramus and Thisbe (IV. 55-166), a part of Ovid's narrative context which Beaumont, doubtlessly familiar with the treatment this subject had received at the hands of Shakespeare's "rude mechanicals," avoids.[34] But Leuconoë follows with the story of Phoebus's love for Leucothoë (IV. 167-270), a myth which Beaumont has already alluded to in the account near the beginning of the poem of Phoebus's love for Hermaphroditus (ll. 35-37). Leuconoë's story also provides the major hint for Phoebus's wooing of Salmacis here in the second digression, and this contributes to the ironic parallelism established throughout the poem between the sexual attractiveness of the two protagonists. Leuconoë prefaces her tale with a brief account of Vulcan's discovery of Venus and Mars, whose adulterous love affair Phoebus was the first to see (IV. 170-189).[35] The importance of this story for Beaumont's first digression is obvious. Finally, it is Alcithoë's turn, and after tantalizing her sisters by mentioning several stories she will pass by (including the story of how Sithon, "the natural laws reversed, lived by changing sex, now woman and now man," IV. 279-280), she promises to "charm your minds with a tale that is pleasing because new" (IV. 284). This is the story of Salmacis and Hermaphroditus, and most classical scholars agree that it is indeed Ovid's own mythic invention.[36] The motif in Alcithoë's story of an ultimately destructive denial or repression of erotic energy, which links Hermaphroditus's fate with the fates of Hippolytus, Adonis, Narcissus, and Daphnis (another of the tales mentioned briefly by Alcithoë at the beginning of her discourse—IV. 276-278), also emerges, ironically, in the fate of the Minyades themselves. For Bacchus eventually appears to the three sisters who have defied him and, as terrible proof of his divinity, transforms them into the grotesquely shrivelled forms of bats (IV. 389-415). The presence in Beaumont's second digression of "light-headed

Bacchus" (l. 409), his brow "chaf'd with the bleeding vine" (l. 422), may therefore be seen as a "sportive" yet subtly foreboding allusion to the thematically relevant Ovidian narrative which frames the primary source of *Salmacis and Hermaphroditus*. Beaumont's surface playfulness disguises a complex formal and thematic unity created through the multiple use he makes of the *Metamorphoses*.

In the second digression Beaumont moves even more clearly into full-blown mythological burlesque than he had in the first digression. It is particularly important to note, therefore, that this digression begins with an episode that leads directly back to *Hero and Leander*. The idea for the figure of "light-headed Bacchus" clearly came from Ovid's framing narrative in the *Metamorphoses*, but the model for Bacchus's wooing of Salmacis is Marlowe's account of Mercury's wooing of the country maid, along with a few salient details from the wooing of Hero and Leander themselves:

> The Nymph was taken with his golden hooke:
> Yet she turn'd backe, and would have tript away;
> But *Bacchus* forc't the lovely mayd to stay,
> (ll. 438-440)

> Here blusht the maid,
> And faine she would have gone, but yet she staid.
> *Bacchus* perceiv'd he had o'ercome the lasse,
> And downe he throwes her in the dewy grasse,
> And kist the helplesse Nymph upon the ground,
> And would have stray'd beyond the lawful bound.[37]
> (ll. 455-460)

Just at this enticing moment we are told that Phoebus, whose "glittering eye / Sees all" (ll. 461-462), has been jealously spying on Bacchus and Salmacis. In addition to the fierce passion for Hermaphroditus recounted at the beginning of the poem, Phoebus also bears "an old affection" for Salmacis. When he interrupts the love-making of Bacchus and Salmacis and "gainst her wil . . . sav'd her maiden-head" (l. 468), Bacchus turns for help to Mercury, his old friend and Phoebus's perennial arch-enemy.

Mercury, of course, is Hermaphroditus's father, and his appearance in the second digression balances Venus's appearance in the first. Mercury's presence also signals a turn towards an almost cartoon-like mythological burlesque. He is found "Drinking with theeves and catch-poles on the earth" (l. 472), and when he recalls how successful he had been in tormenting Phoebus in the past—first stealing his cattle and then,

upon being threatened with revenge, stealing his famous arrows as well
(ll. 497-506)—he decides to help Bacchus get his revenge:

> . . . whilst the Sun wonders his Chariot reeles,
> The craftie god had stole away his wheeles,
>   (ll. 523-524)

There are three main points to be made about Beaumont's writing in this
section of the poem. First, although his "sportive Muse" has finally led
him into what can only be described as mythological burlesque, his
relation to Ovid is still playfully comic and not derisive in the manner of
later seventeenth-century *Ovides travestis*. Secondly, the kind of mythological burlesque developed in the account of Mercury's theft of
Phoebus's chariot wheels evolves directly out of Beaumont's emulation of
Marlowe's comic mythological inventions. Beaumont's comic burlesque
is subject to more sustained narrative elaboration than Marlowe's, but it is
no more extravagantly playful in conception than, for example, the
account of Cupid's response to Hero's weeping with the pain of love:

> And as she wept, her tears to pearl he turn'd,
> And wound them on his arm, and for her mourn'd.
>   (I. 375-376)

Thirdly, even at his most whimsical, Beaumont's concern for formal
integrity remains firm, and he continues to tie his digressive elaborations
to the main narrative with virtuoso inventiveness: Phoebus retaliates
against Bacchus and Mercury by asking Salmacis to help him recover his
wheels, promising her as a reward that "she should enjoy / The heavenly
sight of the most beauteous boy / That ever was . . ." (ll. 537-539). The
particular way in which the etiological function of the digression is
completed has been carefully prepared for by the earlier account of
Phoebus's passion for Hermaphroditus.

One further point about Beaumont's excursions into mythological
burlesque may be made with reference to the final section of the second
digression: the sheer fun of writing in this vein could present a danger for
the fluently gifted poetic virtuoso. Even a sympathetic reader may find his
attention flagging somewhat as the vignette about Phoebus's wheels is
spun out for another seventy lines or so. It is not that Beaumont loses
sight of his major themes, or that he ceases to be concerned with formal
integration. He continues to dramatize the idea of cosmic erotic disorder
by reworking some of the familiar loves of the gods into comically
original etiologies (Jove's "treble night" of love with Alcmena occurred,

we are told, while Phoebus's wheels were "amending," ll. 566–572). But the initial burlesque motif begins to wear thin and fails to provide an adequate narrative line for the subsidiary mythological wit Beaumont tries to work in. It is as if a Marlovian conceit had been prolonged beyond the limits of its capacity to surprise and amuse.

Despite this falling off towards the end of the second digression, Beaumont's two extended additions to Ovid's narrative are among the most fertile creations of the Elizabethan epyllion. And their interest lies, as we have seen, as much in their connections back to Marlowe as in their anticipation of the mythological burlesques and travesties which will come to predominate in later seventeenth-century mythological poetry. One aspect of Beaumont's indebtedness to Marlowe which is central to his success in the digressions, and indeed throughout the poem, is his ability to handle the Marlovian couplet with far greater assurance and resourcefulness than Weever. In the opening lines of *Salmacis and Hermaphroditus* the narrator asks Venus to

> Commaund the god of Love that little King,
> To give each verse a sleight touch with his wing,
> That as I write, one line may draw the tother,
> And every word skip nimbly o're another.[38]
>
> (ll. 9–12)

This request itself demonstrates the self-conscious fluency and facility of much of Beaumont's couplet writing. But fluency and facility are not ends in themselves: what one admires is Beaumont's ability to vary his couplets and adapt them to the pressures of the narrative moment. When extraordinary fluency is appropriate, as in the introduction of "Swift Mercury" in the second digression, Beaumont's own metaphor of "melting" ("That every Lovers eye may melt a line," l. 8) aptly suggests the way in which the phrases and clauses flow through an extended period without the slightest impediment from metrical requirements or rhyme. Notice, however, the modulation to a more angular cadence as attention shifts to Mercury's "acute wit":

> The quaint-tongu'd issue of great *Atlas* race,
> Swift *Mercury*, that with delightfull grace,
> And pleasing accents of his fayned tongue,
> Hath oft reform'd a rude uncivill throng
> Of mortals; that great messenger of *Jove*,
> And all the meaner gods that dwell above:
> He whose acute wit was so quicke and sharpe
> In the invention of the crooked Harpe:
>
> (ll. 485–492)

In the more overtly comic and dramatic moments, Beaumont varies his couplet technique to take advantage of dislocated syntax and of abrupt colloquial phrasing:

> But a faire Nymph was bathing when he wak'd,
> (Here sigh'd great *Jove*, and after brought forth) nak'd,
> (ll. 245–246)

> In limpt the Blacke-smith, after stept his Queene,
> Whose light arrayment was of lovely greene.
> (ll. 325–326)

There are stylistic flaws in *Salmacis and Hermaphroditus* of the kind one might expect from an eighteen-year-old poet: the overworked resumptives "which" and "which when," for example; the occasional weak or forced rhyme.[39] But on the whole the writing is inventive, supple, and deftly controlled. It is the consistently high level of verbal imagination, along with the comic resourcefulness and the intricate but unobtrusive ties to the main narrative, which make Beaumont's two digressions more than simply occasions for indulging a "sportive Muse."

The scene for the meeting of Salmacis and Hermaphroditus is set in the brief return to the main narrative between the two digressions. There, in a passage which recalls the symbolism at the end of Shakespeare's epyllion of Venus plucking and coveting the flower which has sprung from Adonis's blood, we observe Salmacis as she is rewarded with her first "heavenly sight" (l. 538) of Hermaphroditus:

> Sometimes by her owne fountaine as she walkes,
> She nips the flowres from off the fertile stalkes,
> And with a garland of the sweating vine,
> Sometimes she doth her beauteous front in-twine:
> But she was gathering flowres with her white hand,
> When she beheld *Hermaphroditus* stand
> By her cleare fountaine, . . .
> (ll. 391–397)

We return to this scene at line 625 after having been shown in the second digression that the meeting of Salmacis and Hermaphroditus is, paradoxically, both pre-determined and yet ultimately fortuitous. Although Phoebus fulfilled his promise to Salmacis that she "should enjoy / So lovely faire, and such a well shap't boy" by sending "the boy that way, / Where the cleare fountain of the fayre Nymph lay" (ll. 619–624), the agreement arose in the first place from "an uncouth accident of love" (l. 407)—the amorous rivalry of Bacchus and Phoebus. As in *Hero and Leander*, what lesser beings experience as fate and destiny derives ultimately from the machinations of gods and cosmic powers as subject as are mortals to the chaos and irrationality of love. If Salmacis and Hermaphroditus are "crost by the sad starres of nativitie," the poem shows that nativity itself may depend on nothing more than an "accident of love."

In the two hundred lines devoted to Salmacis's wooing of Hermaphroditus (ll. 625–826), Beaumont continues the controlling idea of the opening portraits by forecasting, in detail after detail, the final contradictory yet ironically fitting union of his protagonists:

> Wert thou a mayd, and I a man, Ile show thee,
> With what a manly boldnesse I could woo thee:
> (ll. 715–716)

Not all the forecasts of the eventual merging of Salmacis and Hermaphroditus are as obvious as this. In the most elaborate conceit in this section of the poem, Hermaphroditus is prevented from responding to the beauty of Salmacis when he sees his own even more beautiful image reflected in her eye:

> For long he look'd upon the lovely mayd,
> And at the last *Hermaphroditus* sayd,
> How should I love thee, when I doe espie
> A farre more beauteous nymph hid in thy eye?
> When thou doost love, let not that Nymph be nie thee;
> Nor when thou woo'st, let the same Nymph be by thee:
> Or quite obscure her from thy lovers face,
> Or hide her beauty in a darker place.[40]
> (ll. 689–696)

This passage must be seen within the context of Beaumont's sequential development of the convergence of the myth of Salmacis and Hermaphroditus with that of Narcissus.[41] We have already learned that Salmacis's fountain is the very place where Narcissus died out of frustrated self-love (ll. 399–402) and where she narcissistically admires her own image (ll. 382–386). Now, by reflecting Hermaphroditus's image back to him and thus undermining the power of her own beauty, Salmacis is placed in a position simultaneously analogous to Narcissus's pool (on which

metaphorical level Hermaphroditus takes over Salmacis's role as
Narcissus) and to Echo, Narcissus's spurned lover. By metaphorical
implication, then, she becomes an agent both of Hermaphroditus's
destruction and of her own frustration. The irony is further complicated a
few lines later when Salmacis makes the parallel with the Narcissus myth
explicit but shows herself to be aware only of Hermaphroditus's
involvement in the analogy, and not of her own:

> Remember how the gods punisht that boy
> That scorn'd to let a beauteous Nymph enjoy
> Her long wisht pleasure; for the peevish elfe,
> Lov'd of all others, needs would love himselfe.[42]
>
> (ll. 703-706)

Other features of the conceit in lines 689-696 also look forward to the
final sexual merging. Hermaphroditus, like Edwards' Narcissus, interprets his reflected image as that of a nymph, and he sees that image in the
eye of Salmacis—both details anticipate Hermaphroditus's eventual
effeminization and physical union with Salmacis. And Hermaphroditus's
concluding advice to Salmacis, that she hide the beauty which is
diminishing her own "in a darker place," hints at the dark and disturbing
aspect of the final alteration of his beauty in the strange union in the pool.

Having failed to win Hermaphroditus with her verbal and physical
blandishments, Salmacis pretends to go away but instead hides near her
pool. The poem's ambiguous symbolism of water and bathing culminates
in the account which follows of Hermaphroditus's dive into the pool.
One pattern of emphasis encourages the reader to see the scene as an
entirely innocent display of youthful energy:

> He then supposing he was all alone,
> (Like a young boy that is espy'd of none)
> Runnes here, and there . . .
>
> (ll. 827-829)

The imagery of whiteness which pervades the poem—of skin described in
terms of ivory, snow, lilies—is especially conspicuous here and lends
support to the purity and innocence of the experience from Hermaphroditus's point of view. But there is another, more powerful perspective
operating in the scene which charges the most innocent gesture with
erotic significance:

> Then with his foote he toucht the silver streames,
> Whose drowzy waves made musike in their dreames,
> And, for he was not wholy in, did weepe,
> Talking alowd and babbling in their sleepe:
> Whose pleasant coolenesse when the boy did feele,
> He thrust his foote downe lower to the heele:
>
> (ll. 831-836)

The sexual suggestiveness of Hermaphroditus's apparently innocent bathing could hardly be made more emphatic. The entire scene is strongly reminiscent of the scene in Chapter 11, Book II of Sidney's *New Arcadia*, where the nude bathing of Pamela and Philoclea arouses the river, "cold Ladon," as violently as it does the disguised Pyrocles.[43] In Beaumont's poem not only the water but the sun (ll. 839-842) and the moon (ll. 843-850) respond erotically to Hermaphroditus, as if the entire physical universe were conspiring against his chastity. And Salmacis, watching Hermaphroditus from her hiding place, is "almost mad" and "scarce her selfe contaynes" (l. 858). Hermaphroditus's final gesture before he dives into the water, an epitome of the way in which the scene has transformed innocent exercise into tantalizing eroticism, is certain to overcome any lingering restraint Salmacis might feel:

> . . . young *Hermaphroditus* as he stands,
> Clapping his white side with his hollow hands,
> Leapt lively from the land, . . .
>
> (ll. 859-861)

This final gesture is taken over directly from Ovid and is an indication of the extent to which Beaumont's scene may be understood as a consistent elaboration of the more condensed ambivalence of the scene in the *Metamorphoses*.[44]

In a passage echoing details from the description of Hermaphroditus's dive, Salmacis casts "her light garments . . . from off her skin" and "so leapt lively in" (ll. 867-868).[45] The conclusion of the narrative extends Beaumont's commitment to retell Ovid's episode in a way which is both true to the complexity of the original and yet cleverly free and "sportive." Beaumont alters the tone and even some of the details of Ovid's ambivalent conclusion, but in so doing he creates his own highly sophisticated version of the ironic contradictoriness which is at the heart of the episode in the *Metamorphoses*. In describing Salmacis's love-making, for example, Ovid combines some of the most overtly erotic

writing in the *Metamorphoses* (IV. 358-360)[46] with three similes, two of
them surprisingly savage and grotesque: Salmacis's embrace is compared
to a serpent whose coils entangle and entrap an attacking eagle (IV. 362-
364), to ivy which twines itself around the trunks of trees (IV. 365), and to
"the sea-polyp" which "holds its enemy caught beneath the sea, its
tentacles embracing him on every side" (IV. 366-367). Beaumont is less
graphic than Ovid in his description of Salmacis's love-making, a clear
indication that he was not interested in any crudely obvious exploitation
of the sensationalistic possibilities of his subject. And he adopts only the
second of Ovid's three similes, thus reducing the explicit savagery which
Ovid associates with Salmacis's embraces. But just as Lodge eliminated
certain grotesque details from Ovid's account of Scylla's metamorphosis
in order to focus on another range of irony,[47] so Beaumont tones down the
savagery of Salmacis's love, and gives her a long speech of very
conventional erotic persuasion (ll. 875-894), in order to draw attention to
the ironic implications of her union with Hermaphroditus. For the point
about Salmacis's prayer is that it is not a conscious request to be joined
physically to Hermaphroditus, but rather a conventional lover's hyperbole which the gods interpret in a grotesquely literal way:

> So graunt, just gods, that never day may see,
> The separation twixt this boy and mee.
> The gods did heare her pray'r and feele her woe;
> And in one body they began to grow.
>
> (ll. 899-902)

As this passage continues, it becomes increasingly apparent that
Beaumont sees the union of Salmacis and her lover as a gruesome parody
of the traditional language of love-poetry:

> She felt his youthfull bloud in every vaine;
> And he felt hers warme his cold brest againe.
> And ever since was womans love so blest,
> That it will draw bloud from the strongest brest.
>
> (ll. 903-906)

Beaumont has not eliminated the darker element in Ovid's account. He
has, however, re-projected it as a grotesque subversion of the poetic cliché
in which lovers melt into a single being. If Lodge's irony at the end of
Glaucus and Scilla was generated at the expense of the Petrarchan lover
and his cold, unrelenting mistress, Beaumont's irony reflects upon those
lovers who, like Spenser's Scudamour and Amoret, are imaged as having

"growne together quite." The particular kind of ironic literary self-consciousness characteristic of the Elizabethan epyllion from the beginning transforms but does not dissipate the haunting ambivalence of Ovid's episodes.

Beaumont also takes a playfully subversive approach to Hermaphroditus's prayer to the gods that his fate be shared by anyone who enters the pool. In a plea recalling most of the principal figures of the two digressions (Mercury, Venus, Vulcan, Phoebus) and thus reminding us of the irrationality of the powers who control the fate of this "lucklesse payre," Hermaphroditus asks that his "latest breath be blest" (1. 913) and that whoever enters the pool

> May nevermore a manly shape retaine,
> But halfe a virgine may returne againe.
> (ll. 917–918)

Readers familiar with Ovid's Latin have wondered about Beaumont's "halfe a virgine," since it looks at first like a mistranslation of Ovid's "semivir" ("half-man," IV. 386). But surely the change is a deliberately ambiguous maneuver, designed to point simultaneously to the ironic effeminization of this youth whose former androgynous beauty could hardly be described as a "manly shape," and to the incomplete spoiling of Hermaphroditus's sexual purity in a union which begins as a lustful embrace but which makes genuine sexual consummation impossible. Hermaphroditus is now "halfe a virgine" in both senses of the phrase.

A second key to Beaumont's subversive irony here at the end is the word "blest"—"Let your poore offsprings latest breath be blest" (1. 913). Hallett Smith has argued that in Beaumont's poem "the original theme that the effeminizing quality of the spring was something dreadful and unfortunate is glossed over,"[48] and on one level this is indeed the case. Beaumont actually appears to celebrate the effeminizing power of the spring in direct contradiction to the traditional moralized interpretation of the tale:

> His parents hark'ned to his last request,
> And with that great power they the fountaine blest.
> (ll. 919–920)

A moment's reflection on the word "blest," however, will reveal that Beaumont's final presentation of the union in the pool is ambivalent in a way which recalls those late-classical statues of the sleeping hermaphrodite, ideally beautiful because they are posed so as to conceal an essentially monstrous physical reality [Fig. 14]. Beaumont has in fact given the reader good reason to be suspicious of the word "blest," for it was applied with repeated satirical irony to Astraea's sanctioning of Jove's lustful bargain with Salmacis:

> *Jove* onely thankt her, and beganne to show
> His cause of comming . . .
> Telling *Astraea*, It might now befall,
> That she might make him blest, that blesseth all:
> (ll. 229-234)

> He seeing lov'd, the Nymph yet here did rest,
> Where just *Astraea* might make *Jove* be blest,
> (ll. 247-248)

Both digressions have shown that the "blessings" of the gods whom Hermaphroditus calls upon flow from lust and selfishness and have consequences which are at best ambivalent, at worst chaotic and brutal. The charming of the spring satisfies nothing except the impulsive vindictiveness of Hermaphroditus and perpetuates the gods' perversely literal response to Salmacis's prayer. It stands as a final manifestation of the irresponsible sexual whimsy which has dominated the poem. It also adds a disturbing dimension to what might otherwise be read simply as a clever young poet's parting sally against the received moralized interpretations of Ovid's episode. Beaumont's conclusion recapitulates the tension established in the opening address to the reader between the witty celebration of Hermaphroditism ("I hope my Poeme is so lively writ, / That thou wilt turne half-mayd with reading it") and the lament for "a lucklesse payre, / Whose spotlesse soules now in one body be."

Conclusion

The Epyllion and the Poetry of the 1590s—Alternatives to the Spenserian Synthesis

❧

The central argument of this study has been that at its best the Elizabethan epyllion encourages not a frivolous and merely entertaining escape into erotic fantasy, but rather an awareness, often through a witty or comic perspective, of the turbulence and contradiction in erotic experience. I have also argued that the main expressive concerns of the epyllion are deeply characteristic of the final and most productive decade of Elizabethan poetry. The simple fact that Spenser's *Faerie Queene* was published in the 1590s—Books I-III in 1590, Books IV-VI in 1596— suggests that one appropriate way of concluding these arguments would be to review the claims I have made for the epyllion in the context of what we can all agree is the culminating achievement of Elizabethan literature.

The possibility of a significant interplay between Spenser's great poem and the epyllia of Shakespeare, Marlowe, and their contemporaries has been explored only briefly in previous studies: in Paul Alpers' brilliant formal comparison of the "dramatic" verse in Marlowe's *Hero and Leander* to Spenser's "undramatic," formulaic verse;[1] in Donald Cheney's suggestion that "Shakespeare, writing his narrative poems in 1592-93 . . . saw *The Faerie Queene* as his principal challenge";[2] and, to shift the terms of the comparison, in Roger Sale's contrast between what he sees as the disruption of Spenser's unified poetic vision in Books V and VI of *The Faerie Queene* and "the shouted triumph of Marlowe's plays and the playful wit of his poem. . . . "[3] Responding to these observations will enable us to extend a contrast suggested recurrently in earlier chapters. In the epyllion there is a self-consciously ironic tendency to heighten the contradictions and tensions inherent in narrative materials adapted from Ovid and a wryly subversive relationship to moral orthodoxy. In the synthesizing poetry of *The Faerie Queene,* on the other

219

hand, contradictions and tensions between different perspectives on experience are relaxed so that they can be reconciled in Spenser's inclusive mythic transformation of what he saw as Christian man's "traditional wisdom about himself."[4]

Recent critics of *The Faerie Queene* have given us a fuller sense of the generosity and complexity of Spenser's poetry by emphasizing his ability to deal with the perplexing diversity of earthly existence, with drives and weaknesses which are no less human because they conflict with that "vertuous and gentle discipline" of which he speaks in the Letter to Raleigh. At the same time, however, these critics have continued to affirm Spenser's commitment to celebrating a traditionally Christian and ideally harmonious universe. Alpers, for instance, shows how Spenser's sensitivity to "the realities of human psychology" and to "moral understanding" or "awareness" rather than "moral judgment" allows him "to treat the elements of a complex moral case as distinct and self-contained moral perspectives," "to see all around a complex issue" without narrowing the reader's experience to a matter of enforced decision.[5] Yet the flexibility and openness of Spenser's manner serve ultimately to secure a harmonious reconciliation among kinds of experience which the poet and his readers have traditionally valued. The "major issue" in Book III is still, for Alpers, "the compatibility of sexual desire and spiritual value in human love."[6] In Book VI "the conflict between active knighthood and pastoral retirement is . . . presented in a way that shows the attractiveness of pastoral ease" as well as "the problem of choosing between it and heroic action."[7] The very conduct of the verse in Book VI allows us "to have our pastoralism both ways,"[8] to see the virtue as well as the danger in pastoral delight and retirement without insisting that we choose one perspective or the other. Alpers' view of Faerie Land is more, not less, inclusive for the "psychological" complexity he finds represented there.

Roger Sale's reading of *The Faerie Queene*, particularly in the ways it diverges from Alpers', carries even more interesting implications for the thesis that the Elizabethan epyllion is a significant poetic alternative of the 1590s. More emphatically than Alpers, Sale affirms the confident, synthesizing inclusiveness of Spenser's imagination. As an essentially "undramatic work," *The Faerie Queene* "emphasizes likenesses, usually harmonies."[9] Spenser's dominant concern was to "reveal the relation between men and an ordered universe";[10] his "task was . . . not to explore the edge of the unknown, but to embody and make imminent the endless aliveness of his received universe."[11] So far, then, Sale's reading follows Alpers' in establishing a contrast between Spenserian synthesis and the Ovidian irony and dissonance of the epyllion. But for Sale, Spenser's deepest poetic powers and commitments reveal themselves primarily, or most successfully, in the first three Books of *The Faerie Queene*, published in 1590 and written during the 1580s, and in parts of Book IV, much of which was also probably written by 1590. In the years between 1590 and 1596, Sale argues, something "happened" to Spenser and to his poem. New elements of strain manifest themselves in Book V, where Spenser's preoccupation with harsh political reality leads eventually to the brutality of Talus, "Artegall's one-man police force,"[12] and in Book VI, where retreat into pastoral retirement becomes the only way of sustaining integrity in a world ravaged by the Blatant Beast. Without going into Sale's biographical and historical speculations about "what happened to *The Faerie Queene*," we may consider his summary judgment of the poetic consequences: "Faerie Land no longer exists as a viable way to describe the moral nature of action in a harmonious universe; it is now a part of a larger, fragmented, dramatic way of seeing."[13]

It should already be apparent that the movement Sale traces in Spenser towards a more disturbed and fragmented poetic vision has something to do with the movement we have traced in the epyllion from the Ovidian ambivalence of Shakespeare and Marlowe to the heightened tendency towards satire and parody in the poems of Marston, Weever, and Beaumont. When Sale locates a "new, marring, and troubling" "impulse to satire" in Spenser's "dour" contrast between the antique world and the present in the Proem to Book V,[14] he connects Spenser with that same impulse which runs throughout the epyllia of the 1590s and becomes dominant around the turn of the century. Following out these parallels ultimately confirms, however, a basic contrast between Spenser and the Ovidian poets. Whatever the deep-lying causes of the cultural and literary instability of the 1590s, its consequences were quite different for *The Faerie Queen* than for the epyllion. Spenser's poem was grounded in his confidence in an ultimately harmonious, ordered universe where, ideally, "we need feel no split between the sensual and the moral. . . . "[15] It was inevitable that Spenser's synthesizing inclusiveness would be threatened, fragmented, and narrowed by the historical and literary pressures of the 1590s. Lodge, Shakespeare, and Marlowe began with less commitment—personal and poetic—to order, harmony, and tradition. For one thing, they were younger and more directly involved in those aspects of life in London where the historical and literary circumstances we have noted were concentrated. But more importantly, as authors of epyllia they drew their inspiration from the poetic world of Ovid, a world founded upon sophisticated irony as the inevitable response not only to change, but to the violence, disorder, and contradictoriness of experience. Thus, during the years when Spenser was striving, at times unsuccessfully, to accommodate his sense of the turbulence of life within *The Faerie Queene,* Shakespeare and Marlowe were writing poems filled from their conception with an awareness of that turbulence. The "impulse to satire" reflected in later epyllia exaggerates and in some respects impoverishes the Ovidian ambivalence of Shakespeare and Marlowe, but it does not contradict and threaten their poems in the way that the unity of Books I-IV of *The Faerie Queene* is contradicted and threatened by the dissonance and "impulse to satire" Sale discovers in Books V and VI.

The sense in which Alpers' and Sale's readings support the contrast I have been developing between *The Faerie Queene* and the epyllion could be extended in terms of the conclusions of other recent critics. But it might be more useful at this point to look at two or three instances where Spenser and the authors of epyllia draw upon the same Ovidian source and deal in distinctly different ways with the realities which these sources suggest. Although Spenser's Garden of Adonis has been commented on at great length, the fundamental difference between his adaptation of the myth of Venus and Adonis and Shakespeare's has never been clearly brought out. This difference is especially apparent in the two poets' relationship to Ovid's handling of the myth in Book X of the *Metamorphoses.* Ovid, as we have seen, places a delicate but unrelieved tragic emphasis on the fact that at the end of the episode the most beautiful of mortals has been taken away from Venus. Venus herself sees the enduring monument ("monimenta manebunt/semper") which she causes to spring up from Adonis's blood not as the reappearance of Adonis, but as "an imitation of my grief" ("plangoris . . . simulamina nostri") (X. 725–727). And in the magnificent concluding lines of Book X this enduring monument is itself shown to be short-lived, doomed as beautiful flowers are to be shaken from their stalks by the wind and destroyed. In Spenser's climactic adaptation of the myth, much of Ovid's poignant irony disappears: Adonis's mortal fictional identity as Venus's lover merges into his supernatural mythic identity as a nature god who dies and is reborn in a seasonal cycle:

> There wont faire *Venus* often to enjoy
>   Her deare *Adonis* joyous company,
>   And reape sweet pleasure of the wanton boy;
> There yet, some say, in secret he does ly,
>   Lapped in flowres and pretious spycery,
>   By her hid from the world, and from the skill
> Of *Stygian* Gods, which doe her love envy;

> But she her selfe, when ever that she will,
> Possesseth him, and of his sweetnesse takes her fill.

> And sooth it seemes they say: for he may not
>   For ever die, and ever buried bee
>   In balefull night, where all things are forgot;
>   All be he subject to mortalitie,
>   Yet is eterne in mutabilitie,
>   And by succession made perpetuall,
>   Transformed oft, and changed diverslie:
>   For him the Father of all formes they call;
> Therefore needs mote he live, that living gives to all.
>   (III.vi.46–47)

Spenser's poetic interests are simply different from Ovid's—whatever gains in mythic breadth and resonance one finds in Spenser's adaptation have to be set against the loss of precisely those elements which make Ovid's episode so moving. The phrases "some say" (st. 46, l. 4) and "it seemes they say" (st. 47, l. 1) do more than "remind us," as Alpers has observed, "that the myth is a creation of many men and has taken on a life of its own, independent of, but still obviously capable of nourishing, an individual poet."[16] They also suggest a strategic tentativeness and humility on Spenser's part in taking up a view of the myth which draws its ultimate authority and justification from a conceptual premise rather than from the immediate human ramifications of the story, from what Adonis *represents* rather than from what he *is* to Venus:

> For him the Father of all formes they call;
> Therefore needs mote he live, that living gives to all.

The mythopoeic logic by which Spenser plays down the tragedy and loss of the story runs directly counter to Shakespeare's approach in his epyllion, where the logical consequences of Adonis's identity are reversed:

> For he being dead, with him is Beauty slain,
> And, Beauty dead, black Chaos comes again.
>   (ll. 1019–1020)

Shakespeare's fidelity to Ovid is inseparable from his preoccupation with the tragic contradiction between love and beauty inherent in his view of the myth. In Spenser's "joyous Paradize" (III.vi.29.1) Venus and Adonis still enjoy each other as they always have; in the tangled, steamy wood of

Shakespeare's poem Venus and Adonis have never enjoyed each other, a reality we are ironically reminded of in Venus's final gesture of plucking and smothering the flower which has sprung from Adonis's blood before she flies away "through the empty skies" (l. 1191).

It is not that Spenser was unaware of the expressive dimensions of Ovid's episode. His earlier appropriation of the Venus and Adonis story in the description of Malecasta's tapestries (III.i.34-38) is much closer to Ovid and emphasizes the very features of the story which are suppressed in Canto vi. But both the context and the internal articulation of these Venus and Adonis scenes in Castle Joyous reinforce our sense of how different Spenser's ultimate interest in the myth is from Ovid's and from Shakespeare's. By making Venus's rapturous enjoyment and unrelieved loss of Adonis the central decoration in a chamber of "superfluous riotize" (st. 33), "untimely ease" (st. 39), and "lascivious disport" (st. 40), Spenser places his Ovidian version of the myth in a moral framework which does not cancel out but certainly qualifies our valuing of that version. If the pathos of the tapestry scenes complicates our response to Castle Joyous, Spenser's presentation of the castle exerts a control over our response to the tapestries. Like Shakespeare, Spenser is alert to the ironic possibilities of Venus's causing a flower to spring from Adonis's blood. But he uses the irony not so much to deepen our sense of the desperation of Venus's loss, as Shakespeare does, as to make us aware that in Malecasta's tapestries, in contrast to the Garden of Adonis, such consolation is in part an artificially achieved illusion:[17]

> But when she saw no helpe might him restore,
> Him to a dainty flowre she did transmew,
> Which in that cloth was wrought, as if it lively grew.
>   (III.i.38.7-9)

One might add that Spenser's "Ovidian" perspective on the myth takes him even further from Shakespeare's epyllion since, as we observed in Chapter III, he stresses the very feature of the episode which Shakespeare so significantly reverses in pointing up the muted conflicts of Ovid's version—the joyful erotic bliss of "Venus and her Paramoure" (III.i.34.4).

A similar contrast emerges when we set Spenser's interest in Ovid's tale of Salmacis and Hermaphroditus beside that of Beaumont. More than any other Elizabethan poet, Spenser draws upon the complex tradition of hermaphroditic symbolism which we examined briefly in the last chapter, and he makes repeated but highly selective use of Ovid's episode itself. The fountain from which the Red Cross Knight drinks before he is defeated by Orgoglio in Canto vii of Book I is a variation on the fountain of Salmacis:

11. Johannes Sambucus, "In sponsalia Johannes Ambii Angli & Albae Rolleae D. Arnoldi Medici Gandavensis filiae" (woodcut). *Emblemata*, Antwerp, 1564, p. 124.

12. Nicholas Reusner, "Amor Conjugalis" (woodcut). *Aureolorum Emblematum*, Strasburg, 1587, Emblema 50, sig. D 1^V. Photo British Museum.

> Thenceforth her waters waxed dull and slow,
> And all that drunke thereof, did faint and feeble grow.[18]
>
> (I.vii.5.8-9)

The Venus and Adonis scenes in the tapestries of Malecasta's castle contain a key motif borrowed from Ovid's Salmacis and Hermaphroditus episode:

> And whilest he bath'd, with her two crafty spyes,
> She secretly would search each daintie lim,[19]
>
> (III.i.36.5-6)

The original conclusion of Book III presents the final embrace of Amoret and Scudamour in terms of the figure of the hermaphrodite as a conventional metaphor for the ideal union of complementary selves:

> Had ye them seene, ye would have surely thought,
> That they had beene that faire *Hermaphrodite,*
>
> (III.xii.46.1-2)

And finally, in Book IV, when Scudamour visits the Temple of Venus and describes the veiled statue of the goddess he finds there, we see Spenser drawing upon the symbolic tradition of the hermaphroditic Venus, the *Venus biformis,* whose identity includes complete sexual self-sufficiency:

> The cause why she was covered with a vele,
>   Was hard to know, for that her Priests the same
>   From peoples knowledge labour'd to concele.
>   But sooth it was not sure for womanish shame,
>   Nor any blemish, which the worke mote blame;
>   But for, they say, she hath both kinds in one,
>   Both male and female, both under one name:
>   She syre and mother is of her selfe alone,
> Begets and eke conceives, ne needeth other none.[20]
>
> (IV.x.41)

With the possible exception of the cancelled conclusion to the 1590 version of Book III, the thematic function of each of these appropriations of hermaphroditic myth and symbolism is clear. And the remarkable thing is the way Spenser lets the reader know that he is aware of the erotic sensationalism associated with the hermaphrodite while at the same time placing that awareness within a pervasively sustained moral or philosophical perspective. In Book IV, for instance, when he almost coyly has Scudamour emphasize that the reason for the statue's veil "was not sure for womanish shame," he moves close, if only for an instant, to the sort of piquant interest in the hermaphrodite exploited in Antonio Becadelli's notorious *Hermaphroditus* (1426). In fact the wit of "But sooth it was not sure for womanish shame" has the effect of obviating any humor that might undermine the serious import of the symbolic description of the statue. But what one does not get in this or in any of the other allusions to the myth of the hermaphrodite in *The Faerie Queene* is an evocation of the troubling pathos of Ovid's episode.

This is true even of the stanzas in the 1590 conclusion to Book III. As Cheney has argued, Spenser's account of the embrace of Scudamour and Amoret is ambiguous—perhaps deliberately so.[21] The narrator first assures us that

> No word they spake, nor earthly thing they felt,
> But like two senceles stocks in long embracement dwelt.
> (III.xii.45.8-9)

But in the stanza which follows, where the reference to "that faire *Hermaphrodite*" appears, the verse encourages a different range of associations:

> Had ye them seene, ye would have surely thought,
> That they had beene that faire *Hermaphrodite*,
> Which that rich *Romane* of white marble wrought,
> And in his costly Bath causd to bee site:
> So seemd those two, as growne together quite,
> (III.xii.46.1-5)

The language at the end of both stanzas 45 and 46 recalls those sixteenth-century emblems in which the hermaphrodite appears as an embodiment of sacred married love [Figs. 11 & 12].[22] The phrases "two senceles stocks" and "growne together quite" recall specifically the emblem entitled *Matrimonii Typus* in Aneau's *Picta Poesis* (1552), where the bodies of two embracing lovers merge to form the trunk of a tree which branches out over their heads [Fig. 8].[23] But the striking allusion in stanza 46 to "that faire *Hermaphrodite*, / Which that rich *Romane* of white marble wrought" evokes those late antique statues of the hermaphrodite which delighted the worldly and sophisticated Renaissance collector much as they had the Roman and Hellenistic patrons for whom they were originally carved [Fig. 14].[24]

Cheney's suggestion that Spenser was using the ambiguous allusion to the Hermaphrodite in the 1590 version of *The Faerie Queene* "to call

13. Nicholas Reusner, "Forma viros neglecta decet" (woodcut). *Emblemata*, Frankfurt, 1581, p. 136.

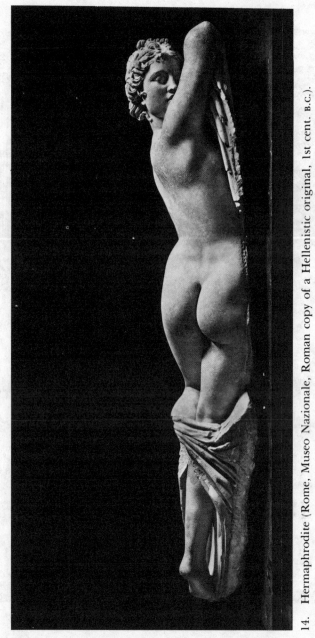

14. Hermaphrodite (Rome, Museo Nazionale, Roman copy of a Hellenistic original, 1st cent. B.C.).

Photo Alinari.

attention to apparent contradictions in celebrating sexual union within the context of a Book devoted to chastity"[25] is well-taken. Certainly Spenser's shift from the initial perception of the unearthliness of the embrace to the subsequent emphasis on how that embrace might look to an observer—"Had ye them seene"—supports such a suggestion. But Cheney's further argument, that Ovid's episode of Salmacis and Hermaphroditus is the "most pervasive source" for Spenser's original conclusion to Book III and that "Spenser's stanzas provide an extraordinarily rich and felicitous recapitulation of Ovid's story,"[26] may not be warranted by the details of the passage. Spenser does not allude to Salmacis or Hermaphroditus by name, and there is no evocation of the secluded forest pool which provides the crucial setting for their encounter in the *Metamorphoses*. More importantly, the struggle between the bashful, love-hating Hermaphroditus and the lascivious Salmacis stands in sharp antithesis to the mutual passion of Scudamour and Amoret. Spenser would certainly have known what we observed in the last chapter, that in contrast to the consistently positive meanings invested in the hermaphrodite itself, the prevailing sixteenth-century interpretations of Ovid's story were negative. Aneau uses one type of hermaphroditic figure with no explicit connection to Ovid's story as an image of *Matrimonii Typus*, and another, quite different woodcut showing Hermaphroditus trying to flee from the clutches of a lustful Salmacis [Fig. 10] to illustrate the motto "Fons Salmacidos, Libido Effoeminans."[27] Ovid's story presented complications which were not to Spenser's purpose and carried moral associations which were irrelevant to his celebration of the love of Scudamour and Amoret, even though their love (or our perception of it) may be otherwise qualified by the allusion to the Roman statue of the hermaphrodite. Spenser deals selectively with the myth of Salmacis and Hermaphroditus in *The Faerie Queene*, much as he deals selectively with the myth of Venus and Adonis. In both cases he depends upon our willingness to attend faithfully to what the verse tells us about these myths and not to insist upon aspects of Ovid's episodes which lie outside his meaning. And it is precisely those aspects that are given emphasis in the epyllia of Shakespeare and Beaumont.

I have argued throughout this study that the authors of Elizabethan epyllia involve us, often with a witty subversiveness, in those disturbing but hauntingly expressive dimensions of Ovid's episodes which earlier writers, committed to the traditional moral and allegorical view of the *Metamorphoses*, either had to reject completely or present as images of sin and vice. Those aspects of Ovid's poetry most important to the epyllion are also suppressed, restricted, or morally "placed" in Spenser's poetry, even though Spenser's appropriations from Ovid constitute a major demonstration of his synthesizing mythopoeic imagination.[28] I am not of course claiming that the achievement of the epyllion is comparable overall to *The Faerie Queene*. Spenser reaches out to a vast range of value and experience which is never touched upon in the epyllion. It is in dealing with human sexuality that the Ovidian poets offer something more than piquant entertainment—though they offer that as well—to challenge Spenser's vision of the "glorious fire" of love ideally realized in the creative chastity of marriage.[29] But it is not too much to claim, I think, that the epyllion—along with Shakespeare's plays and sonnets of the 1590s, Donne's earliest lyrics, and the savage satire examined in the preceding chapters—reflects an openness to the turbulence of experience, and to the ironic and dramatic ways in which that turbulence can be expressed, which is deeply important to late Elizabethan and Jacobean literature. Recognizing that Spenser's poetry, for all its generous inclusiveness, does not completely satisfy the need to find an artistic way of valuing the compelling, irreducible disorder of erotic experience can help us see the significance of poetry which, largely because of its attentiveness to the example of Ovid, does.

Notes and Index

Notes

CHAPTER I

1. William S. Anderson, in *The American Journal of Philology*, 89 (1968), 93. Anderson goes on to say that the difficulty posed by the *Metamorphoses* is only in part that of assessing Ovid's tone—that basic questions about narrative and thematic structure also remain unanswered.

2. "Chapman's 'Hero and Leander,'" *English Miscellany*, ed. Mario Praz, V (1954), 41: "Certainly 'Ovid' and 'Ovidian' have been used in too simple ways about Elizabethan poems."

3. See Beaumont's *Salmacis and Hermaphroditus*, "The Author to the Reader."

4. See Hermann Fränkel, *Ovid: A Poet Between Two Worlds* (Berkeley, 1945), pp. 17-18; L. P. Wilkinson, *Ovid Surveyed: An Abridgement of Ovid Recalled* (Cambridge, 1962), pp. 85-88; Charles Paul Segal, "Ovid's *Metamorphoses*: Greek Myth in Augustan Rome," *SP*, 68 (1971), 372-380.

5. *The Sense of an Ending* (New York, 1967), pp. 39 ff.

6. See Wilkinson, *Ovid Surveyed*, p. 86.

7. Ibid., p. 90.

8. *Elizabethan and Metaphysical Imagery: Renaissance Poetic and Twentieth Century Critics* (University of Chicago Press, Phoenix paperback, 1965), p. 157.

9. "Venus and Her Nun: Portraits of Women in Love by Shakespeare and Marlowe," *SEL*, 5 (1965), 254.

10. See Segal, "Greek Myth in Augustan Rome," 383.

11. Wilkinson, *Ovid Surveyed*, pp. 67, 112-116.

12. "Lascivia" means, primarily, "sportiveness," "playfulness," but also "wantonness," "lewdness." See Lewis and Short, *A Latin Dictionary* (Oxford, 1969).

13. *Landscape in Ovid's Metamorphoses* (Wiesbaden, 1969), p. 1. See also Hugh Parry, "Ovid's *Metamorphoses*: Violence in a Pastoral Landscape," *Transactions of the American Philological Association*, 95 (1964), 268-282.

14. See William S. Anderson, "Multiple Change in the *Metamorphoses*," *Transactions of the American Philological Association*, 94 (1963), 9.

15. See Segal, "Greek Myth in Augustan Rome," 382.

16. *Landscape in Ovid's Metamorphoses*, p. 1.

17. See Wilkinson, *Ovid Surveyed*, p. 71.

18. Ibid., p. 17.

19. *Ovid as an Epic Poet*, pp. 14, 16.

20. See Wilkinson, *Ovid Surveyed*, p. 51.

21. *Ovid as an Epic Poet*, p. 104.

22. *Ovid Surveyed*, pp. 53-54

23. *Ovid: A Poet Between Two Worlds*, p. 3; Otis, *Ovid as an Epic Poet*, p. 276, n. 1.

24. *Ovid Surveyed*, pp. 94, 95; see also p. 7.

25. Ibid., p. 95.

26. Otis, *Ovid as an Epic Poet*, p. 277; see also pp. 268-272.

27. See Douglas Bush, *Mythology and the Renaissance Tradition in English Poetry*, rev. ed. (New York, 1963), p. 86; Elizabeth Story Donno, "The Epyllion," *English Poetry and Prose 1540-1674*, ed. Christopher Ricks, vol. II in the *Sphere History of Literature in the English Language* (London, 1970), p. 91.

28. *Ovid as an Epic Poet*, pp. 215-230, 325, 327, 330, 352, 365.

29. Ibid., pp. 169, 276.

30. Otis uses this phrase to designate Books VI-XI of the *Metamorphoses* (see Chs. VI and VII of *Ovid as an Epic Poet*).

31. See Wilkinson, *Ovid Surveyed*, p. 37, and Charles Sears Baldwin, *Ancient Rhetoric and Poetic* (Gloucester, Mass., 1959), pp. 71-72.

32. *Ovid as an Epic Poet*, p. xiii.

33. I am referring particularly here to Otis's reading of the *Metamorphoses*. For a concise indication of the distinctions his approach rests upon, see the opening of his first chapter on "The Pathos of Love," *Ovid as an Epic Poet*, pp. 166 ff.

34. Compare Otis, in *Ovid as an Epic Poet*, who argues that the Cephalus and Procris episode, along with the episode of Ceyx and Alcyone, represents "the most adequate instance of Ovid's amatory ideal" (p. 270), "the normal, human, heterosexual love of affianced or married lovers" (p. 272).

35. See *Elizabethan Critical Essays*, ed. G. Gregory Smith (Oxford, 1904), I, 101, 234.

36. *Ovid Surveyed*, pp. 9-13.

37. Ibid., p. 147.

38. *Ovid as an Epic Poet*, pp. 332-333.

39. Ibid., p. 335.

40. Ibid., p. 338.

41. *Coleridge's Writings on Shakespeare*, ed. Terence Hawkes (New York, 1959), p. 61.

42. *Mythology and the Renaissance Tradition*, p. 73.

43. See Hallett Smith, *Elizabethan Poetry: A Study in Conventions, Meaning, and Expression* (Cambridge, Mass., 1952; Reprint ed. 1964), pp. 74-75.

44. See *The Works of Christopher Marlowe*, ed. C. F. Tucker Brooke (Oxford, 1966), p. 554, and Frederick S. Boas, *Christopher Marlowe* (Oxford, 1940), p. 30.

45. For an excellent assessment of the strengths and weaknesses of Marlowe's translation, see Roma Gill, "Snakes Leap by Verse," *Mermaid Critical Commentaries: Christopher Marlowe*, ed. Brian Morris (London, 1969), pp. 135-150.

46. Quotations are from the Penguin edition of *The Poems of Christopher Marlowe*, ed. Stephen Orgel (London, 1971).

47. See Tucker Brooke, *Marlowe*, p. 555. Miss Gill disagrees here and argues that Marlowe's imagination was not always fully engaged in the translation

(*Mermaid Critical Commentaries*, pp. 135, 143); but see Orgel's comment, *Marlowe*, p. 233.

48. See Tucker Brooke, *Marlowe*, p. 553: "Marlowe's translation of the Elegies of Ovid survives in at least six early editions. All are undated and all claim—with probable untruth—to have been printed at Middleburgh in Holland."

49. See Boas, *Marlowe*, pp. 30-31.

50. For the text of the edict, see *A Transcript of the Registers of the Company of Stationers of London*, 1554-1640, ed. Edward Arber (London, 1875), III, 677.

51. See the notes in the editions of Marlowe's poetry edited by L. C. Martin (1931) and by Millar MacLure (1968), and Douglas Bush, "Notes on Marlowe's *Hero and Leander*," *PMLA*, 44 (1929), 760-764.

52. See Boas, *Marlowe*, pp. 31-32 and Gill, *Mermaid Critical Commentaries*, pp. 145-148.

53. "False horns" is Marlowe's translation of "cornua falsa," which appeared in sixteenth-century editions of the *Amores*. Modern texts give the line as "virginea tenuit cornua vara manu"—"she grasped with virgin hand his bended horns" (Loeb Library edition, trans. Showerman, pp. 326-327).

54. See Robert Bell, ed., *The Poems of Robert Greene, Christopher Marlowe, and Ben Jonson* (London, 1889), pp. 8, 18.

55. *The Repentence of Robert Greene* (1592), in vol. XII of *The Life and Complete Works of Robert Greene*, ed. Alexander B. Grosart (London, 1881-1883), p. 172.

56. Quotations are from Bell's edition of Greene's poems, cited above, n. 54.

57. *Greene's Vision* (1593), in *Life and Complete Works*, XII, 274.

58. See *The Heroycall Epistles* ed. Frederick S. Boas (London, 1928). For Turberville's career at Oxford and the Inns of Court, see the *DNB*, LVII (1899), 321.

59. *John Marston of the Middle Temple: An Elizabethan Dramatist in His Social Setting* (Cambridge, Mass., 1969), p. 61.

60. Edward Andrews Tenney, *Thomas Lodge* (Ithaca, N. Y., 1935), p. 64.

61. Thomas Lodge, *Scillaes Metamorphosis: Enterlaced with the unfortunate love of Glaucus* (London, 1590). This is the British Library's copy of the first edition. For a discussion of the 1590 date, see Ch. II, n. 5.

62. Edmund W. Gosse, "Memoir of Thomas Lodge," pp. 3-4 in vol. I of *Works*.

63. See Frederick S. Boas, *Thomas Heywood* (London, 1950), pp. 12-13; Arthur Melville Clark, *Thomas Heywood* (Oxford, 1931), p. 8 and n. 2; and Joseph Quincy Adams, ed., *Oenone and Paris* (Washington, D. C., 1943), p. xxxii.

64. Finkelpearl, *Marston*, p. 86.

65. *DNB*, XX, 1060.

66. *Beaumont the Dramatist: A Portrait* (New York, 1914), p. 26.

67. See Clyde Barnes Cooper, *Some Elizabethan Opinions of the Poetry and Character of Ovid* (Menasha, Wisc., 1914); Leo Rick, *Ovids Metamorphosen in der englischen Renaissance* (Münster, 1915); T. W. Baldwin, *William Shakespere's Small Latine & Lesse Greeke*, 2 vols. (Urbana, Ill., 1944); Davis P. Harding,

Milton and the Renaissance Ovid (Urbana, Ill., 1946); Frederick S. Boas, *Ovid and the Elizabethans* (London, 1947); Douglas Bush, *Mythology and the Renaissance Tradition*, esp. Ch. IV, "Ovid Old and New."

68. The relevance of Elizabethan attacks on and defenses of poetry to the status of Ovid in the late sixteenth century has been stressed by Cooper, *Ovid*, pp. 8 ff., and by Donno, "The Epyllion," *Sphere History*, II, 82–85.

69. Quotations are from *A Reply to Stephen Gosson's Schoole of Abuse in Defence of Musick and Stage Plays* in vol. I of the *Complete Works*. To facilitate the reading of this poorly printed text, I have expanded all abbreviations and modernized the punctuation. The works in the edition are separately paginated; this passage appears on p. 19 of the *Reply*.

70. Ibid., p. 21.

71. Ibid., p. 11.

72. Smith, *Elizabethan Poetry*, p. 76.

73. See J. W. H. Atkins, *English Literary Criticism: The Renaissance*, 2nd ed. (London, 1955), p. 112. For more recent confirmation of the story, which has sometimes been dismissed as apocryphal, see Elizabeth Story Donno's edition of Harington's *The Metamorphosis of Ajax* (London, 1962), p. 4.

74. Quoted from *Ludovico Ariosto's "Orlando Furioso," Translated into English Heroical Verse by Sir John Harington* (1591), ed. Robert McNulty (Oxford, 1972), p. 11. For the "Exact and Necessarie Table," see pp. 579–588 of this edition.

75. *The Kindly Flame: A Study of the Third and Fourth Books of "The Faerie Queene"* (Princeton, 1964), pp. 3–31. See Bush's remark that "Opposed attitudes toward Ovid existed side by side, even within the same mind" (*Mythology and the Renaissance Tradition*, p. 78).

76. See Holofernes' well-known speech on "Ovidius Naso" as "the man . . . for smelling out the odoriferous flowers of fancy, the jerks of invention" in *Love's Labor's Lost* (IV. ii. 119–124). See also T. W. Baldwin's comment on this speech in *Shakespere's Small Latine & Lesse Greeke* (II, 405), which contains the fullest account of Ovid's importance in Elizabethan pedagogy. For briefer accounts of the subject see Wilkinson, *Ovid Surveyed*, pp. 200–201, 211, and R. M. Ogilvie, *Latin and Greek: A History of the Influence of the Classics On English Life from 1600 to 1918* (London, 1964), pp. 1–33.

77. See *Epistolae obscurorum virorum*, trans. Francis Griffin Stokes (London, 1921), p. 343.

78. See *The Five Books of Gargantua and Pantagruel*, trans. Jacques Le Clercq (New York, 1944), p. 5.

79. *Mythology and the Renaissance Tradition*, p. 69, n. 1.

CHAPTER II

1. Bush, *Mythology and the Renaissance Tradition*, p. 81.

2. James P. Reardon, "Shakespeare's *Venus and Adonis* and Lodge's *Scilla's Metamorphosis*," *Shakespeare Society Papers*, III (1847), Art. 16, 143–146.

3. *Landscape in Ovid's Metamorphoses*, p. 93.

4. See Tenney, *Thomas Lodge*, pp. 73, 94–95, 100; Gosse, "Memoir of Thomas Lodge," *Works*, I, 13, 17.

5. See the dedicatory epistle to *Scillaes Metamorphosis* addressed to Lodge's friend, Raphael Crane. Tenney (*Lodge*, p. 100) says that the printer who pirated Lodge's poem was Richard Jones, a figure already notorious for such dishonesty. This seems doubtful, however, since it was Jones who eventually published *Scillaes Metamorphosis*, and it is highly improbable, to say the least, that he would have printed an attack on himself. It is more likely that some other printer got hold of one of a pair of poems (Lodge refers in the dedicatory epistle to a companion piece to "Scilla," "Charybdis") and that before this pirated work reached the press Lodge had Jones publish *Glaucus and Scilla* under his own name, together with the other poems which make up the volume entitled *Scillaes Metamorphosis*. This volume was entered in the Stationers' Register on 22 September 1589, under the title *The history of Glaucus and Scilla* (see Arber, II, 248b). In some copies of the first edition, such as the one in the British Library, the date is changed from 1589 to 1590, possibly because the typography of the title-page was "improved" during the course of the first printing, which extended into 1590. See Alexander, *Elizabethan Narrative Poetry*, p. 317, and Fredson Bowers, *Bibliography and Textual Criticism* (Oxford, 1964), p. 132.

6. *Mythology and the Renaissance Tradition*, p. 81.

7. "The Influence of Thomas Watson on Elizabethan Ovidian Poetry," *Studies in the Renaissance*, 6 (1959), 244–245.

8. See Gosse, "Memoir of Thomas Lodge," *Works*, I, 63–64.

9. See Staton, "Influence of Thomas Watson," 246–248. For an example of the sort of writing Lodge might have found attractive, see ll. 28–38 of "Querela prima" in the edition of Watson's *Amyntas* and Fraunce's English translation, ed. Staton and Franklin M. Dickey (Chicago, 1967).

10. Fraunce's translation first appeared in *The Countesse of Pembrokes Ivychurch Conteining the affectionate life, and unfortunate death of Phillis and Amyntas: That in a Pastorall, This in a Funerall: both in English Hexameters* (London, 1591).

11. See Rufus Putney, "Venus and Adonis: Amour with Humor," *PQ*, 20 (1941), 542–543.

12. See Bush, *Mythology and the Renaissance Tradition*, p. 85, n. 41; Walter F. Staton, Jr., "Ovidian Elements in *A Midsummer Night's Dream*," *HLQ*, 26 (1962–1963), 172.

13. L. E. Kastner, "Thomas Lodge as an Imitator of the French Poets," *The Athenaeum*, No. 4017 (22 October 1904), 552.

14. *Oeuvres de P. de Ronsard*, ed. Charles Marty-Laveaux (Paris, 1889), II, 285–286.

15. See ll. 22–30 of Ronsard's poem; Lodge's references to Glaucus's "hallowed heares" (l. 8), "mossie coat" (l. 11), and "heavy head" (l. 43) correspond to Ronsard's description of Glaucus's "chef de longs cheveux diforme, / Et . . . corps monstrueux. . . . "

16. *English Literature in the Sixteenth Century*, p. 488.

17. Quotations are from *The Complete Works of George Gascoigne*, ed. J. W. Cunliffe, 2 vols. (Cambridge, 1907-1910).

18. M. M. Reese, ed., *Elizabethan Verse Romances* (London, 1968), pp. 3, 14-15.

19. See above, p. 37.

20. *Mythology and the Renaissance Tradition*, p. 86. Bush is quoting V.M. Jeffery, "Italian and English Pastoral Drama of the Renaissance," *MLR*, 19 (1924), 180.

21. See Rudolf B. Gottfried, "Spenser and the Italian Myth of Locality," *SP*, 34 (1937), 107-125.

22. *The Complete Works of Sir Philip Sidney*, ed. Albert Feuillerat (Cambridge, 1912), I, 217: ". . . when cold *Ladon* had once fully imbraced them himselfe was no more cold to those Ladies, but as if his cold complexion had bene heated with love, so seemed he to play about every part he could touch."

23. *Shakespeare and Elizabethan Poetry: A Study of his Earlier Work in Relation to the Poetry of the Time* (Peregrine Books Penguin edition, 1964), pp. 55-56.

24. T. W. Craik, ed., *Sidney: Selected Poetry and Prose* (London, 1965), p. 12. Craik points out that "Ovid's song" in l. 87 probably refers to *Amores* I. iv, where Corinna's naked beauty is praised (p. 233, n.). William A. Ringler, Jr., in his edition of *The Poems of Sir Philip Sidney* (Oxford, 1962), p. 410, comments on the popularity of this poem and notes that Marston and Weever are among the many writers who quoted or imitated it.

25. Quotations are from Ringler's edition.

26. The idea for the ride on the dolphin's back may have come from *Metamorphoses* II. 236-237: "quo saepe venire / frenato delphine sedens, Theti, nuda solebas"—"to which often, riding your bridled dolphin, O Thetis, naked did you used to come" (note that in Lodge's epyllion Glaucus's mother is called Thetis). More generally, the dolphin commonly had amorous associations in the visual arts of the Renaissance and was often depicted with Cupid riding on its back. Glaucus himself alludes to the amorousness of dolphins in ll. 261-263.

27. *Landscape in Ovid's Metamorphoses*, pp. 28-29.

28. Ibid., p. 28.

29. The most detailed examination of Lodge's influence on Shakespeare's *Venus and Adonis* is that of C. Knox Pooler, ed., *Shakespeare's Poems* (London, 1911), pp. xvi-xx.

30. For Ovid's use of the ironically appropriate metamorphosis, see Anderson, "Multiple Change in the Metamorphoses," 4 ff.

31. Reardon (*Shakespeare Society Papers*, III, 145) argued that Lodge was referring here to his having abandoned the theatrical profession, both as author and actor.

32. For the Alciati emblem see the edition of 1550, p. 76. The emblem is entitled "Impudentia" and appears under the general heading "Superbia." E. S. Donno ("Epyllion," *Sphere History*, II, pp. 97-98, n. 8) suggests that Lodge may have been influenced by Ovid's story of Anaxarete, which appears later in Book

XIV of the *Metamorphoses*. Anaxarete was changed into a statue for disdaining her lover; Golding glosses the tale in the "Epistle to Leicester": "The tale of Anaxaretee willes dames of hygh degree / To use their lovers courteously how meane so ere they bee" (ll. 280-281).

CHAPTER III

1. *Venus and Adonis* was entered in the Stationers' Register on 18 April 1593 (Arber, II, 297b). For arguments placing the composition of the poem in late 1592–early 1593, see T. W. Baldwin, *On the Literary Genetics of Shakespeare's Poems and Sonnets* (Urbana, Ill., 1950), p. 45; Prince, ed., *The Poems*, p. xxvi; Muriel Bradbrook, "Beasts and Gods: Greene's *Grotsworth of Witte* and the Social Purpose of *Venus and Adonis*," *Shakespeare Survey*, 15 (1962), 63. Shakespeare had written several plays before *Venus and Adonis*, but of course the writing of plays was not considered a genuine literary achievement in the sixteenth century.

2. Henry Wriothesley, Third Earl of Southampton, was not quite twenty years old when Shakespeare dedicated *Venus and Adonis* to him—yet he had already graduated M.A. at the age of sixteen from St. John's College, Cambridge, and had entered his name as a student at Gray's Inn (1589). For accounts of Southampton's early career and relationship to Shakespeare, of his flamboyant appearance and behavior, and of his literary interests, see *DNB*, XXI, 1055-1061; A. L. Rowse, *Shakespeare's Southampton* (New York, 1965), esp. pp. 54-61; G. P. V. Akrigg, *Shakespeare and the Earl of Southampton* (Cambridge, Mass., 1968), esp. pp. 31 ff. There is little concrete evidence to support Esther Cloudman Dunn's claim in *The Literature of Shakespeare's England* (New York, 1936, p. 39) that Southampton "collected *erotica* as many a later exquisite has done" and that "*Venus and Adonis* was a deliberate contribution to the Earl's *erotica*." It is possible, however, that Thomas Nash wrote *The Choise of Valentines* (1594) for Southampton (see *DNB*, XXI, 1056).

3. The story of Venus and Adonis had been a popular literary subject as early as Sappho and Praxilla in the sixth century B.C. Theocritus had written of the worship of Adonis in his *Idylls*, and Bion's *Lament for Adonis* was one of the best-known Greek poems (Shakespeare seems to have been indebted to Bion for his imagery of contrasting red and white). The best account of Continental adaptations of the myth in the Renaissance is that of Sir Sidney Lee, *Shakespeare's Venus and Adonis* (Oxford, 1905), pp. 22-25.

4. *Coleridge's Writings on Shakespeare*, ed. Hawkes, p. 59.

5. *Mythology and the Renaissance Tradition* (Minneapolis, 1932), p. 149. I quote from the first edition of Bush's book because it was the harsher judgment articulated there that influenced all but the most recent criticism. In the revised edition Bush softens his attack somewhat; the phrase I have quoted becomes: "For a sensual orgy it is too intellectual and serious, for a metaphysical fable it is too Ovidian" (p. 148). My summary of earlier criticism, including my interpretation of the role Bush's argument has played, is indebted to J. W. Lever, "The Poems," *Shakespeare Survey*, 15 (1962), 19-22.

6. The "comic" approach was first argued by Rufus Putney, *"Venus and Adonis*: Amour with Humor," *PQ*, 20 (1941), 534–548 and "Venus Agonistes," *University of Colorado Studies: Series in Language and Literature*, No. 4 (1953), 52–66. A number of subsequent studies have incorporated Putney's extremely valuable perceptions. Moral and allegorical readings have been proposed by Lu Emily Pearson, *Elizabethan Love Conventions* (New York, 1933), p. 285; Franklin M. Dickey, *Not Wisely But Too Well: Shakespeare's Love Tragedies* (San Marino, Cal., 1957), pp. 19–53; R. P. Miller, "Venus, Adonis, and the Horses," *ELH*, 19 (1952), 249–264, and "The Myth of Mars' Hot Minion in 'Venus and Adonis,'" *ELH*, 26 (1959), 470–481; Don Cameron Allen, "On *Venus and Adonis*," *Elizabethan and Jacobean Studies Presented to Frank Percy Wilson*, ed. Herbert Davis and Helen Gardner (Oxford, 1959), pp. 100–111. Of previous studies which have brought out the problematic ambivalence of *Venus and Adonis*, the three most helpful to me have been W. B. C. Watkins, "Shakespeare's Banquet of Sense," *The Southern Review*, 7 (1941–1942), 706–734; revised and reprinted as Chapter 1 in *Shakespeare and Spenser* (Princeton, 1950); A. C. Hamilton, *"Venus and Adonis*," *SEL*, 1 (1961), 1–15; Eugene B. Cantelupe, "An Iconographical Interpretation of *Venus and Adonis*, Shakespeare's Ovidian Comedy," *SQ*, 14 (1963), 141–151.

7. *Landscape in Ovid's Metamorphoses*, pp. 8–10 and *passim*; also Parry, "Violence in a Pastoral Landscape," 269.

8. Quoted by Bush, *Mythology and the Renaissance Tradition*, p. 143, n. 15.

9. See Pooler's comment on Spenser's conflation of the stories of Adonis and Hermaphroditus in the tapestries of Castle Joyous in *The Faerie Queene* (III. i. 35); Arden edition, p. xxx.

10. Quotation from *The Life and Complete Works*, VII, 88–90. Several critics have dealt with Greene's romance and its relation to *Venus and Adonis* (Bush, *Mythology and the Renaissance Tradition*, p. 142; Baldwin, *Literary Genetics*, pp. 88–90; Hamilton, "Venus and Adonis," 7), but they have paid little attention to the context of Greene's lyric and to the contrast it affords with Shakespeare's epyllion.

11. Erwin Panofsky, *Problems in Titian, Mostly Iconographic* (New York, 1969), p. 153. Panofsky notes that Titian was criticized by a late sixteenth-century writer, Raffaelo Berghini, "for his departure from Ovid in 'depicting Adonis fleeing from Venus . . . whereas he very much desired her embraces' . . . " (p. 151, n. 36). Panofsky also remarks that the "illustrated Ovid editions . . . contain, as a rule, only two Adonis scenes: Venus and Adonis as happy lovers, she holding him in her lap; and her lament after his death" (p. 152).

12. Panofsky says "the painting ordered by Philip II remained in England for several years and was widely accessible in sixteenth-century prints by Giulio Sanuto (dated 1559) and Martino Rota (died 1583) . . . " (*Titian*, p. 153). The earliest record of its presence in Spain is 1636; see Antonio Onieva, *A New Complete Guide to the Prado Gallery*, trans. Patricia May O'Neill, rev. ed. (Madrid, 1966), p. 51.

13. One might compare the piquantly alert and armed Cupid in the left

foreground of Bartholomeus Spranger's *Venus and Adonis* [Fig. 4] which, though clearly indebted to Titian's treatment of the leave-taking, shows Adonis in an amorous, affectionate pose.

14. Baldwin, *Literary Genetics*, p. 12, and Cantelupe, "An Iconographical Interpretation," 143, emphasize the temporal structure, from the first morning through noon and night to the second morning when Venus discovers Adonis's body. Rufus Putney, "Venus Agonistes," 58, suggests that Shakespeare conceived it like a play as "a series of dramatic episodes, which may conveniently if not accurately be compared to acts."

15. Bradbrook, *Shakespeare and Elizabethan Poetry*, pp. 60–61.

16. "On *Venus and Adonis*," pp. 102–106.

17. Hamilton, "*Venus and Adonis*," 9.

18. Robert Sumner Jackson, "Narrative and Imagery in Shakespeare's *Venus and Adonis*," *Papers of the Michigan Academy of Science, Arts, and Letters*, 43 (1958), 315–320, notes the double conflict, but he does not bring out the mutual dependence of the two or the way in which Shakespeare's changes in Ovid's narrative affect the female/male, goddess/mortal polarities.

19. "An Iconographical Interpretation of *Venus and Adonis*," 151. Hamilton ("*Venus and Adonis*," 9) says that the Platonic relationship of love and beauty is "treated with a sophisticated play of wit"; Cantelupe goes further and argues that it is openly travestied (145, 148).

20. Shakespeare's parody of love-poetry conventions is discussed in detail by Helmut Castrop, *Shakespeares Verserzählungen: Eine Untersuchung der ovidischen Epik im elisabethanischen England* (Marburg, 1964), pp. 39 ff.

21. Cf. Eric Partridge, *Shakespeare's Bawdy* (New York: Dutton Paperback, 1960), p. 192.

22. "The Myth of Mars' Hot Minion," 470.

23. According to Prince ed., *The Poems*, p. 9 n., Malone was the first to compare Shakespeare's line to the opening of Ronsard's "Odelette": "Les Muses lièrent un jour / De chaisnes de roses, Amour ... *(Oeuvres*, Marty-Laveaux, II, 360). No one seems to have noticed that in Ronsard's poem "Amour" (here Cupid, not Venus) is *led by* a chain of roses, rather than doing the leading himself. Malone noted that Ronsard was imitating Anacreon; Baldwin, *Literary Genetics*, p. 15, argues that Anacreon's Ode 30, or a Latin translation of it, was the direct source of Shakespeare's image. Bush, *Mythology and the Renaissance Tradition*, p. 138, n. 2, quotes an English translation of Ronsard's line by Thomas Watson (*Poems*, ed. Arber, Sonnet 83, p. 119) which was apparently written before *Venus and Adonis*. Miller, "The Myth of Mars' Hot Minion," 478, n. 26, submits that the "source of the figure is not Ronsard but a commonplace tradition expressed by Boethius as the *rosae catena* of temporal delights (*de consolatione Philosophiae*, III, met. 10, 1–3)."

24. Cf. Dickey, *Not Wisely But Too Well*, p. 49, and Miller, "Venus, Adonis, and the Horses," 255–257.

25. Geoffrey Bullough, *Narrative and Dramatic Sources of Shakespeare* (New York, 1961), I, 164.

26. *Shakespeare's Poems*, ed. Carleton Brown in The Tudor Shakespeare (1913), pp. xiii-xiv.

27. See articles 10 and 11 under "pride" and 7.b and 8 under "proud" in the *OED*. "Pride" meaning "sexual desire" was usually associated with animals, as in *Othello* III. iii. 404; "As salt as wolves in pride." But even here the simile is applied to human beings. "Proud" was even more commonly used to describe human lust. The *OED* cites Spenser, *FQ* I. x. 26: "In ashes and sackcloth he did array / His daintie corse, proud humors to abate."

28. For more detailed discussion of this imagery, see Hereward T. Price, "Function of Imagery in *Venus and Adonis*," *Papers of the Michigan Academy of Science, Arts and Letters*, 31 (1945), 289-292 and Cantelupe, "An Iconographical Interpretation of *Venus and Adonis*," 149.

29. Allen, "On *Venus and Adonis*," pp. 100-101.

30. Otis, *Ovid as an Epic Poet*, p. 370, characterizes the subject of Orpheus' song as "boys loved by gods; girls deserving the penalty that comes from the indulgence of illegitimate or unnatural desire." He describes the song as "'un-epic' or Callimachean-elegiac" in mode, and goes on to remark: "It is not merely that the amours of Apollo and Jupiter with Cyparissus, Ganymede and Hyacinthus are homosexual (they are in fact quite parallel with the heterosexual amour of Venus and Adonis) but that the amours are frustrated . . . " (p. 371). Sensitivity to the subject matter of Book X on the part of traditional Elizabethan moralizing and allegorizing readers is suggested in Golding's comment ("Epistle to Leicester," ll. 213-215).

31. See Castrop, *Shakespeares Verserzählungen*, p. 20.

32. Cf. *Metamorphoses* III. 351-355: "For the son of Cephisus had reached his sixteenth year and might seem either a boy or a young man. Many youths and many maidens desired him; but in that delicate form was pride so unyielding that no youth, no maiden touched him." Narcissus's effeminacy, even more than Adonis's, was emphasized in late Renaissance paintings and illustrations; see Fig. 5.

33. Watkins, "Shakespeare's Banquet of Sense," 716.

34. Prince, *The Poems*, p. xxxii.

35. *Narrative and Dramatic Sources of Shakespeare*, I, 163. The idea could also have come from the pseudo-Theocritean "The Dead Adonis" (Idyll 30), in which Adonis is said to be "beautiful as a statue." See below, n. 54.

36. J. W. Lever, "Venus and the Second Chance," *Shakespeare Survey*, 15 (1962), p. 82, connects these arguments with the idea of "Venus Genetrix, the cosmic force of *natura naturans*," but overemphasizes, I think, the extent to which Shakespeare's Venus is presented as a straightforward embodiment of "the Lucretian and late-Renaissance vision of 'the whole realm of Nature in growth and fertility'" (Lever is quoting Miss Bradbrook, *Shakespeare and Elizabethan Poetry*, p. 51). See Murray Krieger's comment on Venus's arguments in *A Window to Criticism: Shakespeare's Sonnets and Modern Poetics* (Princeton, 1964), pp. 92-93.

37. *Coleridge's Writings on Shakespeare*, p. 61; Edward Dowden, *Shakespeare: A Critical Study* (London, 1875), pp. 49-51. See Castrop on this point,

Shakespeares Verserzählungen, pp. 51–83.

38. *Coleridge's Writings on Shakespeare*, pp. 61–62.

39. See Bush, *Mythology and the Renaissance Tradition*, pp. 141, 144, 147–148; Smith, *Elizabethan Poetry*, pp. 88–89.

40. Bush, *Mythology and the Renaissance Tradition*, p. 147.

41. Prince ed., *The Poems*, p. xxvii.

42. *Mythology and the Renaissance Tradition*, p. 140.

43. *Coleridge's Writings on Shakespeare*, p. 56.

44. *Shakespeare and Elizabethan Poetry*, p. 64.

45. Cf. the final stanza of *Venus and Adonis*: "Thus weary of the world, away she hies, / And yokes her *silver doves*, by whose swift aid / Their mistress mounted through the empty skies . . . (ll. 1189–1191; my italics).

46. *Shakespeare and Elizabethan Poetry*, p. 64.

47. "On *Venus and Adonis*," p. 109.

48. "*Venus and Adonis*," 14.

49. See Panofsky, p. 152, who comments on the popularity of the subject and points out that it was one of the two scenes which commonly appeared in illustrated Renaissance editions of Ovid. Erwin and Dora Panofsky, "The Iconography of the Galerie Francois 1er at Fontainebleu," *Gazette des Beaux-Arts*, series 6, 52 (1958), 139–144, discuss the traditional subject in relation to Rosso Fiorentino's *Death of Adonis* at Fontainebleu. In poetry, Bion's *Lament for Adonis* was well-known and often imitated in the Renaissance; see n. 3 above.

50. "*Venus and Adonis*—and the Boar," *MLR*, 41 (1946), 355–356.

51. Quotations are from *The Works of Geoffrey Chaucer*, ed. F. N. Robinson, 2nd ed. (Boston, 1957).

52. Hatto, "*Venus and Adonis*—and the Boar," 353–354, makes the same general point but does not show how other details in the poem support it.

53. Prince ed., *The Poems*, p. 59 n. Ovid does not mention the boar's kiss, but he does say that Adonis was gored in the groin: "trux aper insequitur totosque sub inguine dentes" *(Metamorphoses* X. 715).

54. J. M. Edmonds' translation of the relevant passage in the Greek poem reads as follows: "To which the beast 'I swear to thee, Cytherean,' answered he, 'by thyself and by thy husband, and by these my bonds and these thy huntsmen, never would I have smitten thy pretty husband but that I saw him there beautiful as a statue, and could not withstand the burning mad desire to give his naked thigh a kiss'" (Loeb Library edition of *The Greek Bucolic Poets*, pp. 481 and 483). The stanza from Tarchagnota's *L'Adone* (ed. Angelo Borselli [Naples, 1898], p. 16) follows the Greek poem closely:

> Ti giuro, che il voler mio non fu mai
>   Di offender questo tuo si caro amante:
>   Ben è egli il ver, che tosto, ch'io mirai
>   Nel corpo ignudo sue bellezze tante,
>   Di tanta fiamma accesso mi trovai,
>   Che cieco a forza mi sospinsi avante,
>   Per baciar la beltà, che il cor m'opria,
>   Et ismorzar l'ardor, che in me sentia.
>
> (stanza 65)

55. Baldwin lays great stress on these lines in arguing that disorder or chaos, understood in a metaphysical tradition which he traces through Hesiod, Plato, Ovid, and many later writers, is the theme of the poem (*Literary Genetics*, pp. 49–73). My view is that Shakespeare is more interested in the disorder existent in the world while Adonis is alive than after he is dead.

56. "*Venus and Adonis,*" 8.

57. See the previous discussion in Ch. I, pp. 13–14.

58. My attention was drawn to Shakespeare's handling of these similes by William Empson's brief remark on them in the introduction to the Signet Classic edition of *The Narrative Poems*, ed. William Burto (London, 1968), p. xx.

59. *An Essay on Shakespeare's Sonnets* (Cambridge, Mass., 1969), pp. 162–172.

CHAPTER IV

1. See John Bakeless, *The Tragicall History of Christopher Marlowe* (Cambridge, Mass., 1942) II, 100–101. For the entry in the Stationers' Register see Arber, II, 300 b. See also J. C. Maxwell's recent statement in support of the idea of simultaneous composition in his edition of Shakespeare's *Poems* (Cambridge, 1966; paperback ed. 1969), p. xi.

2. See Bakeless, *Marlowe*, I, 161–163. Edward Blunt, printer of the 1598 edition of *Hero and Leander*, dedicated Marlowe's work to Sir Thomas Walsingham.

3. *Amintas Dale* (London, 1592), p. 46.

4. Can we assume that Marlowe followed Scaliger and other sixteenth-century writers in believing "divine Musaeus" (I. 52) to be not an Alexandrian writer of the late fifth century A.D., but one of the legendary founders of Greek poetry, the son or pupil of Orpheus himself? If he did, an interesting parallel emerges between the principal source of Marlowe's epyllion and the song of Orpheus in Book X of the *Metamorphoses* which contains the narrative basis for *Venus and Adonis*. Both Marlowe and Shakespeare chose subjects which sophisticated sixteenth-century readers might have associated with the mythical origins of classical poetry.

5. See T. W. Baldwin, "Marlowe's Musaeus," *JEGP*, 55 (1955), 478–485. It was long believed that Marlowe had access to Musaeus through the Latin translation of F. Paulinus, published in 1587 as part of *Centum Fabulae ex Antiquis*, but Baldwin shows that Musurus's translation was the one which Marlowe and his contemporaries were most likely to have known.

6. The origins of the Hero and Leander story go back to pre-Homeric folklore. A version of the myth was known to Virgil *(Georgics* III. 258–263), to Ovid *(Heroides* XVIII and XIX; *Amores* II.xvi. 31–32), to Statius *(Thebaid* VI. 542–547), and to an Alexandrian poet of the first century A.D. who, five centuries before Musaeus, made Hero and Leander the subject of a poem in Greek hexameters, a fragment of which is preserved in the so-called Ryland Papyrus. See *Musée: Héro et Léandre*, ed. Pierre Orsini (Paris, 1968), pp. x–xi; and Christopher Marlowe, *The Poems*, ed. L. C. Martin (New York, 1931), p. 5.

7. Baldwin argues that Marlowe worked directly with the Greek text; he relies mainly on derivations from the Greek-Latin dictionaries of the day (Crispinus-Constantinus, Stephanus, Scapula) and from the standard Elizabethan English-Latin dictionary, Thomas Cooper's *Thesaurus Linguae Romanae & Britannicae* (1565), to support his case. But Millar MacLure remains dubious: "I think it impossible to establish, from *Hero and Leander*, whether or not Marlowe knew Greek" *(The Poems*, p. xxvi, n. 1).

8. I refer to and quote from the text in the Loeb Library volume containing the works of Callimachus and Musaeus (London, 1975). The text of Musaeus is edited by Thomas Gelzer.

9. "Hero and Leander," *Proceedings of the British Academy*, 38 (1952), 23–37. See also Lewis's account of the poem in his *English Literature in the Sixteenth Century*, pp. 485–489.

10. D. J. Gordon's sensitively learned defense of the appropriateness of Chapman's "continuation," in "Chapman's 'Hero and Leander,'" *English Miscellany*, ed. Mario Praz, V (1954), 41–91, does not deal with the way in which the massive elaborations of the "continuation" relate to the pace and structure of Musaeus's poem.

11. *Mythology and the Renaissance Tradition*, p. 122.

12. Clifford Leech, "Marlowe's Humor," *Essays . . . in Honour of Hardin Craig*, ed. Richard Hosley (London, 1963), pp. 69–81; Brian Morris, "Comic Method in Marlowe's *Hero and Leander*," *Mermaid Critical Commentaries: Christopher Marlowe*, ed. Brian Morris (London, 1968), pp. 115–131.

13. J. B. Steane, *Marlowe: A Critical Study* (Cambridge, 1964), pp. 302–333, has come closer than anyone else to articulating the element of violence and ruthless exposure in Marlowe's epyllion.

14. Wilkinson, *Ovid Surveyed*, pp. 201, 207; Fränkel, *Ovid: A Poet between Two Worlds*, p. 196. Gelzer (Loeb ed., pp. 304–305) argues that Musaeus did not know Ovid and that the similarities between them derive from "conventional elements in erotic narrative."

15. See G. Lazarus, *Technik und Stil von Hero and Leander* (Bonn, 1915), pp. 77, 94, 101, and Douglas Bush, "Notes on Marlowe's *Hero and Leander*," *PMLA*, 44 (1929), 760–761.

16. There are several parallels to this passage in the *Ars Amatoria:* see, for instance, II. 723–724. But MacLure claims that the "sentiment was suggested . . . by Musaeus, ll. 131–132: 'Whenever a girl threatens a man, those very threats are a sign of yielding.'"

17. Cf. *Amores* I. v.24 ("I cling'd her naked body, down she fell") and *Amores* III.vi. 81–82 ("With that her loose gown on, from me she cast her, / In skipping out her naked feet much grac'd her").

18. For a fuller discussion of Marlowe's use of Musaeus's phrase, see my "Marlowe's Hero as 'Venus' nun,'" *ELR*, 2 (1972), 307–320. I quote from the Greek text because I think it likely that Marlowe consulted the original on such key points as this and because there are no significant shifts in meaning in any of the translations. Musurus renders "Κύπριδος ἦν ἱέρεια . . . . "Veneris erat sacerdos,"

Marot as "Estoit nonnain, a Venus dediée." Marot's line has sometimes been cited as the immediate source for Marlowe's "Venus' nun," but this is unnecessary: see below, p. 90 and n. 24.

19. Whitman's translation, which appears in the Loeb Library edition cited in n.8, follows the Greek text far more closely than does Chapman's version, *The Divine Poem of Musaeus: Hero and Leander* (1616), printed in E. S. Donno's *Elizabethan Minor Epics*, pp. 70–84.

20. ἀλλ' αἰεὶ Κυθέρειαν ἱλασκομένη Ἀφροδίτην
πολλάκι καὶ τὸν Ἔρωτα παρηγορέεσκε θυηλαῖς
μητρὶ σὺν Οὐρανίῃ φλογερὴν τρομέουσα φαρέτρην.

(ll. 38–40)

21. See, for example, MacLure ed., *The Poems*, p. 7 n.; Baldwin, "Marlowe's Musaeus," 481; Clifford Leech, "Venus and Her Nun: Portraits of Women in Love in Shakespeare and Marlowe," *SEL*, 5 (1965), 257, 266.

22. Paul W. Miller, "A Function of Myth in Marlowe's Hero and Leander, *SP*, 50 (1953), 164 n. 16.

23. Κύπριδος ὡς ἱέρεια μετέρχεο Κύπριδος ἔργα·
δεῦρ' ἴθι, μυστιπόλευε γαμήλια θεσμὰ θεαίνης·
παρθένον οὐκ ἐπέοικεν ὑποδρήσσειν Ἀφροδίτῃ,

(ll. 141–143)

See the articles on Aphrodite and Venus in *The Oxford Classical Dictionary*, ed. M. Cary *et al.* (Oxford, 1953), pp. 67, 941; in W. Roscher, *Ausführliches Lexikon der griechischen und römischen Mythologie* (Leipzig, 1884–1886), I, 390–419 and VI, 183–207; and in Oskar Seyffert, *A Dictionary of Classical Antiquities*, rev. and ed. Henry Nettleship and J. E. Sandys (London, 1898), pp. 39–40, 681.

24. See article 1.b under "nun" in *OED* and Eugene B. Cantelupe, "*Hero and Leander*, Marlowe's Tragicomedy of Love," *CE*, 26 (1963), 297. Chapman translates " Κύπριδος ἦν ἱέρεια" as "Was Venus Priest" (Donno, *Elizabethan Minor Epics*, p. 71).

25. The relevant passage in *Hamlet* is, of course, Hamlet's "Get thee to a nunnery" (III. i. 122); see John Dover Wilson's note on this passage in the Cambridge edition, 1934 (paperback 1961), p. 192. See article 1.c under "nun" in *OED* and the comments of Paul H. Kocher, *Christopher Marlowe: A Study of His Thought, Learning, and Character* (Chapel Hill, N. C. , 1964), p. 295; Steane, *Marlowe*, pp. 307–308; Alexander, *Elizabethan Narrative Verse*, p. 11.

26. *The School of Abuse*, ed. J. P. Collier (repr. by London Shakespeare Society, London, 1841), p. 26.

27. *The Works of Thomas Nashe*, ed. R. B. McKerrow (London, 1950), III, 405 (l. 48). See article 3 under "nun" in the *OED*. Maurice Charney has pointed out to me that Randle Cotgrave, in his *Dictionarie of the French and English Tongues* (1611), defines French "vestales" as "The Vestall virgines, the Nunnes of the Heathenish Romans."

28. One wonders whether Marlowe and his readers would have known about the sacred prostitution practiced in some ancient cults of Aphrodite. See *The Oxford Classical Dictionary*, pp. 67, 940; Seyffert, *Classical Antiquities*, p. 39.

29. See Cesare Ripa, *Iconologia* (Siena, 1613), p. 170. W. S. Heckscher, "Aphrodite as a Nun," *Phoenix*, 7 (1953), 106–109, shows that the figure of this woodcut derives from a lost statue of the *Aphrodite Ourania* described in Pausanias VI. 25 and in Plutarch's *Moralia* 142. Heckscher's assumption that the gown and veil of Ripa's figure constitute the habit of a nun may be unwarranted; see "Marlowe's Hero as "Venus' nun," 310, n. 9.

30. Edgar Wind, *Pagan Mysteries in the Renaissance* (London, 1958), pp. 73–76.

31. See Wind, p. 75.

32. "Venus and Her Nun," 267. Compare ll. 751–755 of *Venus and Adonis*, where Shakespeare's Venus urges Adonis to procreate " . . . despite of fruitless chastity, / Love-lacking vestals and self-loving nuns. . . ."

33. Cf. Musaeus, ll. 33, 66–68.

34. See Emile Legouis, *The Middle Ages and the Renaissance*, trans. Helen Douglas Irvine, vol. I of *A History of English Literature*, by Legouis and Cazamian (New York, 1929), p. 327; and Philip Henderson, *And Morning in His Eyes: a Book About Christopher Marlowe* (London, 1937), p. 336.

35. Cf. II. 103–105: "But what the secret trusty night conceal'd, / Leander's amorous habit soon reveal'd; / With Cupid's myrtle was his bonnet crown'd."

36. *The Overreacher: A Study of Christopher Marlowe* (Cambridge, Mass., 1952), p. 163. See also Henderson, *Marlowe*, p. 335.

37. It is interesting that this passage echoes the speaker of Ovid's *Amores*, whose praise of Corinna's beauty in I.v includes the following phrases in Marlowe's own rendering: "How smooth a belly under her waist saw I? / How large a leg, and what a lusty thigh?" (ll. 21–22).

38. "Comic Method in Hero and Leander," p. 117, n. 5.

39. *Mythology and the Renaissance Tradition*, p. 130.

40. "Comic Method in Hero and Leander," pp. 116–117. See Sandys, *Ovid's Metamorphosis English'd . . .* (1632), sig. Mmm.

41. On the "loves of the gods" as a subject capable of being treated in a witty and ironic way at the end of the Renaissance, see Charles Dempsey, "'Et nos cedamus amori': Observations on the Farnese Gallery," *Art Bulletin*, 50 (1968), 363–374.

42. Cf. Martin ed., *Poems*, p. 28 n.; Tuve, *Elizabethan and Metaphysical Imagery*, pp. 273–274.

43. *Elizabethan Narrative Verse*, p. 11.

44. αὐτὴ δ', ὡς ξυνέηκε πόθον δολόεντα Λεάνδρου,
χαῖρεν ἐπ' ἀγλαΐησιν· ἐν ἡσυχίῃ δὲ καὶ αὐτὴ
πολλάκις ἱμερόεσσαν ἑὴν ἐπέκυψεν ὀπωπὴν
νεύμασι λαθριδίοισιν ἐπαγγέλλουσα Λεάνδρῳ,
καὶ πάλιν ἀντέκλινεν.

(ll. 103–107)

45. "Venus and Her Nun," 256.

46. See MacLure's notes on these lines and on I. 255–256 and I. 267–268.

47. *Elizabethan and Metaphysical Imagery*, p. 278.

48. For "service" see *OED* 6.c and Partridge, *Shakespeare's Bawdy*, p. 185; for

"procure," *OED* 5.b; for "use," *OED* 3.b and *Shakespeare's Bawdy*, p. 244; for "deed," *Shakespeare's Bawdy*, pp. 99, 103.

49. See *Metamorphoses* II. 708-832; also Otis, *Ovid as an Epic Poet*, pp. 120-121.

50. Miller notes a number of the parallels in "A Function of Myth in Marlowe's *Hero and Leander*," 158-167.

51. See Miller, pp. 161-162, for the traditional association of Mercury with eloquence, learning, gain or profit, subtlety and deceit, and theft. See also MacLure's notes on this passage, *The Poems*, pp. 25-26. MacLure observes that the poverty of scholars was "a commonplace . . . of satire and complaint in the 1590s." Marlowe, like Lodge at the end of *Glaucus and Scilla*, appears to be appealing in these lines to his readers at the universities and Inns of Court.

52. Cf. Steane, *Marlowe*, p. 322 and M. C. Bradbrook, "Hero and Leander," *Scrutiny*, 2 (1933), 61.

53. Marlowe was also thinking here of his own translation of *Amores* III. vi. 21-22: "Pure rose she, like a nun to sacrifice, / Or one that with her tender brother lies." This second line is echoed four lines later in II. 51: "And as a brother with his sister toy'd."

54. See Bush, "Notes on Marlowe's 'Hero and Leander,'" 763, and *Mythology and the Renaissance Tradition*, p. 126, n. 17; Leech, "Venus and Her Nun," 252 n. 5.

55. at tibi flammarum memori, Neptune, tuarum
nullus erat ventis inpediendus amor—
(*Heroides* XIX. 129-130)

56. Martin Williams, "The Temptations in Marlowe's *Hero and Leander*," *MLQ*, 16 (1955), 229-230, n. 12, compares Neptune's wooing of Leander with the account of Jove's wooing of Ganymede at the beginning of *Dido Queen of Carthage*. He also documents a long tradition extending from the *Odyssey* and the *Aeneid* up through *The Faerie Queene* of Neptune as a temptation to baseness and an embodiment of sensuality and lechery (pp. 227-228). See also Levin, *The Overreacher*, p. 164, and Morris, "Comic Method," p. 127. "Ganymede" was an Elizabethan slang term for "homosexual": see Akrigg, *Shakespeare and the Earl of Southampton*, p. 181. One might also compare Richard Barnfield's "Ganymede" sonnets in *The Affectionate Shepherd* (1594).

57. See Ch. I, p. 9.

58. *Marlowe, a Critical Study*, p. 327.

59. Ibid., p. 326.

60. "Comic Method," p. 128.

61. Ibid., p. 124.

62. *Marlowe*, p. 327.

63. See Williams, "The Temptations in Marlowe's *Hero and Leander*," 227.

64. See Martin ed., *Poems*, p. 59 n. There are several references to the myth of Helle and Phrixus in Ovid's *Heroides*: e.g. XIX. 136-142 and 163-164.

65. See Steane, *Marlowe*, pp. 331-332.

66. καὶ χρόα πάντα κάθηρε, δέμας δ' ἔχρισεν ἐλαίῳ
εὐόδμῳ ῥοδέῳ, καὶ ἀλίπνοον ἔσβεσεν ὀδμήν.
εἰσέτι δ' ἀσθμαίνοντα βαθυστρώτοις ἐνὶ λέκτροις
νυμφίον ἀμφιχυθεῖσα φιλήνορας ἴαχε μύθους·
"Νύμφιε, πολλὰ μόγησας, ἃ μὴ πάθε νυμφίος ἄλλος,
νυμφίε, μολλὰ μόγησας· ἅλις νύ τοι ἁλμυρὸν ὕδωρ
ὀδμή τ' ἰχθυόεσσα βαρυγδούποιο θαλάσσης·
δεῦρο, τεοὺς ἱδρῶτας ἐμοῖς ἐνικάτθεο κόλποις."
"Ὣς ἡ μὲν τάδ' ἔειπεν, ὁ δ' αὐτίκα λύσατο μίτρην,
καὶ θεσμῶν ἐπέβησαν ἀριστονόου Κυθερίης.

(ll. 264–273)

67. Paul Cubeta, "Marlowe's Poet in *Hero and Leander*," *CE*, 26 (1965), 502.

68. See U. M. Ellis-Fermor, *Christopher Marlowe* (London, 1927; repr. Hamden, Conn. 1967), p. 125; Kocher, *Marlowe*, pp. 294–297.

69. See Bakeless, *Marlowe*, II, 112–114.

70. Gordon ("Chapman's Hero and Leander," 42, 85–92) argues that the "aims and intentions" of Marlowe and Chapman are not as incongruous as they might at first seem, that in many instances Chapman draws "out themes already present in Marlowe's beginning," and that his goal "was not to contradict, but to complete" Marlowe's version. But Gordon's own admission that "Chapman in fact 'moralized' Marlowe" (85) indicates the fundamental difference between the two visions of the story. Gelzer's reading of Musaeus's poem "as a Christian Neoplatonist allegory" (see Loeb ed., esp. pp. 316–322) carries very interesting implications for Chapman's "continuation" in relation to Marlowe's narrative. Gelzer's forthcoming book on the subject will be extremely important.

CHAPTER V

1. See Ch. XV of Bush's *Mythology and the Renaissance Tradition*, esp. pp. 299–300.

2. E. S. Donno makes a similar point in the introduction to *Elizabethan Minor Epics* when she speaks of "Marston's hope that if he intensified the ironic tone set by Marlowe, he might freshly appeal to the young men of the Inns of Court" (p. 17.)

3. Louis Lecocq, *La Satire en Angleterre de 1588 à 1603* (Paris, 1969), p. 184.

4. See the notes in MacLure's edition of the *Poems*, pp. 17–18.

5. For the relevant passages in *Cephalus and Procris* (ll. 118–128 and ll. 679–705) see Donno, *Elizabethan Minor Epics*, pp. 158, 172–173. See also Lecocq, *La Satire*, pp. 156 ff. and *passim*.

6. See the discussion in the Arden edition, ed. Henry Cunningham (London, 1922), pp. xxi–xxxv.

7. The dedication of Gale's poem to "D. B. H." is dated 1596, but the earliest known edition is 1617. See Bush, *Mythology and the Renaissance Tradition*, p. 323. The text from which I quote is the facsimile reprint of the 1617 edition in *Seven Minor Epics of the English Renaissance*, intro. Paul W. Miller (Gainesville, Fla., 1967).

8. Ovid is, of course, much more deftly indirect in his treatment of the lover's attempts to kiss: "sub noctem dixere 'vale' partique dedere / oscula quisque suae non pervenientia contra," IV. 79–80 ("at night they said goodbye and printed, each on his own side of the wall, kisses that did not go through").

9. The dialogue between Theseus and Philostrate preceding the "rude mechanicals'" performance anticipates the literary satire of the performance itself; see *MND* V. i. 44–55. Walter F. Staton, Jr. has attempted to show that in many other aspects of the play "Shakespeare was drawing upon and to some extent parodying Ovid" and Elizabethan Ovidian poetry ("Ovidian Elements in *A Midsummer Night's Dream*," *HLQ,* 26 [1962-1963], 165-178).

10. *STC* 24477. "Tyro, T. Tyros roring megge, planted against the walles of melancholy. 4. V. Simmes, 1958." See John Peter, *Complaint and Satire in Early English Poetry* (Oxford, 1956), p. 162.

11. *Works of Thomas Nashe,* ed. McKerrow, III, 200. Hereafter as "McKerrow."

12. *Amintas Dale,* p. 46. See Ch. IV. p. 85 and n. 3.

13. McKerrow, III, 195. Nash is alluding of course, to *Hero and Leander* I. 51–52: "Amorous Leander, beautiful and young, / (Whose tragedy divine Musaeus sung)."

14. McKerrow ed., III, 195.

15. See the discussion in vol. II (p. 131) of the Herford and Simpson edition of Jonson's plays (Oxford, 1938). Quotations are from this edition.

16. See Jonas Barish, *Ben Jonson and the Language of Prose Comedy* (Cambridge, Mass., 1960), pp. 232-234. Although Barish speaks of the "revulsion in Jonson's own generation" against the "glut of mythological poems that poured from the English presses in the 1590s," he does not mention Marlowe's poem in particular and appears instead to be thinking of the Hero and Leander story as it figured in the popular imagination. He calls it "an archetypal myth for earlier Elizabethans" (p. 233).

17. O. J. Campbell, *Comicall Satyre and Shakespeare's "Troilus and Cressida"* (San Marino, Cal., 1938) p. 44.

18. Quotations are from *The Collected Poems of Joseph Hall,* ed. Arnold Davenport (Liverpool, 1949).

19. On "Ganymede" as Elizabethan slang for "homosexual,"see Ch. IV, p. 105 and n. 56.

20. Quotations are from *Micro-Cynicon. Sixe Snarling Satyres* (London, 1599); reprinted (Isle of Wight: Beldourne Press, 1842) for Edward V. Utterson, sig. C4^v . The author is only designated as "T. M." and has sometimes been identified as Thomas Moffat, but most scholars now favor Middleton. See Richard Hindry Barker, *Thomas Middleton* (London, 1958), pp. 29-30, 158.

21. Quotations are from Everard Guilpin, *Skialetheia, 1598,* foreword by G. B. Harrison, Shakespeare Association Facsimile No. 2 (London, 1931).

22. See Campbell, *Comicall Satyre,* pp. 37-38 and Alvin Kernan, *The Cankered Muse* (New Haven, 1959), pp. 64-80. For the influence of Martial's epigrams on Elizabethan satire, see John Peter, *Complaint and Satire,* pp. 116, 165-169, and Campbell, pp. 49-50.

23. *Cankered Muse*, pp. 24–25.

24. Quotations are from the British Museum's copy of the first edition (London, 1611) sig. [A3^v].

25. *Anatomy of Melancholy* I.ii. 3. 7, quoted from the edition of Floyd Dell and Paul Jordan-Smith (New York, 1938), p. 230.

26. Quotations are from *Epigrammes: in the Oldest Cut, and Newest Fashion*, ed. R. B. McKerrow (London, 1911).

27. See Lecocq, *La Satire*, pp. 303–315; also Bridget Gellert Lyons, *Voices of Melancholy* (London, 1971), p. 70.

28. See Kernan, *Cankered Muse*, pp. 54–58, and Campbell, *Comicall Satyre*, pp. 24–28. For a fuller and more recent discussion of Renaissance theories of satire, see Lecocq, *La Satire*, pp. 236–296. The ultimate source of the confusion between satire and the Greek satyr-play seems to have been an essay on the history of comedy and tragedy by the fourth-century grammarian Aelius Donatus which was prefaced to most sixteenth-century editions of Terence. Donatus's theory and the Renaissance concepts of satire indebted to it were not shown to be erroneous until 1605, when Isaac Casaubon published *De Satyrica Graecorum et Romanorum satira, Libri duo*.

29. *Cankered Muse*, p. 6; see also pp. 58–61, 108–110, 114.

30. Lecocq, *La Satire*, pp. 276–291.

31. Quotations are from *Seven Satires* (1598), ed. Arnold Davenport (London, University Press of Liverpool: 1948).

32. *Voices of Melancholy*, pp. 58–62. See also Lecocq, *La Satire*, pp. 74–80.

33. See Ch. I, p. 33.

34. Ed. Arber (London, 1868), p. 19.

35. Lecocq, *La Satire*, (p. 94, n. 170, and p. 266) points out that in *The Steel Glass* George Gascoigne had applied the image of the hermaphrodite to the satirist himself in commenting ironically on his own prudence and restraint: "I am not he whom slaunderous tongues have told, / . . . To be the man, which ment a common spoyle / Of loving dames, whose eares wold heare my words / . . . I am in dede a dame, / Or at the least a right *Hermaphrodite" (Complete Works*, ed. Cunliffe, II, 144).

36. For the text of the edict, see Arber, III, 677. See Lecocq, *La Satire*, pp. 134–155 and Peter, *Complaint and Satire*, pp. 148–150.

37. Arber, III, 678.

38. Peter, *Complaint and Satire*, p. 150.

39. Lecocq, *La Satire*, p. 139.

40. Signet edition of the *Narrative Poems*, p. xix; also Maurice Charney, *Shakespeare's Roman Plays* (Cambridge, Mass., 1961), p. 205.

41. See Davenport's introduction to his edition of Marston's *Poems* (Liverpool, 1961), pp. 1–2.

42. See Anthony Caputi, *John Marston, Satirist* (Ithaca, N.Y., 1961), pp. 7–9.

43. See Finkelpearl, *Marston*, pp. 55–58.

CHAPTER VI

1. See Morse Allen, *The Satire of John Marston* (Columbus, Ohio, 1920), pp. 88-92; Hallett Smith, *Elizabethan Poetry*, p. 99; C. S. Lewis, *English Literature in the Sixteenth Century*, pp. 472-474; Samuel Schoenbaum, "The Precarious Balance of John Marston," *PMLA*, 67 (1952), 1074-1075; A. José Axelrad, *Un malcontent Elizabéthain: John Marston* (Paris, 1955), pp. 20-36; John Peter, *Complaint and Satire*, pp. 158-159.

2. *Mythology and the Renaissance Tradition*, pp. 182-183. Bush's position was accepted by John Bakeless in his biography of Marlowe, II, 117-119.

3. "Marston's 'Metamorphosis of Pigmalion's Image': a Mock-epyllion," *Études Anglaises*, 13 (1960), 331-336. Much of Cross's argument is anticipated by Louis Zocca in *Elizabethan Narrative Poetry* (New Brunswick, 1950), pp. 279-283, who was also extending Bush's position. Another case for the poem as "a coherent, extremely ingenious, if not altogether satisfactory, burlesque" is argued by Caputi, *John Marston, Satirist*, pp. 17-22.

4. "From Petrarch to Ovid: Metamorphosis in John Marston's *Metamorphosis of Pigmalions Image*," *ELH*, 32 (1965), 334. A shorter and only slightly altered version of this article appears in Chapter VII of Finkelpearl's book on Marston (see Ch. I, p. 32 and n. 59). I have referred in this chapter to the earlier and fuller account.

5. *La Satire en Angleterre*, pp. 432-448.

6. "'Opinion' and the Reader in John Marston's *The Metamorphosis of Pigmalions Image*," *ELR*, 3 (1973), 221-231.

7. *The Poems of John Marston*, p. 7.

8. "From Petrarch to Ovid," 335.

9. See Pauly-Wissowa, *R.-E.*, XXXIX, 104-181; *Oxford Classical Dictionary*, p. 824.

10. *Ovid as an Epic Poet*, pp. 189-192.

11. See Ch. III, pp. 66-67.

12. "Sunt tamen obscenae Venerem Propoetides ausae / esse negare deam pro quo sua numinis ira / Corpora cum fama primae vulgasse feruntur," (X. 238-240).

13. Fränkel (*Ovid: A Poet Between Two Worlds*, p. 97) notes the parallel with Orpheus, who had rescued his beloved Eurydice from the world of the dead through the power of his art only to see her die again (the reverse of Pigmalion's good fortune).

14. Ed. G. C. Macaulay (Oxford, 1899-1902), I, 312-313.

15. See John Fleming, *The "Roman de la Rose": A Study in Allegory and Iconography* (Princeton, 1969), pp. 91-92.

16. See Fleming's excellent discussion of the entire episode, pp. 228-237.

17. Quotation from *Poems and "A Defence of Ryme*," ed. Arthur Colby Sprague (University of Chicago Press, 1930; Phoenix paperback, 1965). The key source for this lyric tradition is Petrarch's Sonnet 78 *In Vita*: "Pigmalion, quanto lodar ti dei / De l'imagine tua, se mille volte / N'avesti quel ch'i' sol una vorrei!"

Finkelpearl quotes this passage ("From Petrarch to Ovid," 340 n. 7) but does not make clear that for Petrarch and his followers Pigmalion ultimately represents a contrast to, not an equivalent of, the eternally unrequited lover.

18. See Lecocq, *La Satire*, p. 444, who quotes ll. 561–568 of Golding's "Epistle to Leicester."

19. See Otis, *Ovid as an Epic Poet*, p. 191.

20. Lodge may have been thinking of a similar ironic literalization of a Petrarchan conceit in his handling of Scilla's transformation into a sea rock; see Ch. II, pp. 48–50.

21. See *OED* 1 and 6 under "image"; 1, 2, 3, 4, 7, and 8 under "imagery." Puttenham seems to be consciously formulating a new rhetorical concept when he talks about "imagery" in *The Art of English Poesie* (1589), III. 19, ed. G.D. Willcock and Alice Walker (Cambridge, 1936), pp. 203–204.

22. See *OED* 1, 7, 8. Marston's use of "conceit" may also take up *OED* 6, "An overweening opinion of oneself"; the earliest example given is from Joseph Hall's *Meditations and Vows* (1605).

23. I. iv. 3, ed. William Aldis Wright (Oxford, 1885), p. 30.

24. "From Petrarch to Ovid," 339.

25. Cf. St. 1, ll. 5–6: "Yet Love at length forc'd him to know his fate, / And Love the shade, whose substance he did hate." The movement from stanza 1 to stanza 28 vaguely suggests Ovid's theme, that the "shade" or "shadow" of human reality provided by art enables Pigmalion to move from "hate" (st. 1) to "bliss" (st. 28). But Marston does not develop this theme.

26. Thomas Cranley, *Amanda: or, The Reformed Whore* (London, 1635), p. 32, st. 50.

27. For a different interpretation of Marston's religious allusions and imagery, see Lecocq, *La Satire*, pp. 440–441.

28. See *OED* 2 under "imagery": "The use of images in worship; idolatry."

29. Davenport suggests that Marston is alluding to the Biblical account of how Elijah brought life back into a widow's dead son (1 Kings 17:17–23).

30. Marston's technique here anticipates the sensationalistic and deliberately shocking contrasts of Jacobean drama. Lecocq (*La Satire*, p. 440) compares the sacrilegious allusions of Marston's narrator to Giovanni's speech in I. iii of Ford's *'Tis Pity She's a Whore*. But Lecocq sees these allusions as evidence of the moral depravity of Marston's narrator and allows them no positive poetic function.

31. "From Petrarch to Ovid," 343.

32. Colley, "'Opinion' and the Reader," 230, 228.

33. Lecocq, *La Satire*, p. 432, n. 16. Weever will also use the device in *Faunus and Melliflora*, ll. 459–460: "But what he saw, tis needlesse for to say, / Heere shall your thoughts, and not my pen bewray."

34. Ibid., p. 440.

35. Ibid., pp. 437–438.

36. See Peter, *Complaint and Satire*, pp. 168–170.

37. See Lewis, *English Literature in the Sixteenth Century*, p. 472; Davenport ed., *Poems*, p. 7; Reese, ed., *Elizabethan Verse Romances*, p. 23.

38. Lecocq, *La Satire*, p. 437.

39. *The Art of English Poesie* III. 19, ed. Willcock and Walker, pp. 203-204. Shakespeare uses the figure several times in *Venus and Adonis*; e.g. ll. 4, 77-78, 479-480, 497-498. The italics in the quoted passages are mine.

40. Lecocq, *La Satire*, p. 437.

41. For lists of possible echoes, see Bush, *Mythology and the Renaissance Tradition*, pp. 183-184, n. 10, and Bakeless, *Marlowe*, II, 118-119. Davenport deals much more critically with possible echoes in his notes to *Pigmalions Image* and, quite rightly I think, rejects some of those advanced by Bush.

42. Finkelpearl ("From Petrarch to Ovid," 336) observes that "By the use of 'seeme,' 'conceit,' and 'thinks,' Marston has shifted the tone [of Marlowe's passage] to stress the conceited, mental quality of Pigmalion's perceptions."

43. See Ch. IV, pp. 93-94.

44. See Finkelpearl, "From Petrarch to Ovid," 336, n.4: "Certainly Marlowe's poem was on Marston's mind during the composition of *Pigmalion*. He appropriates lines from it and distorts them in meaningful ways. . . . But the main use Marston makes of *Hero and Leander* is as a standard of comparison; the actions of Marlowe's protagonists are a measure of Pigmalion's absurd conduct."

45. See Ch. IV, p. 111 for a brief discussion of Marlowe's use of this passage.

46. For comments on the fictional identities of Rufus and Luxurio in Marston's satire, see Davenport's note, *Poems*, p. 215. "Salaminian" is the adjectival form of "Salaminia," one of the alternate names of Venus.

47. Lecocq, *La Satire*, p. 435, notes that "swaggering" was a new word in the 1590s and draws attention to early examples where it and the variants "swagger" and "swaggerer" appear to have mainly negative connotations. But note the example cited by the *OED* from Beaumont and Fletcher's *Cupid's Revenge* II.i (1611): "He . . . looks the swaggeringst, and has such glorious clothes."

48. These lines clearly echo Leander's praise of Hero in Marlowe's poem (I. 287-288): "But you are fair (aye me) so wondrous fair, / So young, so gentle, and so debonaire." The narrator had not in fact used this Marlovian language in "To his Mistres," but he may be alluding in ll. 7-8 ("Thy favours like *Promethean* sacred fire, / In dead and dull conceit can life inspire") to *Hero and Leander* II. 255-257: "Whose lively heat, like fire from heaven fet, / Would animate gross clay, and higher set / The drooping thoughts of base declining souls. . . . " See Davenport's note, *Poems*, p. 211.

49. Davenport sets out his argument in greatest detail in his edition of Hall's *Collected Poems*, pp. xxix-xxxi. Marston had attacked Hall's *Virgidemiae* in Satire XIV, "Reactio," of *Certaine Satyres*. Hall responded by writing an epigram on *Pigmalions Image and Certaine Satyres* and pasting it into all copies of Marston's book sold in Cambridge, where Hall was residing and lecturing as fellow of Emmanuel College. The epigram runs as follows (quoted from Davenport's edition, p. 101):

> I ask't Phisitions what their counsell was
> For a mad dogge, or for a mandkind Asse?

They told me though there were confections store
Of Poppie-seede, and soveraigne Hellebore,
The dog was best cured by cutting & kinsing,
The asse must be kindly whipped for winsing.
Now then S.K. I little passe
Whether thou be a mad dog, or a mankind Asse.

"S.K." in line 7 stands for "Sir Kinsayder." Marston himself printed this epigram in the second edition of *The Scourge of Villanie* (1599) and said in a note on "kinsing" ("Cutting") in line 5: "Mark the witty allusion to my name." It is highly unlikely that Marston would have done this if he had already replied to Hall's epigram, as Davenport suggests. Finkelpearl ("From Petrarch to Ovid," 344 and n. 8) rejects Davenport's arguments for reasons similar to those offered here.

50. See Davenport's note, *Poems*, pp. 215-216. Book II of the *Ars Amatoria* begins "Dicite 'io Paean!' et 'io' bis dicite 'Paean!' / Decidit in casses praeda petita meos; / Laetus amans donat viridi mea carmina palma . . . " ("Cry 'Hurrah! Triumph!' and 'Hurrah! Triumph!' cry once more: the prey I sought has fallen into my toils; joyously does the lover crown my poem with green palm-leaves . . . "). This is very close to ll. 1-10 of Marston's "The Authour in prayse."

51. Marston's prose introduction to *The Scourge of Villanie* ("To those that seeme judiciall perusers") is signed "W. Kinsayder." It is unlikely that Marston is responding specifically to Hall's epigram in the opening lines of Satire VI. The fact that Marston had not expanded the initials of his satiric pseudonym from "W.K." to "W. Kinsayder" until the first edition of *The Scourge* suggests that Hall's epigram, which plays upon the name "Kinsayder," was not written until after *The Scourge* appeared. It was not until the second edition of *The Scourge* that Marston printed and commented on Hall's epigram. Davenport points out that "butterfly" was a familiar term of contempt for court fops, which Marston also uses in Satire IV, l. 84 (p. 323).

52. Davenport (*Poems*, pp. 323-324) notes that ll. 33-34 echo a more specific attack on Nash's poem by Hall (*Virgidemiae* IX, ll. 21-23) but concludes that "M.'s lines are applicable to so many Elizabethan poets that is is impossible to say whom he had in mind. . . ." Davenport suggests William Smith's *Chloris* (1596) or Hall himself as the referent of ll. 37-38, but Edwards had invoked the example of "Colin Clout" at several points in *Cephalus and Procris*.

53. Once again Marston's ambiguous relation to Ovid is apparent: Davenport (*Poems*, p. 325) notes that several details in this passage seem to be derived from Ovid's account of spontaneous generation after the cosmic flood in *Met.* I. 422 ff.

54. McKerrow ed., I, 10. See Lecocq, *La Satire*, pp. 184-185.

55. Gabriel Harvey refers to Nash's having written indecent poems as early as 1593, but the first explicit reference to *The Choise of Valentines* is in *The Trimming of Thomas Nashe* (1597). Hall also alludes to Nash's poem in *Virgidemiae* (1597); see note 52 above.

56. Quotations of *The Choise of Valentines* are from the text in McKerrow

ed., III, 403-416. The poem was apparently never printed until the end of the nineteenth century and is known to us only through three corrupt seventeenth-century manuscripts. See the discussion in vol. V of McKerrow's edition, pp. 398-402.

57. The usual assumption is Southampton; Nash had dedicated *The Unfortunate Traveler* to him in 1594. But McKerrow says that "surely Lord Strange is a much more likely person" because of the reference to the dedicatee's "matchless Poetrie" (l. 1) and to his connection with the royal family (l. 2).

58. *Voices of Melancholy*, p. 24.

59. See Davenport ed., *Poems*, p. 10: "One thing that all critics have agreed on is that the young Marston was avid for literary fame."

60. Schoenbaum, "Precarious Balance," 1070.

61. Davenport ed., *Poems*, p. 11.

62. See Davenport ed., *Poems*, pp. 24-27, who in addition to Marston's own Malevole mentions Webster's Bosola, Tourneur's Vendice, and Shakespeare's Hamlet, Lucio, Angelo, Lear, and Timon. See also Eudo C. Mason, "Satire on Woman and Sex in Elizabethan Tragedy," *Essays and Studies*, 31 (1950), 1-10.

CHAPTER VII

1. See Ch. I, pp. 32-33 and n. 66.

2. See *DNB*, XX, 1060-1061.

3. Ed. R. B. McKerrow (London, 1611).

4. Ed. Arnold Davenport (London, 1948). All quotations are from this edition. *Faunus and Melliflora* itself is reprinted in Donno's *Elizabethan Minor Epics* (pp. 253-280), with no indication that the mythological account of the origin of satire at the end of the poem is resumed later in Weever's volume.

5. See Ch. II, p. 37. The *Forbonius and Prisceria* volume contains a satire called *Truth's Complaint over England; Scillaes Metamorphosis* contains *The Discontented Satyre*.

6. Davenport provides continuous line numbering beginning with *Faunus and Melliflora* and running through all the inset satires up to "A Prophesie," as well as separate numbering for each individual poem. I have referred to the continuous numbering. "A Prophesie" is numbered separately, apparently because the word "Finis" appears at the end of the resumed mythological fiction integrated with the Juvenal fragment.

7. Davenport ed., *Faunus*, p. vi.

8. Ibid., p. vi. Lecocq is the only critic who has suggested, albeit very sketchily, that the various elements in Weever's mythological narrative may have something to do with the satire which follows it (*La Satire*, p. 352).

9. This poem is signed "T. H."; Davenport speculates that the author was either a member of the Houghton family, perhaps a brother or son of Sir Richard Houghton to whom Weever had dedicated his *Epigrammes*, or Thomas Holecroft, the addressee of one of Weever's friendly epigrams.

10. On Faunus's double identity, see Pauly-Wissowa, *R.-E.*, VI, 2054-2073, and

Smith, *Dictionary of Greek and Roman Biography and Mythology*, II, 137-138.

11. These three sixains are signed "I. F."; Davenport offers no guess at an identity but points out (p. 71) that "I. F." also contributed a commendatory poem to Weever's *The Whipping of the Satyre* (1601). Why not John Fletcher, who would have been twenty-one, three years younger than Weever, in 1600, and who had entered Cambridge (Bene't, later Corpus Christi, College, of which his father had been president) in 1591, three years before Weever enrolled in Queen's College?

12. See Bush, *Mythology and the Renaissance Tradition*, p. 86.

13. Actually Weever is already drawing details from Sidney's "Zelmane" portrait, which provides the model for the account that follows of Faunus's attire. Compare Weever's ll. 35-38 with Sidney's description of "Zelmane's" hair: "Well might he perceave the hanging of her haire in fairest quantitie, in locks, some curled, & some as it were forgotten, with such a carelesse care, & an arte so hiding arte . . . " (I.12.2; ed. Feuillerat, I. 75).

14. Cf. *Hero and Leander* I. 69-70: ". . . but my rude pen / Can hardly blazon forth the loves of men. . . . "

15. See Davenport ed., *Faunus*, p. 72.

16. See Mark Rose, "Sidney's Womanish Man," *RES*, 15 (1964), 353-363.

17. For the story of Hercules and Omphale symbolizing masculine capitulation to love, see Dickey, *Not Wisely But Too Well*, pp. 38-40.

18. "Murrey" means "Mulberry-red" (Davenport ed., *Faunus*, p. 73); Sidney has "crimson."

19. On Marlowe's problematic passage, see Ch. IV, p. 97.

20. For playfully self-conscious and virtuoso borrowing from previous works as a feature of "mannerism" in the visual arts, see John Shearman, *Mannerism* (Harmondsworth, England, 1965).

21. *Elizabethan Poetry*, p. 99.

22. Castrop, *Shakespeares Verserzählungen*, p. 169: ". . . eine hochst gekonnte Parodie."

23. Book I, Ch. 13 (Feuillerat ed., *Sidney*, I, 90). Davenport points out (*Faunus*, p. 74) that Weever is also borrowing details from Sidney's much later description of the six maidens who lure Zelmane, Pamela, Philoclea, and Miso into a trap laid for them by Cecropia (Book III, Ch. 2; Feuillerat ed., I, 360.)

24. See Ch. IV, pp. 90-93. In light of the later episode in *Faunus and Melliflora* involving Venus and Adonis, it is worth recalling that Ovid's Venus put on the garb of Diana so she could accompany Adonis while he hunted (*Met.* X. 535-537).

25. The parallel irony in *Hero and Leander* is, as we have seen, more complex: Leander kneels down and prays not to Venus herself, but to "Chast Hero," "Venus' nun" (I. 177-178).

26. Cf. Book I, Ch. 13-14 (Feuillerat ed., *Sidney*, I, 91-92).

27. The table in Basilius's dining hall "was set neere to an excellent water-works" and was able to "turne rounde, by meanes of water which ranne under, and carried it about as a Mille" (Feuillerat ed., *Sidney*, I, 92). Weever just says that

underneath the nymphs' summer hall "a river rode" (l. 257). For Weever's following description of this river and of the nymphs bathing in it (ll. 258-270), compare Sidney's account of Ladon in Book II, Ch. 11 (Feuillerat ed., *Sidney*, I, 216-218).

28. For commentary on the Faunus episode in *The Faerie Queene* (VII.vi.37-35) see the volume including Books VI and VII of the Variorum edition, pp. 285-91, and William Nelson, *The Poetry of Edmund Spenser* (New York, 1963), pp. 302 ff. The "Mutabilitie Cantos" were not published, of course, until 1609.

29. See Davenport ed., *Faunus*, p. 75. Texts of Sidney's poem appear in Feuillerat ed., *Sidney*, II, 214-228 and in Ringler's edition of Sidney's poem, pp. 242-256. See also Ringler's notes, pp. 493-494. Weever borrows from the poem throughout *Faunus and Melliflora*: see ll. 437-439 and Sidney's ll. 51-52; l. 130 and Sidney's l. 108; ll. 640-641 and Sidney's ll. 123 ff.; l. 18 and Sidney's l. 149; ll. 448-450 and Sidney's ll. 396-400; ll. 742-744 and Sidney's ll. 407-408.

30. Compare, for example, Weever's puns on the word "hell" (ll. 371-376) with Nash's more obviously scurrilous usage in *The Choise of Valentines* (ll. 276-278). "To put the devil in hell" can mean "To have sexual connexion," according to Eric Partridge, *A Dictionary of Slang and Unconventional English* (London, 1961), I, 386. Partridge claims that the use of "hell" for the "female pudend" was not common until the eighteenth century, even though he notes that this meaning derives ultimately from Boccaccio. But the passage from Nash is clear evidence that this usage existed in the sixteenth century. See also the last line of Shakespeare's Sonnet 129: "To shun the heaven that leads men to this hell." Compare this with Weever's ll. 372-374. Other sexual puns in this section include "ease" (l. 342), "sport" (ll. 383, 397), and "gamesome" (l. 417).

31. Feuillerat ed., *Sidney*, I, 119-120; see Davenport ed., *Faunus*, p. 75.

32. Feuillerat ed., *Sidney*, I, 120.

33. Cf. *Venus and Adonis*, ll. 89-90, ll. 121 ff. See Davenport ed., *Faunus*, p. 75.

34. Cf. *Hero and Leander* I. 12: "Where Venus in her naked glory strove."

35. See Lyons, *Voices of Melancholy*, pp. 4, 62.

36. The reference, of course, is to Mantuan's fourth eclogue. See Lecocq, *La Satire*, p. 213.

37. Compare Weever, ll. 767-768 and *Venus and Adonis*, ll. 17-18; Weever, l. 769 and *Venus and Adonis*, l. 366. See Davenport ed., *Faunus*, p. 76.

38. Davenport (*Faunus*, p. 78) places great emphasis on a few undeniable borrowings from *Love's Labor's Lost*, but he fails to point out that many of the ideas and phrases in Faunus's speech come from *Hero and Leander* and that in some instances where Shakespeare and Marlowe express similar ideas, Weever's phrasing is closer to Marlowe than to Shakespeare. Weever's borrowings raise the question of the relationship between Shakespeare's play and Marlowe's epyllion. If Alfred Harbage is right (*"Love's Labor's Lost* and the Early Shakespeare," *PQ,* 41 [1962], 18-30) and Shakespeare's play was originally written for a 1588 performance and revised ca. 1596-1597, then Marlowe may be echoing Shakespeare. On the other hand, if the traditional view is correct and the play was written in 1593-1594, hence at about the same time or just after the composition of

Venus and Adonis and *Hero and Leander,* then it is possible that Shakespeare could be echoing Marlowe.

Davenport also notes (*Faunus,* pp. 77-78) some interesting but rather faint parallels between Faunus's speech and Hamlet's "Get thee to a nunnery" speech to Ophelia (III.i. 88 ff.). It is conceivable, but highly unlikely, that *Hamlet* was written and performed before *Faunus and Melliflora;* it is much more likely, Davenport argues, that Shakespeare was echoing Weever's poem, which he might have made a point of reading because Weever had praised him in one of his *Epigrammes.* But again Davenport fails to point out that Faunus's "A Votaresse, a Secluse, and a Nunne" was probably suggested by Leander's "Venus nun" (I. 319) and by Shakespeare's own reference to "Love-lacking vestals, and self-loving nuns" in *Venus and Adonis,* l. 752.

39. Davenport (*Faunus,* p. 78) notes that Weever's etymology is a variant of the one Hall offers in *Virgidemiae* ("De suis Satyris," Davenport ed., *Collected Poems,* p. 10): "Dum Satyrae dixi, videor dixisse Sat irae. . . ."

40. See Davenport ed., *Faunus,* p. 79.

41. In his *Epigrammes* Weever had complimented Hall and had offered Marston some rather dubious praise: "Marston, thy Muse enharbours *Horace* vaine, / Then some Augustus give thee *Horace* merit" (11th epigram for the 6th week, ll. 1-2; McKerrow ed., *Epigrammes,* p. 96). Both Davenport (*Faunus,* p. viii) and Peter (*Complaint and Satire,* p. 180) take the lines as straightforward praise. But as Davenport later admitted in the introduction to his edition of *The Whipping of the Satyre* (see n. 51 below), "An ironical interpretation of that is not impossible . . ." (p. viii). The key word "merit" appears to be deliberately ambiguous. McKerrow glosses it as "reward," and this was a common sixteenth-century meaning (see *OED* 1). But other meanings of "merit" which would make the lines sarcastic were common as well: "the condition or fact of deserving" (*OED* 2) and "claim or title to commendation or esteem, excellence, worth" (*OED* 4). It should also be noted that in one of the prefatory poems to his *Epigrammes,* "Lectores quotquot, quales, quicunque, estis," Weever glances satirically at Marston's dedication of *The Scourge of Villanie* "To Detraction" (see McKerrow ed., *Epigrammes,* p. 11 and p. 114, n.). Weever is also alluding wryly to Marston's dedication in line 1083 of *Faunus and Melliflora:* "*Detracting* nothing from the excellencie . . ." (my italics). Thus, while Weever's disapproval of Marston's satire in *The Whipping of the Satyre* (ll. 241 ff.) is certainly more overt than it is in the *Epigrammes* or in *Faunus and Melliflora,* it is misleading to say that Weever changed his mind about Marston between 1599 and 1601. Weever's attitude is critical from the beginning.

42. See Peter, *Complaint and Satire,* p. 118; Kernan, *Cankered Muse,* pp. 92 ff.; Lecocq, *La Satire,* pp. 298-303.

43. See Kernan, *Cankered Muse,* pp. 28-29: "Savagery, despair, hate, pride, intransigence, prurience, and sadism may be innate in satire, but Horace, Chaucer, Erasmus, and to a lesser degree, Ben Jonson, all manage to soften or find out more acceptable variations of these unpleasant traits by avoiding the extreme forms of indignation and the more shocking varieties of vice. . . . Horace and

Juvenal thus provide us with the two extremes of the satirist. . . ." See also pp. 64-66.

44. An ironic interpretation of those lines from Weever's epigram—"Marston thy Muse enharbours *Horace* vaine . . ."—would appear to be strengthened by the fact that Weever's translations in *Faunus and Melliflora* show Marston to be much closer to Persius and Juvenal than to Horace. See n. 41 above.

45. Davenport ed., *Faunus*, p. viii.

46. Simmes's name is included in the list, issued by the Staioners' Company on 4 June 1599, of fourteen printers to whom the edict of 1 June was "especyaly" directed. See Arber, III, 678.

47. Although Horace's satires had already been translated into English by Thomas Drant in 1566, Juvenal and Persius were not translated until the seventeenth century: Barten Holyday's *Aulus Persius Flaccus his Satires* appeared in 1616; Sir Robert Stapleton's *Juvenal's Sixteen Satyrs* appeared in 1647. See *The Cambridge Bibliography of English Literature*, ed. F. W. Bateson (Cambridge, 1940), I, 803, 805-806.

48. Lecocq, *La Satire*, p. 149: "Il faut donc qu'il bénéficie de protections singulièrement puissantes, ou d'une clémence exceptionelle. . . ."

49. See Philip Gaskell, *A New Introduction to Bibliography* (Oxford, 1972), pp. 183-184, who cites W. W. Greg, *Some Aspects and problems of London publishing between 1550 and 1650* (Oxford, 1956), Ch. IV.

50. The idea of prophecy is also related indirectly to the mythological basis of Weever's subject in *Faunus and Melliflora*, since the classical Faunus was noted for his oracular and prophetic power.

51. Weever further develops the strategies of "A Prophesie" in *The Whipping of the Satyre*, which provides the culminating example for Lecocq's discussion of "La satire du satirique" (*La Satire*, pp. 189–194). Lecocq discusses the conclusion to *Faunus and Melliflora* and "A Prophesie" in an earlier section (pp. 150-152).

52. See Lecocq's analysis of this aspect of Weever's anti-satirical approach, *La Satire*, pp. 151-152, 351-352.

CHAPTER VIII

1. *Mythology and the Renaissance Tradition*, p. 300, n. 5.

2. The copy of the 1602 edition in the Bodleian Library was long thought to be the only one extant. Alexander's text in *Elizabethan Narrative Verse* (pp. 168-191), from which I quote, is based upon this copy. There is another copy, however, in the Folger Shakespeare Library, from which Donno takes the text printed in *Elizabethan Minor Epics*, pp. 281-304.

3. *Poems: By Francis Beaumont, Gent.* (London, 1640), sig. B1^r-E3^v. *Salmacis and Hermaphroditus* is referred to in a table of contents on the title page and in a subtitle as "The Hermaphrodite."

4. See Bush, *Mythology and the Renaissance Tradition*, p. 184, and Smith, *Elizabethan Poetry*, p. 70. n. 20.

5. "The Authorship of 'Salmacis and Hermaphroditus,'" *N&Q*, 214 (October,

1969), 367-368. Beaumont entered Broadgates Hall (now Pembroke College), Oxford, on 4 February 1597, at the age of twelve (see Gayley, *Beaumont*, p. 25). Less than four years later, at sixteen, he followed his brothers Henry and John to the Inner Temple.

6. *The Metamorphosis of Tobacco* is preceded by six lines "In laudem Authoris" signed "F. B." According to the *DNB* (IV, 54-55), these lines are "Francis's earliest known attempts in verse." One of the introductory sonnets to the 1602 edition of *Salmacis and Hermaphroditus* is signed "J. B." (John Beaumont).

7. See, for example, Prince's edition of the *Poems*, p. xxxii, n. 3.

8. See A. B. Taylor, "A Note on Christopher Marlowe's 'Hero and Leander,'" *N & Q*, 214 (Jan., 1969), 20-21.

9. *Pagan Mysteries in the Renaissance*, pp. 211-215. The Platonic tradition has its origins, of course, in Aristophanes' myth of man's divided nature in the *Symposium* (189-193). The Biblical tradition, based upon early Christian exegesis of Genesis 1:27 ("So God created man in his own image, in the image of God created he him; male and female created he them"), begins with Philo and Origen. Parallels between Platonic and Biblical notions of androgyny are developed in the Renaissance by Pico (*Heptaplus*) and Leone Ebreo (*Dialoghi d'amore*) in Italy, and in France most extensively by Antoine Héroët in *L'androgyne de Platon* (1536). In Renaissance alchemical theory, according to Wind, "the Hermaphrodite, called *Rebis*, represents the apex of transmutation" and was seen as a symbol of the convertibility of spirit and matter (pp. 214-215).

10. See Robert Valentine Merrill, "The Pléiade and the Androgyne," *CL*, 1 (1949), 97-112, and Guy Demerson, *La Mythologie Classique dans l'oeuvre lyrique de la Pléiade* (Geneva, 1972), pp. 169-170, 175, 194, 208-209, 213, 240-243, and 355. There is no concrete evidence that Beaumont knew Bäif's elegant couplet translation of Ovid's episode (see *Oeuvres en Rime*, ed. Marty-Laveaux [Paris, 1881-1890], II, 190-195).

11. Book III, ch. 21 (ed. Romano, I, 140-142).

12. *Pictura Poesis* (Lyon, 1552), p. 32 (see Arthur Henkel and Albrecht Schöne, *Emblemata; Handbuch zur Sinnbildkunst des XVI. und XVII. Jahrhunderts* (Stuttgart, 1967), 1628-1629.

13. I quote from the Bodleian Library copy of *The Pleasant fable of Hermaphroditus and Salmacis . . . With a morall in English Verse* (London, 1565). See n. 8 above.

14. *Pictura Poesis*, p. 32 (Henkel and Schöne, *Emblemata*, 1628): "At revera hic fons nihil est aliud, nisi cunnus. . . . "

15. See Wilkinson, *Ovid Surveyed*, pp. 95-97, and Segal, *Landscape in Ovid's Metamorphoses*, pp. 24-26, 52-53.

16. In Elizabethan usage "sportive" often meant "inclined to amorous sport or wantonness" (*OED* 2) as well as "inclined to jesting or to levity" (*OED* 1). The only English writer before Beaumont who displays any sportive distance from the stern moralizing approach to Ovid's episode is Abraham Fraunce in *Amintas Dale*, pp. 48-50. Fraunce also moralizes and allegorizes the myth (he gives a

summary in Italian of the physiological theory recounted by Boccaccio, according to which the womb consists of seven chambers—three of which produce males, three females, and one hermaphrodites). But he first has the shepherd Ergastus narrate the story in deliberately comic doggerel, and he adds some humorous details about Hermaphroditus's effeminate beauty: ". . . so like to a God, to a goddess; / That shee wisht him a God, yet feared that he might be a Goddess. . . . "

17. See the commentary quoted by Reusner in *Picta Poesis Ovidiana* (1580), p. 43 : "Mercurio genitore satus, genitrice Cythere: / Nominis ut mixti; sic corporis Hermaphroditum. . . ."

18. Beaumont's characterization of Diana's sport as "savage and bloudy" is consistent with Ovid's persistent emphasis on her cruelty in the *Metamorphoses;* see, for example, III. 253-254—"aliis violentior aequo/visa dea est."

19. *Shakespeares Verserzählungen,* p. 168.

20. Lecocq, *La Satire,* p. 150.

21. See *Met.* IV. 171-189 and *Ars Amatoria* II. 569 ff.

22. See Ovid's account of Mercury's theft of Phoebus's cattle in *Met.* II. 685 ff.; see also the *Homeric Hymns* IV, "Hymn to Hermes," ed. Allen, Halliday, and Sikes (Oxford, 1936), pp. 267-274 and Horace, *Odes* I.x 272. For Ovid's account of Phoebus's chariot as the work of Vulcan ("Vulcania munera"), see *Met.* II. 106 ff. Beaumont's accounts of the sun's progress through the day (ll. 507-512, 557-614) and his allusion to Phaeton (ll. 550-556) are all derived from this section of Book II of the *Metamorphoses.*

23. See Ch. IV, p. 97.

24. *Met.* I. 149-150.

25. "Queen Elizabeth as Astraea," *Journal of the Warburg and Courtauld Institutes,* 10 (1947), 49. This essay is reprinted in *Astraea: The Imperial Theme in the Sixteenth Century* (London, 1975), pp. 29-87. See also Ch. IV of Donald Cheney's *Spenser's Image of Nature: Wild Man and Shepherd in "The Faerie Queene"* (New Haven, 1966), pp. 146-175.

26. "Queen Elizabeth as Astraea," 56-57. Miss Yates discusses in some detail the anonymous *Histrio-Mastix* (1589?), Peele's *Descensus Astraeae* (1591) and *Anglorum Feriae* (1595), Davies's *Hymnes to Astraea* (1599), the Countess of Pembroke's *Dialogue between two shepherds Thenet and Piers, in praise of Astraea* (1602), as well as allusions to Astraea in Spenser, Shakespeare, and other late sixteenth-century writers.

27. Miss Yates does not mention the Astraea section of *Salmacis and Hermaphroditus.* But she does discuss Shakespeare's distinctly ambiguous use of Astraea in *Titus Andronicus* IV.iii.4 ff. (70-72), and she notes that among recusant writers the virgo-Astraea symbolism was often perverted to discredit the Queen (76-81).

28. See the narrator's account of his dream-visit to Fame's palace in Book III (ed. Robinson, pp. 292-302).

29. See Bush, *Mythology and the Renaissance Tradition,* p. 185.

30. Beaumont might have heard of a play entitled *The Misfortunes of Arthur,* produced in Gray's Inn in 1588, the prologue of which contains some extended

praise of Elizabeth as Astraea. See Yates, "Queen Elizabeth as Astraea," 59.

31. Beaumont is echoing Marlowe's description of the Temple of Venus in *Hero and Leander* I. 143-152 and, in the reference to Venus's "naked pride," the description of the image of Venus embroidered on Hero's gown in I. 11-14.

32. Cf. ll. 869-874.

33. In *Met. I.* 259 Ovid speaks of Jove's thunderbolts as having been made by "Cyclopean hands": "tela reponuntur manibus fabricata cyclopum": The cyclops were Vulcan's traditional helpers.

34. See Ch. V, pp. 121-122.

35. " 'primus adulterium Veneris cum Marte putatur / hic videsse deus; videt hic deus omnia primus . . .' " (IV. 171-172). Cf. Beaumont's ll. 461-462: "This saw bright Phoebus: for his glittering eye / Sees all that lies below the starry skye."

36. See Fränkel, *Ovid: A Poet between Two Worlds*, pp. 126-217.

37. Cf. *Hero and Leander* I. 330 ("Thus having swallow'd Cupid's golden hooke"); II. 4 ("Wherewith, as one displeas'd, away she trips"); I. 339 ("Did charme her nimble feet, and made her stay"); II. 6-7 (" . . . excuses did she find, / To linger by the way, and once she stayd . . ."); I. 405-406 ("As shepheards do, her on the ground he layd, / And tumbling in the grass, he often strayd / Beyond the bounds of shame . . .").

38. Beaumont may be glancing here at Ovid's joking apology for writing elegiacs instead of epic hexameters in *Amores* I.i. 3-4: "The second verse was equal to the first—but Cupid, they say, with a laugh stole away one foot" ("par erat inferior versus—risisse Cupido / dicitur atque unum surripuisse pedem").

39. E.g. ll. 41-42 ("day"/"sea"), ll. 75-76 ("woo"/"snow"), ll. 283-284 ("rayes"/"seas"), ll. 417-418 ("shone"/"Endimion").

40. This passage forms a brilliant metaphorical pendant to the earlier conceit telling how Hermaphroditus came to have Cupid's eyes (ll. 59-74). Both passages are related to the conceit of "babies in the eyes" which appears in *Glaucus and Scilla*, l. 620 ("And how she looks for babies in his eyes"), *Faunus and Melliflora*, l. 842 ("In those two Diamonds prettie babes he spies"), and elsewhere in Elizabethan poetry (see, for example, l. 10 of Sidney's *Astrophel and Stella* 11). As W. C. Bolland demonstrated (*N. & Q.*, Ser. 8, No. 63 [March 11, 1893], 181-183), the conceit of "babies in the eyes" derives in part from a variation on the notion of Cupid's blindness: Cupid's eyes were given to a beautiful woman and thereby heightened her attractiveness. To have "babies in the eyes" came to mean "to have Cupid's eyes" or "to have Cupid in one's eyes," i.e. to excite love and desire. But the older explanation of the conceit, that "babies in the eyes" referred to a miniature reflection of the lover in the eyes of his beloved, should not be completely rejected. Hermaphroditus ironically has Cupid's eyes, but he also falls in love with his own reflection in Salmacis's eyes. Similarly, in *Faunus and Melliflora*, Cupid "on Faunus ey-balls stood" (l. 587) and later Faunus looks into Melliflora's eyes and "prettie babes he spies" (l. 842).

41. These two myths were often treated as a pair in the sixteenth century. In Pontus de Tyard's *Deuze Fables des Fleuves et des Fontaines* (1586), a set of prose descriptions and verse epigrams originally intended as directions for a group of

allegorical paintings in the Château d'Anet, the "Huitiesme Fable de la Fontaine de Narcisse" is followed by the "Neufiesme Fable du Fleuve Salmace," indicating that the two subjects were to be conceived as pictorial pendants (*Oeuvres Poetiques,* ed. Ch. Marty-Laveaux [Paris, 1875], pp. 214-217). See Wind, *Pagan Mysteries* (rev. ed.), p. 75, n. 1, and Francis Yates, *The French Academies of the Sixteenth Century* (London, 1947), p. 135, n. 5. Emblems using illustrations of Salmacis and Hermaphroditus and of Narcissus are also juxtaposed in Nicholas Reusner's *Emblemata* (Frankfort, 1581), pp. 136-137.

42. Here we find the nymph who flouts the law of Diana echoing Venus's warning to Adonis in Shakespeare's epyllion (ll. 161-162).

43. The hyperbolic images evoking nature's erotic participation in the events of the narrative here and elsewhere in Beaumont's epyllion (see, for example, ll. 46-54) are deeply indebted, as are Weever's in *Faunus and Melliflora,* to Sidney's *Arcadia.*

44. Ovid has "ille cavis velox adplauso corpore palmis" (IV. 352). Beaumont may actually be echoing Golding's translation of this line: "He clapping with his hollow hands against his naked sides" (IV. 434).

45. Hermaphroditus is said "To strip his soft clothes from his tender skin" (l. 838) and to have "Leapt lively from the land" (l. 861).

46. See Fränkel, *Ovid,* pp. 216-217: "This is the only passage in Ovid's works, I believe, which has a touch of sultry sensuality. . . ."

47. See Ch. II, p. 50.

48. *Elizabethan Poetry,* p. 73.

CONCLUSION

1. *The Poetry of "The Faerie Queene"* (Princeton, 1967), pp. 78-95.

2. "Spenser's Hermaphrodite and the 1590 *Faerie Queene,*" *PMLA,* 87 (1972), 199.

3. *Reading Spenser* (New York, 1968), p. 184.

4. Alpers, *The Poetry of "The Faerie Queene,"* p. 330.

5. Ibid., pp. 285, 288.

6. Ibid., p. 18.

7. Ibid., p. 293.

8. Ibid., p. 296.

9. *Reading Spenser,* p. 26.

10. Ibid., p. 56.

11. Ibid., p. 59.

12. Ibid., p. 168.

13. Ibid., p. 181.

14. Ibid., p. 165.

15. Ibid., p. 198.

16. *Poetry of "The Faerie Queene,"* p. 328.

17. See Alpers, p. 377.

18. Most editors have noted Spenser's submerged allusion here to the Salmacis and Hermaphroditus story (see, for example, Hugh Maclean's note in the Norton Critical Edition of *Edmund Spenser's Poetry* [1968], p. 76). The allusion is highly selective and very free: Hermaphroditus is never mentioned, and the fountain is cursed with the power of effeminization not because of Hermaphroditus's prayer, as in Ovid, but because of Diana's anger at the nymph who has given up the chase and fallen out of favor.

19. Spenser's introduction of the bathing motif from the Salmacis and Hermaphroditus story into the Venus and Adonis story is interesting for the way in which it extends the pervasive connection in *The Faerie Queene* between sexual gratification and water: "And swimming deepe in sensuall desires" (III.i.39.8).

20. For the sources and allegorical meaning of this passage, see the *Spenser Variorum* edition of Book IV, pp. 230-233. See also Wind's note on the *Venus biformis, Pagan Mysteries,* p. 211, and Roche, *Kindly Flame,* pp. 132-133.

21. "Spenser's Hermaphrodite," 198.

22. Roche, *Kindly Flame,* pp. 134-136, cites two marriage emblems as analogues to Spenser's image: Johannes Sambucus, *Emblemata* (Antwerp, 1564), pp. 124-125 [Fig. 11], and Nicholas Reusner, *Aureolorum Emblemata* (Strasbourg, 1591), sig. Diii [Fig. 12].

23. See Cheney, "Spenser's Hermaphrodite," 193-194, who re-examines Spenser's relation to the emblematic tradition invoked by Roche and introduces Aneau's emblem into the discussion.

24. Cheney rejects the attempt by A. R. Cirillo ("Spenser's 'faire Hermaphrodite,'" *PQ,* 47 [1968], 136-137) to connect Spenser's passage with a classical marble copy of an original bronze upright hermaphrodite in the collection of Cardinal Alessandro Farnese (see n. 6 to Cheney's article). But he acknowledges that the idea of an antique hermaphrodite statue on display in a rich Roman's bath evokes a "sensuality which seems to challenge whatever purely spiritual union might be attributed to the Hermaphrodite image per se" (195).

25. "Spenser's Hermaphrodite," 198.

26. Ibid., 193. As usual, Spenser makes precise judgments about the extent of mythological allusiveness extremely difficult. It could be argued that the reference to a rich Roman's bath recalls, indirectly, Salmacis's pool, and that "two senceles stocks" echoes not only Aneau's marriage emblem but Ovid's simile comparing Salmacis embracing Hermaphroditus to ivy twining around a tree (*Met.* IV. 365). In both instances, however, Spenser's imagery differs significantly from Ovid and is much closer to details from other sources (marriage emblems and the Renaissance connoisseurship of hermaphroditic sculpture). And the fundamental difference between Scudamour's love for Amoret and Hermaphroditus's revulsion from Salmacis remains.

27. *Pictura Poesis* (Lyon, 1552), p. 32 (see Henkel and Schöne, *Emblemata,* 1628-1629). Cheney does not mention this emblem, although he comments brilliantly on Aneau's *Matrimonii Typus* at the end of his article. He does mention, however, an emblem of Nicholas Reusner [Fig. 13] which uses an engraving similar to Aneau's "Fons Salmacidos, libido effoeminans" to illustrate

the motto "Forma viros neglecta decet"—"A casual appearance is fitting for men" (*Emblemata* [Frankfurt, 1581], Emblema 25, p. 136; see Henkel and Schöne, 1629-1630). The connection of the negative moralizing emblems to illustrations of Ovid's episode, and the dissimilarity of both these types of illustrations to hermaphroditic marriage emblems, is borne out in Reusner's "De Hermaphrodito" from *Picta Poesis Ovidiana*, which uses the same woodcut as the 1581 "Forma viros neglecta decet," (Frankfurt, 1580), p. 43^v. So strong was the tradition of interpreting Ovid's episode in negative moral terms that in some sixteenth-century editions of Ovid the illustration contradicts the text by showing Hermaphroditus willingly embracing Salmacis and thus submitting to lust: see the Leipzig edition of the *Metamorphoses* (1582), ed. Jacobus Mycillus, new rescension Gregor Bersmann, p. 168.

28. See Calvin Edwards, "Spenser and the Ovidian Tradition," (Ph.D. diss., Yale University, 1958).

29. See St. 3 of the Proem to Book I of *The Faerie Queene*.

Index